The Book of the
9F 2-10-0s

By
Richard Derry

Irwell Press Ltd.

For Peter Herring, who put me
back on track with railway
writing.

First published in the United Kingdom in 2006
by Irwell Press Limited, 59A, High Street, Clophill,
Bedfordshire MK45 4BE
Printed by Newton Printing, London

CONTENTS

Acknowledgements

My short career of observation and note taking (note care taken to avoid 'spotting') was spent in the heart of Southern territory and the closest any 9Fs came was Feltham. I never caught them there but came across my first one at Southall. My Ian Allan 'Combined Volume' of summer 1961, still with its 'ABC Binder De Luxe' in green, reveals a final total 'bagged' of 73, including, even, one of the Crosti conversions. The great part of these were all observed on the London sheds of Cricklewood, Willesden, Southall or Old Oak. My one photo of a 9F was at Cricklewood, its number, sadly, obscured by steam. I even saw a handful at Top Shed, Kings Cross, but visits never lasted long there before, as many can testify, enforced eviction. Old Oak was the best 'theatre', especially on Sunday afternoons when walking through the four great open roundhouses, a vast building in which the 9Fs seem to dwarf even the Kings.

For the background to the Engine Histories and for an account of the 9Fs' design and development I have ransacked the *Journal* of the Stephenson Locomotive Society, *The Railway Observer*, *The Railway Gazette*, *The Locomotive*, *Railway World*, *Trains Illustrated*, *Steam Classic* and *The Railway Magazine*, as well as odd editions of various society journals. For self-contained accounts I've consulted Atkins (*The British Railways 9F 2-10-0*, Irwell Press 1993), Cox (*British Railways Standard Steam Locomotives*, Ian Allan, 1966), Reed (*Loco Profile 18 German Austerity 2-10-0*, 1971 and *Profile 33 BR Class 9F 2-10-0*, 1973, Profile Publications), Talbot (*Pictorial Record of BR Standard Steam Locomotives*, OPC, 1982), *The Book of the BR Standards* and *The Book of the BR Standards 2*, both Irwell Press, various Ian Allan *ABCs*, Mountford (*Caerphilly Works 1901-1964*, Roundhouse Books), Teal (*BR Motive Power Allocations 1959-1968 1: BR Standards and Austerities*, Ian Allan), Weekes (*BR Standard Class 9F*, Bradford Barton), Fairclough and Wills (*BR Standard Steam in Close-up Vol. 2*, Bradford Barton), Cross (*BR Standard Steam In Action*, Bradford Barton), Rogers (*Riddles and the 9Fs*, Ian Allan), Freeman Allen (*The Riddles Standard Types in Traffic*, Allen & Unwin), Hands (*What Happened to Steam* series).

The usual stalwarts came to the rescue and I would like to thank, in no special order, Eric Youldon, Ian Sixsmith, Peter Groom, Allan Baker, Alec Swain, Bryan Wilson, Malcom Castledine, Keith Miles, Gavin Morrison, Alan Thompson, Julian Peters, George Reeve, Martin Smith, Edward Talbot and Mike Kinder.

The first sighting of the 9Fs was on 21 January 1954 in the yard of the Paint Shop at Crewe, where 92000-92003 were lined up on parade. All were destined for the Western Region and their official 'To Traffic' dates reflect the fact that they had been 'retained temporarily' by the LMR. Note the WR lamp irons but as yet no shed plates. The WR ATC conduit is visible on 92001, strung along the lower edge of the left-hand running plate. They would all have been out on the road for a bit, if only for running in – for proof see the time-honoured dirty top of 92001's boiler where the cleaners could not reach!

THE BOOK OF THE 9F 2-10-0s

The tale of the 9Fs has been told before, certainly – in some instances and in some aspects, to a detail and level of authority that is beyond the scope of this modest account. Yet in this distillation from books, the contemporary press and, crucially, the works records, in the usual style of 'The Book Of' series, it is hoped that a full and enjoyable picture of the 9Fs will emerge. A few snippets, as usual, will be entirely new or will revive some aspects that are half-forgotten. There's always a nugget or two to be had. In many of these previous 'Book Of' volumes, it has been possible to list the detail variations in a single section. This is because largely the modifications were applied to all (or most) of a class over time. They might be tiny (removal of crosshead vacuum pumps on a Jubilee or the application of 'pockets' at the front framing of a rebuilt SR Pacific) or they might be of a wholly different magnitude – the rebuilding of a Royal Scot or Merchant Navy into a locomotive of a comprehensively different outline. With the 9Fs it's a bit different. While detail differences there were, applied over time in the fashion described above, there were not *that* many for a class of over 250. Rather few in fact, given the size of

the class. What there was, by contrast with many other classes, was more or less radical additions made to individuals and the wholesale transformation of ten, the Crostis, so constructed from the very beginning as, really, to constitute a different class. So these matters have been described *within* the number sequence rather than at the beginning, which seems a more logical way of doing things.

****

If you wanted to be unkind, you could claim that many British railway locomotives and the features of their design and construction were, if not exactly obsolescent when contrasted with the best of foreign practice, well, were getting on a bit. The BR Standards, in a way, continued this noble tradition. Bar frames, for instance, had come and gone in North America by the time the plate frame BR Standard engines began to appear in 1951. Bar frames figured in the original BR thinking but had to be abandoned. There were plans for hundreds of 4-6-0s and they soon began to appear from the works; it never occurred to any of us that the rest of the world had long given up

building 4-6-0s... This is not so much a criticism born of hindsight but merely an observation. 'Obsolescent' doesn't mean an engine that can't do the job in the particular conditions for which it was designed. And the BR Standards possessed other features that were remarkably well designed. So it comes as no surprise that Britain was a little 'behind' in developing a 2-10-0. You can trust P. Ransome-Wallis to know something of the European dimension and in a splendid appraisal of the 9Fs in *Trains Illustrated* of September and October 1959 pointed out that ten-coupled locomotives had been at work in Europe since the turn of the century. The type reached its apogee in Germany, with two cylinder '50' class 2-10-0s, the basis of the 'Kreigsloks', appearing in 1938. *Over ten thousand* engines in this group (he says) were built and were at work all over Europe on freight, minerals and express passenger trains.

Yet the two cylinder 2-10-0 was not *entirely* unknown in Britain. Ministry of Supply engines had been produced from 1943 and were at work widely until going overseas. Twenty-five came into BR stock spending their lives in Scotland, the only BR Region where, peculiarly, the 9Fs were *never* allocated. The only exception seems

Cauliflower 0-6-0 58413 was posed alongside in that good old railway tradition of 'David & Goliath', 'Old & New' and so on. It must be said, it was certainly a striking contrast.

The first four in an impressive line-up, all with 'rods down' in traditional style, 21 January 1954. There was obviously no hint of the embarrassment to come in South Wales. The event was reported in a curiously low-key way in most journals – certainly this was the case in *The Railway Observer*, a journal represented on the day by one of the Honorary Editors. Still, it was a different world then, when the unveiling of a new locomotive was a fairly ordinary affair.

A fabulous close-up of the motion on 92000. In these first views it can be seen that the lubricator (with its horizontal drive rod and its vertical component) is in its customary place under the running plate; the access hole was too small and was latterly opened out a bit. The return crank is the original LNER style square pin, later replaced by the LMS pattern. Clear view of the reversing gear disappearing up under the running plate where it joins the reversing shaft.

to have been the inexplicable loan for a few weeks of both Crosti (!) 92023 and 92050, fresh from their test period at Rugby to spend a few weeks at Kingmoor (in England but at the time 68A in the Scottish Region) in 1955. The reasons behind this are unknown; it was presumably done for ScR officers to get a look at the new engines and compare them.

For quite a while the new BR freight engine was to have been a 2-8-2, another type in almost universal mixed traffic use world-wide and another type largely unknown over here. This first manifestation of the intended heavy freight locomotive was E.S. Cox's 2-8-2 outline of June 1948,

Class 6 4-6-2 express passenger
Class 6 4-6-2 mixed traffic
Class 5 4-6-2 mixed traffic
Class 8 2-8-2 freight

These were the existing LMS power classifications, later amended. To iron out the LM's '5X' designation when applying the power classes across BR, 6, 7 and 8 became 7, 8 and 9, with 5 and below remaining the same. The first group of four ended up, through much argument and discussion, quite a bit different. The proposed 'Class 5' light Pacific became the 73000 4-6-0, which was certainly not an 'entirely new design'. The two 'Class 6' Pacifics became the Class 7 Britannias and the

increasing use of fitted stock, it is felt that a standard for the future should have rather better speed capabilities, while retaining the same tractive effort as the existing standard 2-8-0s.

It is interesting to recall that in the 1930s the American Railways found themselves with many thousands of freight locomotives with wheels of around 4'9" dia. which proved to be useless to meet the speeding up of freight which road competition demanded.

There was certainly a debate as to whether the new loco should be a 2-8-2 or a 2-10-0 and in *The British Railways Standard 9F 2-10-0* (Irwell Press, 1993) Atkins furnishes us with much more detail from the period. In a *Memorandum* of 11 August 1950 Cox

The quartet numbered left to right, 92003-92000. In years to come this might be the view presented to the visitor at any number of sheds – but with nothing like this level of cleanliness!

designed to be interchangeable in respect of boiler, cylinders and so on with a second outline, a Class 5 4-6-2 (*First Report on Proposed Standard Steam Locomotives,* June 1948). The influx of WD 2-8-0s and 2-10-0s and the extra Stanier 8Fs built in the War meant heavy freight requirements exercised the minds of Riddles' team over the next few years rather less than repairing the deficiencies in the mixed traffic sphere. Getting on for half of these, Cox estimated, were too long in the tooth. There were twelve Standard types proposed, as is well known, four of which were to be 'entirely new designs'. These were envisaged with bar frames, as mentioned earlier. Cox called it 'a first shot at integrating the remit which we considered had been laid upon us'. One of the four 'entirely new designs' was the putative 2-8-2:

Class 6 Clans. The one we're interested in, the Class 8, became the 9F 2-10-0.

Cox writes that, after the 2-8-2 design had been worked up, Riddles was 'unhappy' and that experience with the WD 2-10-0s (the 2-8-2 offered little, for instance, in adhesion over a 2-8-0) made him settle for that layout instead. The boiler, though very similar, could not be made interchangeable with the Britannia, but most fitments would be standard. Here was the 1948 argument for the 2-8-2:

The 2-8-2 is proposed for heavy freight in preference to the 2-8-0 or 2-10-0 types because of the wish to use a wide firebox in conjunction with a 5'3" dia. coupled wheel. Existing heavy freight engines in all Regions use wheels of about 4'8" dia. but having regard to the very large number of such locomotives which already exist, and considering also that the future trend will be towards faster movement of freight and

laid down a number of good reasons why a 2-8-2 *would be preferable to* a 2-10-0 for the (then) envisaged higher speeds of 35mph with maxima of 50mph, and quite compelling they were. To summarise:

A 2-10-0 'was absolutely limited by the British Loading Gauge to a wheel diameter at 4ft 10in' which meant less tractive effort for what the concept was worth. As it turned out, the 9F ended up with 5ft diameter wheels...

A 2-8-2 would always be faster...

A 2-10-0 boiler would be too restricted in boiler diameter, grate area, firebox volume and ashpan compared to a 2-8-2...

A 2-10-0 lacked, in comparison, adhesion and especially surefootedness in starting...

A 2-10-0 could not make use of standard components, flanging blocks and patterns as would be the case with a 2-8-2...

For good measure Cox then conducted a brief world survey of the 2-10-0 especially in comparison with the

92002 on display – note absence of sand fillers on this left-hand side. The three on the other side each fed two wheels.

2-8-2 and was decidedly dismissive. No country, it seems, thought the 2-10-0 worth a light, even Germany, with thousands of them! So, as late as the summer of 1950, a 2-8-2 it was still likely to be.

Work thus seems to have continued on the 2-8-2 into the next year but by 1951 Cox, presumably at the behest of his master, Riddles, produces a further *Memorandum* which comes down firmly *in favour of* the 2-10-0 *over* the 2-8-2... The U-turn came about through changed predictions as to future working. It was over-optimistic, perhaps, to envisage higher average speeds for coal and mineral trains, for many reasons; more realistically, despite temporarily heightened hopes, speeds would remain for the great part at traditional levels. With this in mind Riddles had plumped for a 2-10-0. So it was that, less than a year after his 2-8-2 case for the defence (or was it the prosecution?) in June 1951 Cox was able to put another powerful case for – a 2-10-0. Existing loads and times were assumed 'for the present time' and the bread and butter of the new engine would be unfitted stock at no greater speed than 40mph, though it should be capable of 50mph when necessary...

Predictions as to future developments could go grievously awry and required subtle evaluation. 'The problem', Cox enumerated, 'is one of reducing overall timings by raising speeds on up grades and on the level rather than by running any faster downhill.' Which assumed in turn that

no special wagon braking problems would arise. The alternatives, as set out in a *Memorandum* and severely paraphrased here, were a 2-8-2 with the same boiler as the Britannia ('5ft 3in wheels, 35,916lb. Tractive Effort and a factor of adhesion of 4.22 with maximum axle weight of 17 tons') and a 2-10-0 ('5ft 0in wheels, 39,666lb. Tractive Effort and a factor of adhesion of 4.5 with maximum axle weight of 16 tons'). The 2-10-0 had the advantage of more tractive effort at all speeds, better adhesion and lower first cost (since weight was less). Wheel diameter was three inches less but 'with modern valve events and roller bearings this was 'no detriment'. 50mph with a 5ft 0in dia. wheel corresponded to 60mph with 6ft 2in wheels. The slightly smaller boiler compared to the Class 7 4-6-2 would 'none the less supply all the steam needed under freight conditions'. A number of new flanging blocks would, however, be required. It had been seen with the WD 2-10-0s that flangeless tyres on the driving wheels meant easy negotiation of curves down to 4½ chains. A slightly increased sideplay was required on leading and trailing coupled wheels. The ashpan arrangement was 'not so good', but its capacity was at least as great as the 2-8-2 and the arrangement of its sloping sides somewhat better than on the LMR Duchess Pacifics, for example.

There was not only the choice between the 2-10-0 and the 2-8-2 to be considered, but also the choice between the proposed 2-10-0 and

existing Regional types. The starting Tractive Effort of the 2-10-0, Cox quotes, was only slightly higher than the bigger home-grown 2-8-0s such as the Stanier 8Fs, but the performance at speed would be higher *pro rata* due to the greater steam producing capacity of the boiler. The principal advantage of the 2-10-0 would be its ability to climb the banks faster. Thus, 'At a speed in the neighbourhood of 20mph, ability to climb 10 mph faster represented a much greater saving in journey time than would the ability to run say 50 mph instead of 40 mph downhill'. This is Cox's 'faster uphill' quality mentioned earlier. The proposed engine should, therefore, 'allow of overall journey times being reduced without increase in maximum speed so far as non-fitted trains are concerned'. This was important, for it allowed the new 2-10-0 to plod wherever it had to in time-honoured fashion or to race a bit whenever better traffic conditions, braking improvements and so on, could be taken advantage of.

All this duly saw the prize go to the 2-10-0, by now of course classified '9'. In the event Riddles retired before the first 9F left Crewe Works and there never had been unanimity, it turns out, at the top-most levels of the Executive; a 2-8-2 might have been better after all, it was felt in some quarters; Atkins quotes Roland Bond from his memoirs of 1975 that, had he been in charge, the BR freight engine would indeed have been a 2-8-2. Ransome Wallis was also aware of this, writing in *Trains Illustrated* of September 1959 that: *even after the proven value of the Class '9' there are many who are still of the opinion that a Mikado would have been a more useful engine.*

****

In accordance with established practice the preliminary design was drawn up at Derby and then sent to another Drawing Office for the detail work, Brighton in this case. Other elements remained the preserve of other works, including Derby. Bar frames were particularly suited to a wide firebox design and were perceived to be more reliable than plate frames, while long experience in the United States of America had shown them to be more or less indestructible, even on vastly larger and more powerful locomotives. Nevertheless they had been jettisoned; work had proceeded on the assumption that bar frames (fairly revolutionary for Britain it must be said) would be used but it soon became clear that expertise and equipment necessary in the production and (almost more tellingly) the handling of such heavy and complex castings or forgings in this country was lacking. So plate frames were used, with complex bracings to thwart fatigue cracking and a thickened part where it narrowed under the firebox.

An almost absolute rigidity was sought, and largely attained. With the possible exception of one or two obscure rebuilds back in the 1840s, remarks Reed, 'No frame structures in history were more rigid than those of the 2-10-0s.'

The cylinders were 'almost indestructible' being made of steel with cast iron liners, American practice which was then, apparently, unusual in this country. Most of the other BR Standards – the Pacifics, Class 5 4-6-0s, Class 3 and 4 2-6-0s and Class 3 2-6-2Ts – had the same arrangement and when worn out the cast iron liners were simply renewed.

The cabs of the Pacifics had come in for some criticism; mounted on the boiler back with floor cantilevered over the tender front proved noisy, draughty and dusty, despite meticulous attention in the wind tunnel and mock-ups for trade union approval. A more conventional cab arrangement with tender fall plate (though the cab was still attached to the boiler back) was adopted, in line with that made for the last ten Britannia Pacifics, 70045-70054.

However akin the 9F was to the Britannia in looks, so much so that the boilers might be *assumed* to have been interchangeable we have seen that they weren't. A new boiler had to be designed for the 9F. *Trains Illustrated* in its unveiling of the class

in March 1954 makes the curious comment that 'for reasons which we were unable to ascertain clearly, the new engines are not now regarded as one of the standard BR types'. And the reasons have been impossible to ascertain ever since!

Whatever the projected uses of the new engine and at whatever speeds, weighed in the balance by Cox back in 1950-51, by the time the first one appeared more adventurous times were being prepared for them. On the appearance of 92000 the accompanying technical brochure was clear:

One of the 2-10-0's features which is immediately noticeable is that its driving wheels are 5ft diameter, some 3 to 6 inches larger than what has hitherto been normal in this country on a heavy freight engine. Behind this change is a plan to use the new 2-10-0s to speed up unfitted block freight workings, such as the daily out-and-home turns with coal from March to the Brimsdown power station, on the Eastern Region's Cambridge main line, returning with empties, and similar duties between New England and Ferme Park, on the East Coast route, which are to be amongst the new engines' duties. For the same reason the engines have the unaccustomed frill for a freight engine of smoke deflectors; these are a decided benefit as far down the speed

92003 on that famous 21 January 1954. The GW style of lamp iron, which slotted into the side of the lamp rather than the rear as everywhere else, can be seen to be quite different. During construction (see page 13 for instance) the lower part of the smoke deflector fitted on first, once the cylinders were complete, then the main part was erected. Only the lower sections were removed along with a panel of the front framing when the valves needed to come out for maintenance. Mounted on top of the vacuum ejector just behind the smoke deflector is the WR ATC brake valve – all the BR Standards (except the Britannias) equipped for the WR system would seem to have had this.

range as 35-40mph and at that rate some of the most important block mineral loads on principal main lines, such as the celebrated Toton-Brent coal run, are often operated. We refer, incidentally, to the normal coal workings between Toton and Brent, not the experiments with a fitted coal train still in progress. The latter are being conducted purely to investigate the problems of braking such loads at high speeds and not to test the capabilities on such work of the engines so far used in the trials; there is as yet no plan to provide dual braking on one of the 2-10-0s for experiments with the fitted coal train..

The wheel balancing was new to Britain; the rotating masses were fully balanced in the normal way, but the reciprocating masses were 'statically balanced to the equivalent of 40 per cent, by placing lead weights in the coupled wheels in the same phase on both sides of the engine'. The arrangement apparently reduced the 'wheel' hammer blow (but not the 'axle'

Cab of 92140, with BR1F tender. The hinged flap is not for ventilation, though it might have come in useful to let a bit of air in; certainly in traffic they are frequently seen to be left open. Whether by design or because they were jammed up most of the time is not known. They were actually there to give access to the bottom corner of the firebox, to a washout plug. The 9Fs, and all BR Standards from 1954 (with the exception of the Class 2 2-6-0s) had this new form of cab to combat the excessive draughtiness (experienced on the Britannias for instance). They differed in having no hand rail pillars and looked very different from the side or rear. Tenders had gangway doors and full width fall plates. Photograph The Transport Treasury.

A flangeless wheelset fallen off, in this case 92026 at Cricklewood shed. See *Not a Word to the Guv'nor* in *British Railways Illustrated* Volume 9 No.6, March 2000, for a step by step account of how this mishap proceeded. 92026 was a Wellingborough engine, the first Crosti conversion in fact, of September 1959. As the 9F went off shed the flangeless wheels 'dropped down' between the rails. The traditional remedy was resorted to – keep going till it re-rails itself and not a word to anyone! Photograph J.G. Walmsley, The Transport Treasury.

92144 late on at New England. Good view of the BR AWS conduit tagged to the lower edge of the running plate; vacuum reservoir below cab along with battery box (the two nuts holding the door to the latter are clear). Photograph Paul Hocquard, The Transport Treasury.

hammer blow) as well as saving approximately two cwts weight. The weights themselves consisted of plates clamped on either side of the coupled wheel spokes to form pockets into which lead was inserted.

The 9F boiler was designated BR9, coincidentally, and as it was a new design, feats of fitting maximum power within the 'universal' L_1 loading gauge had to be accomplished, similar to those that so distinguished the design and construction of the Britannia boiler. A principal reason for the difference was the need to mount the 9F firebox above the 5ft wheels, making it necessarily smaller. On the plus side the BR9 boiler used the same pressings from the same pressblocks as the Clan Pacifics while the front tubeplate used the same pressing as that for the Britannia, which saved a bit. With the BR9 being a little smaller, the theoretical design prospects for optimum efficiency were, it seems, not as good. Yet as Atkins has pointed out, tests on the Rugby Plant later indicated that at the manual firing limit the 9F boiler turned out to be slightly *more* efficient even than the Britannia.

All the by now customary aids to servicing were fitted – rocking grate, self-emptying ashpan and self-cleaning smokebox.

There had been instances of broken and bent coupling rods on the Britannias, and the I section rods had been replaced by fish belly plain section rods which solved the problem. Doncaster, responsible for their

design, wisely thought it best, for the 9Fs, to follow the arrangement of the WD 2-10-0s; the startling sight of 90763 at Doncaster in May 1952 is assumed to be related to the requirements of the Doncaster Drawing Office. Arriving from Carlisle 90763 was put to work on local freights before commencing duty on the main line runs to Peterborough. Doncaster obviously needed more than just a look and when 90763 failed and was despatched to Cowlairs a second WD 2-10-0, 90757, arrived. It was working from Doncaster shed during August 1952 and the principal reason for its presence, it emerges, was to undertake clearance trials for the expected arrival of 9Fs. It does not seem to have gone back north until the following year.

WHEELS

As is well known, the centre, main, driving wheels were flangeless; in this way the 9F got to negotiate tight curves, though in difficult situations the flangeless pair could 'drop off'. The discovery of a BR Motive Power Committee minute of 30 September 1955 indicated that matters were a lot more complicated and had even involved prolonged testing at Willesden (Twyford Abbey). Former BR engineer and author of a number of erudite volumes, as well as long-time contributor to these volumes and to *British Railways Illustrated*, Allan C. Baker, brought clarity to some mystifying technical references:

'Class 9F Tyre Profiles.

There were some concerns by the Civil Engineering fraternity shortly after the engines were first introduced into service, in connection with the effects they were having on the performance of the track. The concerns were on two counts: first the long coupled wheelbase as there was little experience in this country of such engines; secondly the use of flangeless tyres on the intermediate coupled wheel-set. Three potential issues were the concern of the Civil Engineers: in the first instance excessive side wear (leading to the infamous, of more recent times, gauge-corner cracking) on the rail-head when the engines were negotiating tight curves and caused by flange friction; secondly gauge spreading – similarly on tight curves. Thirdly, there was the possibility of the intermediate coupled wheels becoming derailed, either one or both, with the potential to cause a more damaging derailment, or climbing back onto the rail-head again. In the latter case, in all probability some rail damage would occur, with the potential to cause 'stress raisers' in the rail-head, which in some circumstances could lead to a subsequent fracture of the rail.

'Originally the engines had an experimental tyre profile on the intermediate and flangeless coupled axle, rather than the 'standard' variation for flangeless coupled wheels of the British Engineering Standards Association (BESA) 'G' profile. This was as well as the tyre

BR AWS was unmistakable from the front, with that protector plate behind the screw coupling. There was little or no indication of the GW apparatus from the front. The conduit running along the running plate was more or less indistinguishable from the GW version but again at the back the vacuum reservoir and battery box (often mounted on the running plate in other classes) are unmistakable. Compare the condition of these two AWS examples (92200 in the lead) with the 1954 quartet at Crewe! Photograph The Transport Treasury.

width being 5¾ inch as opposed to the 'standard' 5½ inch for coupled wheels on main line locomotives in this country. The 'G' flangeless profile had a 'standard' 1 in 20 taper on the tread for roughly ¾ of the width of the tyre, and a sharp reverse taper for the remaining ¼ - it was known as the 'G2' profile, or sometimes the 'X' profile. The 'G' profile itself was quite normal for coupled wheels other than those in leading or trailing positions as it had a slightly thinner flange. It was 'backed-off' on the inside edge and this gave a design clearance of a new tyre on new rails in a 1¾ inch flange way of five sixteenths of an inch, as opposed to three eighths with the 'A' profile, which was otherwise the 'standard' tyre profile for locomotives and tenders in this country. On the 9Fs the leading and trailing coupled wheels had the 'A' profile, and the second and fourth pairs the 'G' profile. I think I am right in saying that all previous engines used in this country with flangeless coupled wheels, the ex-LNWR eight coupled engines for example and the WD 2-10-0s, had the 'G2' profile on the flangeless wheels.

'The original profile used on the 9Fs differed from the 'G2' as it had a slight concave cone effect (in other words a profile not unlike a worn tread), presumably with the design intention of reducing the tendency of the wheels to derail. However, this profile seems to have had other disturbing effects

(perhaps even the reverse of the intention) and to address the problem a series of tests were conducted in Twyford Abbey Sidings at Willesden in the late summer of 1955. It appears that when passing over curves of six chains radius the behaviour of the later profile, referred to as the 'BR profile' was suspect, and as a result a number of recommendations were made.

'It was agreed that engines with either type of profile should not be permitted to traverse lines with curves sharper than six chains radius, and that engines with the later 'BR profile' should have their intermediate coupled wheel treads re-profiled to the 'G2' profile as and when they passed through main works. However, it was also agreed that periodic inspections should be made of locations with curves of a radius of 15 chains or less to see what, if any, track damage was being done by the engines. And, in the case of the engines with the 'BR profile', and until modified, the Chief Civil Engineer of each Region where the engines were working was to be kept informed, and periodic inspections made of any curves with a radius of 30 chains or less, again to see if any damage was being caused, and until all the engines had been modified.

It is worth noting that the original design specification for the locomotives was an ability to negotiate

six chain radius curves without gauge widening. There may have been a maximum speed attached to this requirement, but if so I have not been able to discover what it was. It may be that the tests were also designed to establish if in fact the engines could safely negotiate sharper curves than those of six chains radius, without gauge widening. If this was part of the process then it would seem six chains was established as the minimum, whatever the profile of the tyres on the flangeless coupled wheels.

'The Motive Power Committee, in a minute dated 30 September 1955, noted that the Chief Civil Engineer was to keep the use of these locomotives under close observation for a period of twelve months, and to make recommendations in the light of experience gained. Presumably this applied to all the locomotives and wherever they were working.

(The Twyford Abbey Sidings were, as far as I know, on the down side between Willesden Junction and Stonebridge Park. The 1938 RCH Handbook of Stations gives Steinway & Sons Twyford Abbey Sidings, Willesden Junction.)
Allan C Baker
28 April 2006'

ATC
Only the Western had ATC (Automatic Train Control) at the time and provision was made for its fitting to

The last steam locomotive built at Crewe, it was decided, should be recorded photographically. Which was just as well, for very little survives of 9Fs being built at Crewe. 92250's boiler floats through the Erecting Shop against a backdrop of intensive diesel shunter production. The one behind will become D3591. Unlike pre-nationalisation designs, foot framing was mounted on the boiler, not the main frames; hence the projecting supports.

Piston and rod standing upright on floor, with radius rods, crosshead, combining lever and union links alongside; firebars a little to the right. All in their own chalked areas. The piston and rod constituted a single piece in the later engines, the length of rod and length of slide bars allowing the piston to come out the front without splitting the crosshead or slidebars. Note piston rings hanging on cylinder cover studs, a favourite resting place.

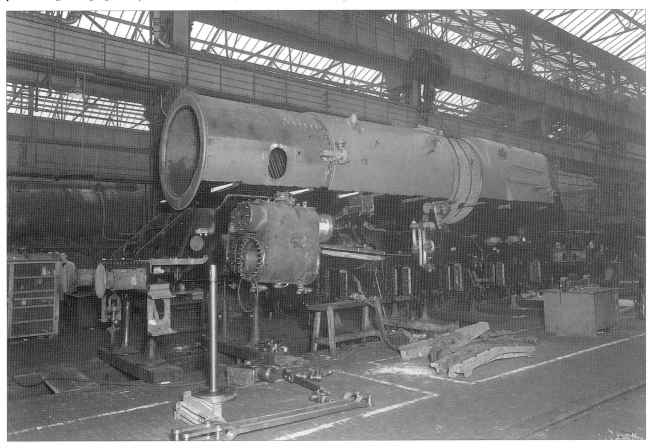

The boiler approaches position above the frames. The resulting 9F was destined to be Crewe's last steam locomotive but it was not the last boiler constructed at the great works – it was building 9F boilers for three more years.

the first ten destined for that Region; two of these in fact were diverted to the LMR in 1954, 92008 and 92009 but, though they thus didn't need the equipment, the conduit at least was fitted to 92009. Not so 92008, however. The third Crewe Lot, E497 from 1958 and the second Swindon Lot, 429 from 1959, saw the resumption of deliveries to the Western Region, so these were fitted with ATC. Unfortunately there is little external indication on a WR ATC fitted engine, apart (on the 9Fs) from the conduit under the left-hand running plate. It might be expected that the Crewe ones would have gone to Swindon for the fitting but, like 92009 the conduit at least was in place when they left the LM, strung under the left-hand running plate.

AWS

AWS, Automatic Warning System, was widely introduced on BR late in the 1950s though by no means all 9Fs received it. Some Eastern Region ones seem to have been among the earliest to be equipped, at Darlington in 1959. Getting on for a hundred might have been fitted with the BR AWS, including one or two (92239 for instance) that originally had been on the Western and then transferred elsewhere. The difference from the WR ATC was that the BR AWS had a prominent protector plate under the buffer beam and cylindrical vacuum reservoir and battery box under the cab on the left-hand side. Those identified from either the Record

Cards (usually marked as 'Job E4983' or, somewhat erroneously, as simply 'ATC') and by examining photographs as carrying BR AWS are as follows, though readers will almost certainly spot more from published pictures of the class. Information welcome!

92020	92097	92175
92033	92098	92176
92034	92099	92177
93035	92122	92178
92037	92128	92179
92038	92135	92181
92039	92138	92182
92040	92140	92183
92041	92141	92184
92042	92144	92185
92043	92145	92186
92049	92146	92187
92060	92148	92189
92061	92149	92190
92062	92150	92191
92063	92155	92192
92064	92163	92197
92065	92166	92198
92066	92168	92199
92069	92169	92200
92076	92170	92211
92077	92171	92223
92078	92172	92231
92092	92173	92234
92094	92174	92239

REGULATOR

The Pacifics had the sensitive multiple valve regulator in the superheater header, tried and tested all over the world. It required external rodding and though the other Standards, including the 9Fs, had the conventional British slide regulator in the dome the external rodding of the Pacifics (together with the regulator in the cab moving to and fro rather than side to side at right angles to the direction of movement) was replicated. The principle was that the Standards' cab layout should be the same from class to class.

LAMP IRONS

Nothing was straightforward when it came to standardisation and every detailed aspect required thought and cogitation. Take lamps. The WR ones had side mountings, the rest had rear mountings. This meant the irons differed, and never the twain could meet. In June 1953 BR's Motive Power Committee recommended that the ex-LNER headlamp, 'suitably modified', should be made standard for British Railways steam locomotives. 'A full-scale trial', it was decided, should be carried out before the final decision. Modified lamps were tried on the Eastern, North Eastern and Scottish Regions and further modifications suggested; ultimately, after the modifications had been incorporated, 1,000 lamps were distributed *for further trials* on all Regions, on BR Standard and Regional locomotives with the exception of ex-GWR types. On ex-SR locomotives a slight modification was made to the lamp brackets to enable the trial to be carried out. Following the trials further modifications were submitted,

The bottle jacks at the front, with two at the rear, would be used to take the weight with the axle boxes in more or less 'running position'. Otherwise the engine would have to be jacked up later, to put the springs and gear in place. The men are positioned to guide the axle boxes into the horns; those in the pit will steady the axle boxes. In some works the practice was to wheel the engine first and then put the boiler on, in others the reverse. Crewe usually put the boilers on first, then wheeled the engine.

Erecting a 9F at Swindon, showing the set up of the reversing gear particularly well. Photograph Roy Wilson, The Transport Treasury.

Lot Nos. and Works
Crewe E487 92000-92014
Crewe E491 92015-92019
Crewe E488 92020-92029
Crewe E489 92030-92049
Crewe E490 92050-92086
Swindon 421* 92087-92096
Crewe E493 92097-92134
Crewe E494 92135-92177
Swindon 422 92178-92202
Swindon 429 92203-92220
Crewe E497 92221-92250
transferred from Crewe 2/54

agreed and the final approved design advised to the Trade Unions. 'No adverse comment' was received. The WR General Manager declared that the expense involved in altering the lamp brackets could not be justified; the SR General Manager stated that 'as the modification to the lamp bracket is only slight, the locomotives should be altered to take the BR headlamp'. It was decided that 'the BR Standard Steam Locomotive headlamp, Drawing SL/DN/YY/243, as subsequently modified', be adopted as standard for use on all locomotives except those of ex-GWR origin. The BR standard headlamp would, it was ordered, supersede the existing pattern lamps, including those on BR Standards on the WR, but despite all the words, trials, consultation, drawings and attention, it never did.

Have a look at the pictures of Crewe's last tender, no.1561 years later, for instance.

BEARINGS
The 9Fs had plain bearings which is hardly surprising, given that even the Britannias and the Class 5s were not wholly roller bearing-fitted. Those later 9F passenger exploits, of course, were not even dreamed of. The tender had Timken roller bearing axleboxes.

SANDING
There was one odd feature of the 9F sanding. It was steam fed to both front and rear of the flangeless middle driving set and to the front of the leading drivers; this was conventional enough but there were only *three* sandbox fillers in total, all on the right-hand running plate only.

Normally there'd be three each side, making a total of six. The Crostis, with special problems of space, were different. They had the fillers and boxes placed more or less conventionally on the left-hand side for the middle driving pair but on the right-hand side they were placed closer together, a little way in front of the boiler-slung chimney. The front fillers were most unusual in being sited at the very front, either side of the 'pre-heater' smokebox door. When the Crostis were modified with the smoke deflector plate on the right-hand, chimney side, a hinged plate was provided so the fillers could be got at, but it remained 'damn awkward'. When the Crostis were rebuilt into conventional form the fillers and boxes remained in place, as accessible as any others.

SMOKEBOX FOOTSTEPS
The 9Fs (except the Crostis) were built with two small footsteps, one inside each frame plate, directly under the smokebox. This was the same arrangement as on the Britannias, providing (to our modern eyes) a somewhat precarious footing for smokebox cleaning. On the Pacifics it proved awkward for the placing of headboards on the top lamp bracket on the smokebox door. From 1955 the steps accordingly began to be replaced by a single large plate between the frames, with a central support. Some time after this, when the ostensible purpose (the fitting of headboards) had perhaps been forgotten, some 9Fs began to get the new platform. It would certainly have made smokebox cleaning easier. The first seem to have appeared around 1958 but BR had given up fitting them, probably, by about 1961, leaving a number still with the original steps.

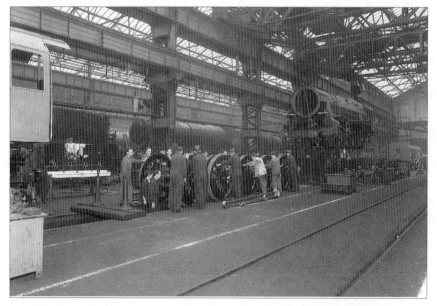

The lads try to look the part (with variable results!) while the photographer does his work. The previous 9F so dealt with, 92249, stands in grey on the left. Behind are a stripped down Black Five 45317, Pacific 46237 and another Black Five, 44744. Connecting rod and eccentric rod on floor.

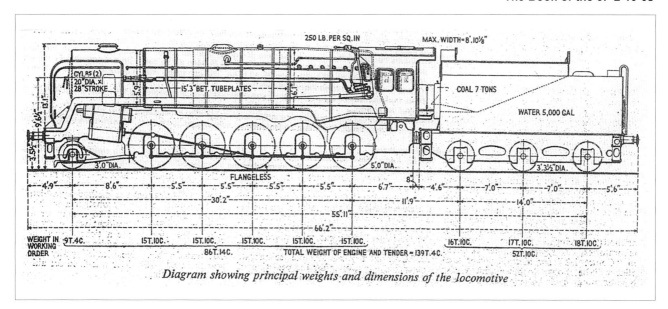

Diagram showing principal weights and dimensions of the locomotive

RETURN CRANK

The return crank, as on the Britannias, was mounted on a square pin, LNER style. As with the Britannias, from the mid-1950s this was gradually replaced by a standard LMS-type four stud design. So it is that, as those numbered in 92040s appear, we see a mix of the two cranks. By the time the 92050s are under way the four stud LMS-type one is universal. You can find plenty of earlier 9Fs subsequently fitted ('retro-fitted' as they say now) with this but

it would not have been by any means universal.

HEADLIGHT
See 92079.

CROSTIS
See 92020-92029.

AIR PUMPS
See 92060-92066, 92097-92099.

GIESL EJECTOR
See 92250.

TENDERS

'A new design of tender' was prepared for the 9Fs. This was the 7 ton BR1G, the 5,000 gallon BR1A but equipped with a fall plate for the cab. BR announced that 'various arrangements' of tender would be fitted as 9F production proceeded, 'to suit the particular divisions on which the locomotives are called upon to work'. It might seem almost like excess subtlety – why not as high a coal capacity as was possible and have done with it? The reason apparently

Crewe built them in lines, Swindon in rows... 92203, 92204 and 92205 (presumably that's 92202 on the left) all with double chimneys nearing completion at Swindon. The secret of erecting locomotives was to gather all the parts together at the right time and of course the various BR works had this process honed to perfection. The unchanged time-honoured features are the trolleys (each works had its own species, it seems) the wooden trestles and so on. Photograph B.K.B Collection, Initial Photographics.

was that, where coal capacity was markedly greater than the amount routinely burned, the stuff at the back merely deteriorated in quality over months and when the time did come to use it up, it could be worse than useless. 'Some Regions' the railway press were informed, *require a high water capacity in relation to coal, particularly for routes where water troughs are infrequent or non-existent,*

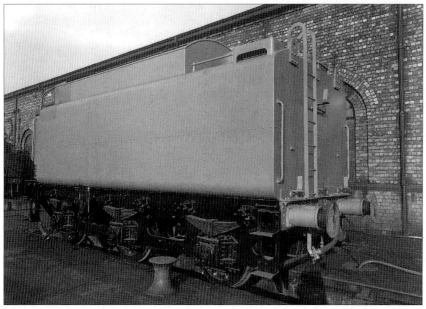

Top and middle left. Two familiar 'record' pictures of a BR1G tender, no.1561 provided for 92250. It was, famously, the last tender constructed at Crewe. It was an odd chance that it should carry *Great Western* lamp irons! The 1G with its fall plate was 'conventional' compared to the BR1 and BR1A; note gangway doors folded back with their rubber anti-draught flaps at the bottom. These could not have had an enduring life in footplate conditions.

Bottom. The BR1B with its reduced coal space (see the divider brought forward) as fitted to the Crostis and the NER air-braked 9Fs, such as 92098 here. That big 1B could be running behind a Duchess, from the look of it. However, by far the most intriguing aspect of this lovely portrait is the fact that one of Tyne Dock's finest is at Haymarket shed, Edinburgh. It was attended at Gateshead shops in 1957 and it may have been appropriated for a job into Scotland. Photograph J. Robertson, The Transport Treasury.

The BR1C tender which (for obvious reasons) characterised the LMR allocation. 92122 has just received its AWS in 1963 at Crewe and is thus in sparkling condition for a 9F at this late time. The AWS battery box under the cab is particularly well shown. And just look at those bright yellow Timken roller bearing tender axle boxes. The red stripe indicated to 'prep' crews that no lubrication was required. Top lamp iron lowered to right, centre buffer beam iron moved to right to correspond. Photograph J.G. Walmsley, The Transport Treasury.

whilst elsewhere, for long distance freight working where troughs are provided at frequent intervals, high coal capacity becomes the important factor.

As it turned out, the 9Fs got *five* different tender arrangements, all distinctive (as BR had indicated, in a way) of a given Region. The process started straight away and in the first batch of twenty 9Fs there were three different tender types. The aforesaid BR1G (externally just like the BR1 and BR1A of most of the Britannias) was married to the first ten, 92000-92007 for the Western Region and 92008 and 92009 for the LMR. The next five, 92010-92014, were for the Eastern Region. These were the first of the 7 ton 5,700 gallon flat-sided BR1F tenders. All the Eastern Region 9Fs got this distinctive flat-sided type with its largely straight top edge.

The last of the first batch of twenty, 92015-92019, were destined for the LMR. At 9 tons and 4,700 gallons, the BR1C fitted to these five looked very much like a Stanier tender, so we can see now how a tender type became more or less diagnostic of the owning Region.

The BR1B was a version of the BR1C in which the rear coal space plate was merely moved forward so that the coal capacity was reduced to 7 tons. It was put behind the Crostis (they were supposed to need less coal after all) and the ten 9Fs later produced for the North Eastern Region. These air pump-fitted NER ones (the Region only ever had this

ten) were for the specialised work on the Consett iron ore trains – they did not get water pick up gear, for the same reason. The fifth type, for the stoker engine-carrying Berkley mechanical stoker 9Fs 92165-92167, was the BR1K, at 9 tons and 4,300 gallons. Before tenders came to be switched around after a few years, the system was a fairly well-ordered one but it went awry in 1957. 92150, for instance, should have got BR1C 1360, but a new tender was required for 71000 DUKE OF GLOUCESTER and 1360 was the first available. 92150 got 71000's original BR1E 1271, modified to 1C with the same number. So, 92150 came out with tender 1C 1271. 71000's '9F' tender 1360 was renumbered BR1J 1528 and another tender was later numbered 1360 and fitted in turn to 92162. In the confusion, with delay to the Stoker fitted engines (originally to be five, 92163-67) 92168, which followed 92162 in the building sequence, somehow got BR1F 1377. This was an error; the last Stoker, 92167, emerged with BR1K 1377 in May 1958 and 92168's had to duly be replated 1374.

DOUBLE CHIMNEY

A number of 9Fs got double chimneys. As the 1950s wore on the coal supply problem that had played such a part in the decision to try out the Crosti boiler only grew worse and it is peculiar that BR largely turned its back on simple, inexpensive improvements to existing steam locomotives. As has been pointed out

innumerable times before, the work of S.O. Ell at Swindon was revealing just how many types were working below their maximum potential – often well below. A notable exception was the Britannia design but the same could not be said for some other BR Standards. When 92178 emerged from Swindon (without smoke deflectors!) in 1957 with a double chimney intended to give a freer exhaust and better draughting, subsequent controlled road tests between Reading and Stoke Gifford in January-February 1958 with passenger stock up to 650 tons (including the dynamometer car) showed a near 200 horsepower increase and a significant saving in coal. The possibilities if this sort of improvement had been extended across many more classes were considerable, but it never got going.

The 9Fs then under construction, from 92183 onwards, as well as stoker-fitted 92165-92167, completed out of sequence, all got the double blastpipe and chimney; the work with 92178 showed that the deflectors were still necessary with the double chimney and they were duly fitted at the end of the tests. The Western equipped a few more of its older 9Fs with the double chimney arrangement – 92000, 92001, 92002, 92005 and 92006 in 1960 – but with this the impetus faded. Neither the LMR or ER fitted any double chimneys on their 9Fs.

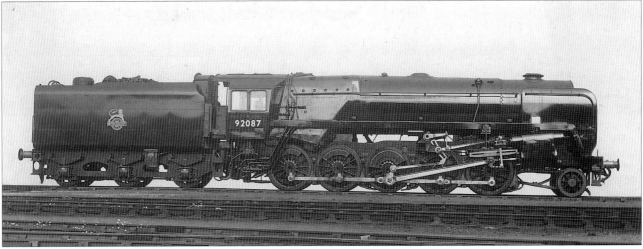

Top and above. The distinctive BR1F of the Eastern Region, first seen on 92010-92014. This was the first Swindon 9F, 92087 which ushered in Lot 421, going into traffic at the end of August 1956. Note there are six washout plugs in a line above the hand rail each side (on the left-hand, the rear-most is obscured by piping) but for efficient washing out, they are not opposite each other but off-set somewhat. By now the prominent four stud LM-style return crank is the standard provision. You might think the tender sides were a bit wobbly but it's just the perfect lighting. In anything like normal condition, with a coat of grime, the Swindon sides looked as flat and solid as any other. No AWS on this Swindon product, destined as it was for somewhere called Yorkshire. Note lightweight pony truck structure.

One of the Eastern Region BR1F 9F tenders, at Peterborough, bursting under Spital Bridge, by the look of it, heading north into the yards. Photograph B. Richardson, The Transport Treasury.

92031 with BR1F tender (note how the coal really *does* go unused and degraded towards the rear) in the spring of 1965. The train has just emerged from under bridge No.430, hauling a train of bogie bolster wagons. The 1 in 176 climb finished a short distance beyond bridge No.429, a farm accommodation crossing just visible at the top of the picture. The crew have the cab roof ventilator open. Photograph M. Kinder.

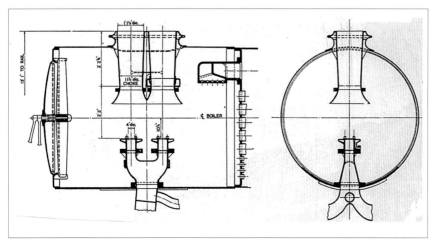

Above. The new double chimney arrangement, which proved so effective. Someone somewhere can doubtless calculate, or has indeed calculated, the coal savings over the years, say, from 1958-1968 for the 9Fs. Extend this across BR to suitable classes (the Crabs apparently were capable of particularly spectacular improvement) and it must add up literally to mountains of coal. Yet there was another side to things. The projected 'mountain' of coal saved assumes optimum conditions of maintenance, suitability of duties and coal supply. The figures for the improvement took some time to emerge but a 'coal saving' over the single chimney engines was reckoned at a good 5%. This was worthwhile, given (critically) the installation costs involved though hardly striking and could well decline out on the road. The type of work and the coal used would also decline, you could expect (even if the locomotives were maintained properly) and so the real saving might only be 2-3% which for a working steam locomotive was near enough beyond sensible measurement. It also needs to be realised that no amount of refinement to draughting saves on coal consumed lighting up and standing idle.

Below. Double chimney WR 9F, 92204 at Old Oak Common on 13 June 1962. It has the WR ATC, invariably invisible at the front and though there was no battery box and vacuum reservoir under the cab, the conduit under the running plate is the same. Photograph Peter Groom.

Double chimney 9Fs. *Top right*. 92233 is at Bath Green Park in company with an S&D 2-8-0, in July 1962. Photograph Norman Preedy. *Below right,* 92239 is at Banbury with 50A York plate on 7 June 1965 (see her in her pomp on page 246). Photograph Colin Stacey, Initial Photographics.

92000 at Swindon for rectification work on the regulator in the dome, 31 October 1954; note operating rod loose, dome cover removed. The 'spell of masterly inactivity' at Ebbw Junction, as *The Railway Observer* termed it, was now coming to an end with 92002 back in service and the others either on the way to Swindon, in the works or on their way back. There is a rare glimpse of the WR ATC – the oblong object beyond the sand pipe. Photograph A.R. Carpenter, The Transport Treasury.

INTO SERVICE

In Cox's writings on the Standards, there is the occasional wince at the reception they were afforded on the Western Region. He must therefore have cursed the hostage to fortune that saw the first eight 9Fs sent to the Western Region. Well, he would at least have had reservations. With only 92000-92005 at Ebbw Junction for iron ore trains and with 92006 and 92007 on their way, problems were found with the regulator throttle sticking open. Under some conditions of working, closing it could be almost impossible. In fact the 'start' for the class at Ebbw Junction in the unpromising conditions of South Wales could hardly have been less auspicious. Two of them, 92004 and 92005, collided in the shed yard, exposing a brake deficiency, too! Add to this the perceived strangeness of these locomotives, the lack of lookout (it was felt) over that huge boiler, an already-acquired animus to anything

'Standard' filtering down from experience with the Britannias and the understandably disliked left-hand drive, then it is not hard to imagine the telephone wires from points west and south beginning to glow...

By mid-July 1954 Ebbw Junction provided the humiliating spectacle of all its new 2-10-0s out of service, mainly in the shed yard with the chimneys sacked over. 92001 was inside the shed, minus its dome cover – the clue to what was going on – while 92002 was absent, stored elsewhere.

The regulator problem was solved by fitting a smaller sliding throttle in the dome. 92002 duly underwent some trial modifications and was put to work successfully on September working iron ore from Newport Docks in September 1954. It completed the job 'without untoward incident', *The Railway Observer* noted. The latest 9F, 92015, was then altered

accordingly and tested at Rugby; in October 1954 results were satisfactory and the modification was effected on the earlier engines as soon as was practicable, with the Ebbw ones sent to Swindon almost immediately; 92000, 92001, 92003 and 92006 certainly by November.

This left the braking problem. Tests with 92002 (the one subject to the regulator modifications) in July revealed that the brake cylinders took much longer to reach the required pressure when cold. The existing unlagged steam pipes feeding the cylinders were replaced by wider bore ones and then lagged, which solved the problem of the delay in effective braking making itself felt. With regulator throttle and brakes duly 'fixed' the WR 9Fs could take up their intended duties by the year's end, or thereabouts, and their 'spell of masterly inactivity' as *The Railway Observer* correspondent termed it, would be over.

Years of iron ore work behind it, 92000 rests inside its home shed Ebbw Junction in April 1961. It was to enjoy a summer away on the Somerset & Dorset that year, operating from Bath Green Park but it left South Wales for good in 1962, going to Old Oak Common. It remained at WR sheds until withdrawal more or less at the very end of steam power on the Region. Photograph Prorail UK (Durrant), The Transport Treasury.

While the WR put an immediate 'stop' on its 9Fs, there is nothing to indicate what the LM and the ER were doing with *their* 9Fs, at Wellingborough and March respectively and it is presumed that they merely operated normally.

In fact, there seems to have remained something of a shadow over the braking of the 9Fs. Atkins, for instance, refers to question marks raised by the Southern and the Eastern Region in 1955, over the braking capabilities of the BR Standards in general; they were considered inferior to Regional types. The operating people, and crews after a while, it must be assumed, just did what they had always done, matching each locomotive type to a job in the light of experience, making brake applications earlier, providing a 'head' of fitted wagons behind the engine or whatever. It was strange

that there were reservations about the braking of the 9Fs, given that superiority in this respect was an argument for the 2-10-0 arrangement over the 2-8-2 in the first place. By the end of that eventful year, 1954, the best part of forty 9Fs were in service.

In November 1954 92030, the first of many to arrive for the coal workings Yorkshire-London and the empties back, arrived at New England. After a few days, and in a sign of things to come, on 18 November it was coupled to a coal train for Ferme Park, to return the same day with seventy empties. With the earlier arrivals at Wellingborough, the classic pattern of 9F working – endless slogging coal trains up to London to feed its domestic hearths and power stations and back with incessant bouncing four wheelers – was set for the Midland main line and the GN. Unfortunately the very nature of the traffic made for low mileages. Engines and crews spent much of their time waiting in loops (or backed up on the permissive block in the case of the Midland) constrained by the various needs of the passenger traffic into and out of London. Actually that is an oversimplification, especially in the case of the ER 9Fs, where their speed and power saw them ousting V2s as well as WDs!

To make the 9F debut in South Wales even more inauspicious, 92004 and 92005 collided in the shed yard at Ebbw Junction which was probably the last straw so far as the WR people were concerned. In December 1954 92004 appears to have just arrived at Swindon in semi-dismantled state but still with the sacking over the chimney which it had borne in the months out of use at Ebbw Junction. 92005 (top) seems to have come off the worst in the clash and is undergoing suitable repairs inside the works. Photographs R. Wilson and Prorail (UK) Durrant, The Transport Treasury.

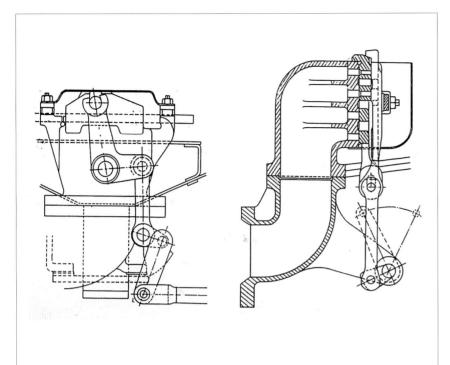

Left. original regulator valve arrangement (with horizontal grid). Right, its more conventional replacement, after the Ebbw Junction *contretemps*.

The up train consists of forty-five loaded wagons and leaves New England at 5.50am arriving at Hitchin at 7.40am; departing from here at 8.36, Ferme Park is reached by 10.10am. The return journey is covered in quicker time with sixty empty wagons. Departing from Ferme Park at 11.15am, Hitchin is passed at 12.50pm and New England is reached at 2.35pm. Braking tests are carried out on the up journey at Huntingdon, Tempsford and Wood Green, whilst for the five miles uphill between Hatfield and Potters Bar, sixteen minutes are allowed. On the down journey the 15½ miles between Huntingdon and Peterborough is timed to take twenty-six minutes. 92032/33 were in the first instance incorrectly allocated to March but this was quickly rectified, although 92032 did arrive at New England via March. 92033 arrived via Doncaster. It is understood that the engines are not popular with the crews at New England or March because they are said to be draughty and to have poor brakes. ['We have heard this view expressed on other Regions', the RO Honorary Editors commented at this point.] *On the very first test run the engine is reported to have overshot the appointed stopping place at Huntingdon by some 1,000 yards.*

92030 ran a number of trials (including braking) during November 1954 and these contributed somewhat to the ER's expressed doubts over 9F braking. An over-run of up to *a thousand yards* was encountered though this, and other alarming instances, may have been due to unfamiliarity with the new locos of course. Remember, a crew was just expected to climb up on a new engine and take it away. Whatever, it was certainly alarming, and masked wider concerns on the Regions. Consider the subsequent *Railway Observer* account of 92030's exploits: *The braking trials with Class 9F 2-10-0 92030 have continued each week (Monday to Friday) for at least the first three weeks of December.*

After Wellingborough new LM 9F 2-10-0s began to go to Toton and all were working to London very soon. There was a 'spectacular sight' (and it must have been spectacular) on 15

Summer Saturday on the Somerset & Dorset:1. 92001, just about to enter Chilcompton tunnel with the Pines Express, Sheffield-Bournemouth on 12 August 1961. Photograph Gavin Morrison.

Left. A new 9F at Swindon, Castle alongside. The threaded tap-like object is a boiler drain valve to which a 'cooling down' hose pipe was attached – where such practices were in force prior to washing out. Not all sheds used this method, so it was not universally present. Compare the shiny new WR 9F here with the standard state of a 9F in traffic, at Carnforth shed (right) in June 1967! Photographs George Heiron and A.W. Battson, The Transport Treasury.

Below. Summer Saturday on the Somerset & Dorset:2. 92006 exiting Chilcompton tunnel with the 7.43 Bradford Forster Square to Bournemouth West, 12 August 1961. Using 9Fs meant that much double heading could be dispensed with. P.W. Smith (*Mendips Enginemen*, OPC, 1972) fondly recalls the debut of the 'Nines' on the line and laments the fact that none of these 'incredible' locomotives was ever fitted with steam heating so that their benefits could be felt all year round. Photograph Gavin Morrison.

October when 92048 headed 48187 on down coal empties.

There were 160 or more 9Fs in service by 1957, nearly all engaged on the coal workings of the LM and ER (GN and GC and, to a lesser extent, the GE Sections). The years 1958 and 1959 saw all but a handful of the WR fleet delivered, and these took up similar duties, though they were perhaps found more on iron ore workings than those on other Regions, except of course the Tyne Dock ones. Yet the work was varied in nature and almost the only non-passenger work the 9Fs *didn't* do on an everyday basis would have been the humble pick-up. The 9Fs were set to tasks hitherto undreamed-of on their owning Regions. Hosts of 2-8-0s, from 28XX to O4s, were made to look pedestrian by comparison...

In 1957 came the startling realisation that the 9Fs were being used – deliberately so – on passenger workings... This remarkable turn of events seems to have come generally to pass in the summer of 1957. The

three main users – the LM, the ER and then the WR, discovered that they had a very useful tool indeed for those extra summer workings, jobs on which it would be unthinkable to employ any 2-8-0s. Nearly brand new 92137 and 92142 worked Sunday excursions out of St Pancras in August 1957 while earlier in the month 92048 worked a holiday train for the West Country from Leicester as far as Bristol. The holidays saw a flurry of East Midlands 9Fs at Blackpool (though Stanier 8Fs turned up too) and even one of Wellingborough's Crostis put in an appearance.

The 2-10-0s were turning up on empty stock duties at Euston, including Toton's 92130 on 18 June 1958. They worked up to London on the LNW on coal trains and 92130 was presumably nicked by Willesden. And if any reader can suggest a less likely role for 92078 in August than pilot at London's Broad Street terminus, it will be interesting to hear it! In the same period Leicester's

92164 was a regular on the 'Master Cutler' from Leicester to Sheffield. Timekeeping was said to be 'excellent'. July and August 1958 saw a positive flowering for 9Fs on GC passenger work, with any number of them on (mainly) Saturday expresses; 92164 worked both the up 'South Yorkshireman' and the down 'Master Cutler' on Monday 4 August. In late July the same engine managed sustained running at 70+ and 80+ mph. A long tradition also began, of 9Fs working trains from the Midlands to Bournemouth. In the same summer of 1958 9Fs were replacing Crabs and 4Fs traditionally used on the August bank holiday relief traffic. *The Railway Observer* reported no less than nine 9Fs on fourteen expresses in one weekend: 92050, 92051, 92086, 92102, 92121, 92122, 92123, 92130 and 92153.

The use of 9Fs on the Eastern Region for passenger work seems to have reached its apogee in the same August bank holiday of 1958. The 2-10-0s, the operators were

In service on the Midland main line, 92009 on the Down Goods passes southbound Cricklewood 8F 48163, being given a run on the Up Main, north of Ampthill tunnel in September 1955. The box in the distance is Millbrook. Pictures of the Cricklewood 8Fs in action are not that common, in fact; this one, on a 1 in 200 up grade and blowing off with a Class 'H' unfitted freight, is showing how it should be done, in no uncertain fashion. Photograph The Transport Treasury.

In service on the Great Northern main line, an unidentified 9F thundering north through Hadley Wood past a new DMU, 18 July 1959. A few years before, you'd have seen a V2 on this job, perhaps. You'd certainly never have seen the predecessors to the 9Fs (the WDs and, before them, the O2s) on a fast fitted freight. Photograph F.W. Goudie, The Transport Treasury.

On of the Ebbw Junction originals, 92005 ended up a York engine and could be found at times on the Great Central; here it is returning north from Woodford Halse with a Class 4 vans train on a glorious morning in September 1964. Photograph Mike Kinder.

discovering, were extremely useful machines to throw into the fray — though they'd have been no use at Christmas, lacking steam heat. They had become familiar on slow passenger trains but the spectacle of 92184 on the 1.52pm Kings Cross-Leeds and 92195 on the 3pm to Newcastle certainly turned heads. About this time 9Fs began to appear on Kings Cross-York parcels vans, while there were repeated reports of them on heroically loaded empty stock trains.

Over on the Western Region it was a similar story as the 9Fs' unexpected usefulness on summer Saturdays dawned. Once again it seems to have begun in 1957 with LM examples working in on holiday trains bound for the West Country but it took a while for the WR itself to cotton on to the 9Fs' unsuspected abilities. The summer of 1958 had passed before a 9F even got as far as Taunton but it must be remembered that apart from the small stud isolated in South Wales the Western only had 9Fs 'at large' from the early part of that year. The Western habitually used the big 47XX 2-8-0s on summer passenger work, as is well known, but it is less well appreciated that the 28XXs were pressed into service too — though usually timekeeping was fairly lamentable. You wouldn't use them if you didn't have to. So it was the

summer of 1959 before 9Fs really got to grips with passenger trains on the Western, notably 92224 from Newton Abbot (destination Swansea) and 92207 on a train from South Wales to Bournemouth. By July they were breasting Dainton with pilots in traditional style and on 4 July there was the astonishing spectacle of Canton's 92249 working an express for its home town out of Paddington. By August Old Oak Common 9Fs, released from their iron ore bondage at Ebbw Junction, were appearing at Snow Hill on passenger trains in the middle of the aptly named Industrial Holiday fortnight and numerous Midland line 2-10-0s were getting to Bristol and beyond on holiday reliefs to the West Country. Cox would surely have allowed himself a small smile of vindication.

It was in 1958 that Dr Tuplin reported *Ninety With a 'Nine'*, in the December issue of *The Railway Magazine*. The recent use of 'the space ships' he declared, was 'naturally a stop-gap procedure, tolerable when no more obviously suitable engine has been available' while noting that sprightly running of 80 mph and more was prompting questions as to why more imaginative use could not be made of them. It was the 'Master Cutler' which had provided the chance for 92164 (on loan from Leicester LM to Leicester

GC shed) to reach a maximum of 86 mph on the GC while 92184 attained 90 mph on the GN. With much detailed reasoning, utilising fearsome equations, Tuplin warned in essence that while there was nothing 'supernatural' about a 9F reaching such speeds (it was all there in the arithmetic) it could only come at the cost of reduced efficiency, an increased risk of running hot and the certainty of greatly increased wear and tear. Using engines that were not in good condition would exacerbate all these negative consequences.

Early in 1959, alarmed at wear and tear in piston and valve rings and the prospect of worse wear and damage should a thoroughly run-down 9F be urged to such dizzying heights under an enthusiastic driver (they rode so well, after all) the LMR produced an edict that conformed with Tuplin's strictures completely, that they should only be used in emergency. The Regional structure of BR still ensured much independence of action and the decision about using the 9Fs on passenger work remained that, a Regional one, though the ER seems to have more or less followed the LM's cautious approach. On the Western, however, which had got the 'space ships' in enough numbers for general use quite a bit later than the LM and ER, it seems to have been a case of making up for lost time.

9Fs at Newton. Two and a half miles north of Rugby the Great Central ran in cuttings near the village and was spanned over a few hundred yards by four graceful overbridges – now it's a footpath and the M6 crosses the track bed beyond the farm bridge… Two 9Fs, 92094 and 92095 approach with an up freight on 9 May 1964; double heading was unusual on the GC main line and this instance is probably explained by getting one of them back home while saving a path. Photograph M. Mitchell.

On Wednesday 24 June 1959 Hall 7916 MOBBERLEY HALL piloted 92006, now of Canton, into Newton Abbot on a Plymouth to Paddington parcels. With 92208, 92209 and 92221-92225 based at Laira by 1959 it was inevitable that they would turn up on passenger work; on 20 June (a Saturday) 92224 duly hauled the 10.20am Penzance-Swansea, on Saturday 27 June 92225 was on the 5.35pm Kingswear-Exeter local and on 3 July (a Friday) 92209 had the 7.55am (MFO) Camborne-Bristol. Throughout the summer the WR was using its 'space ships' on summer Saturday duties, including Plymouth-Paddington; on Saturday 8 August 92206 was on the up 'Mayflower' at Newton Abbot, 92222 had charge of the 10.05 Penzance-Manchester (through working Plymouth-Shrewsbury), 92221 had the 12.05pm Paddington-Plymouth and 92230 was on the 1.25pm Paddington to Kingswear.

The Western, it seems, issued no banishment order for its 9Fs, continuing to use them on passenger work – Old Oak's 92241 on Saturday 6 August 1960, for instance, with the 10.40am Minehead to Paddington, from Taunton onwards. When EVENING STAR went brand new to Canton (such a successful home to the Britannia Pacifics) in 1960 it was afterwards to be found on London expresses, including 'The Red Dragon'.

With diesels coming in, it might have been expected that a high point for 9Fs on regular summer work had been reached. Except… From that summer of 1960, the 2-10-0s were found regularly working the summer passenger trains on the Somerset & Dorset. Tests with 92204 on 29 March 1960 were successful, the 9F running from Bath to Bournemouth and back with eleven coaches. *The Railway Observer* recorded a local observation that the start up the 1 in 80 from Blandford was 'like an engine and brake'. The first 'fleet', in 1960, was made up of 92203-92206, all on loan from St Philip's Marsh and fitted for the season with tablet exchange apparatus. So, for three summers, 1960-1962, Bath Green Park shed got a complement of 9Fs drafted in. The S&D, *The Railway Observer* commented in 1960, 'must be the only

line in the country where engines of this class regularly work passenger trains'.

We of course tend to concentrate overmuch on the passenger workings of the 9Fs. They were startling and linger in the mind and, perhaps more tellingly, they are recorded in some considerable detail. No one was much bothered to note yet another 9F on yet another freight or mineral train. But goods and minerals remained of course the very stuff, the bread and butter of 9F working, which has gone largely unsung. Wherever the work was heaviest and most gruelling, there they would be. They were classically associated with coal and iron ore, steel and oil. Consett is the name that immediately springs to mind but they served most of the iron and steel works in England and Wales. They were concentrated at certain sheds (Ebbw Junction has already figured prominently in these notes) for iron ore, both imported from the coast and from ore fields when we still dug the stuff ourselves. The sheds which had 9Fs can almost be used to plot a simple geography of a Britain that was once heavily industrialised. Even those at sheds not obviously local to iron and steel centres were often involved in the traffic – Doncaster and Banbury for instance.

In a sense, the 9Fs were not really exploited to the maximum extent. They were capable of a prolonged horsepower output far beyond the strength of the mightiest Fireman – beyond even a pair of them maybe, though in truth anything much beyond a Class 4, working flat out, would run away from even the most *Stakhanovite* Fireman. Tests at Rugby showed more than 2,000 indicated horse power at 60 mph and nearly 1,800 i.h.p. at 30-40 mph. These figures were exceeded in many instances out on the road; Reed in his *Profile* for instance declares an indicated horse power approaching 2,900 'being probable' for short distances.

Bulletin No.13 was issued by BR long after Rugby Plant and road tests, in July 1959. Two 9Fs were tested on the Stationary Plant and out on the line with the dynamometer car in 1954 and 1955 while a third underwent limited tests on the Plant. The *Bulletin* succinctly put what we all knew in its concluding paragraph: *The locomotives have proved in service that they are suitable not only for the heavy freight duties originally envisaged but also for working fast fitted freight trains.*

The intractable nature of the traffic put limitations on the use to which the 9Fs could be put. Early dreams of modern bogie wagons, mechanically loaded at the pithead and running fast with continuous brakes, to be again mechanically unloaded at their destination, soon faded. Much of BR's coal traffic continued to operate as a travelling storage facility for the NCB and its many coal merchant customers. It was all very well having a powerful, modern, efficient locomotive that could handle prodigious loads at speed but if these engines spent half their time blowing off in loops and sidings out in the wilds of distant Bedfordshire (in the case of both the GN and the Midland) and beyond then the full 'added value' of the 9Fs would never be got. To the end of steam on these jobs, for instance, the coal ran in the essentially Victorian four wheel box. The point is, an expensive modern 9F which spent the same portion of its time stuck in goods loops as its 4F predecessor was a thing trammelled.

The 9Fs could haul more, faster, than their predecessors but on Britain's railways, in the 1950s it was difficult to realise the advantages. All this meant that annual mileages were low. The 2-10-0s were certainly capable of mileages some way beyond earlier generations of motive power but it was not possible to radically re-cast the nature of their everyday work.

Given their speed, an attribute which at one time was regarded as unnecessary and unlikely anyway, the longer distance fitted freights, such as Saltley's heroic Water Orton-Carlisle trains might have seen the mileages rise. The use of 9Fs on V2 diagrams on the Eastern raised the mileage figures there but by and large new 9Fs went on to the existing coal trains or iron ore trains of a Region. They were a considerable boon for, within the existing pattern of workings they were faster, more reliable and took heavier loads. But the intrinsic nature of the work meant that, in a given day, only relatively short distances were encountered. On innumerable jobs, new 9Fs still worked jobs that had evolved with 0-6-0s. A turn would be worked in time-honoured fashion, the engine coming off and going to shed after forty miles or whatever while another came on and continued the working. The 9F, which could happily have blasted away on the job all day, then sat on shed before ambling back at the designated time.

Regional types could show up better in terms of mileage, if not availability. Take the WR. The eight

The LNW's 'ghost train', a special block train of vacuum braked bogie wagons which fed coal to the railways' own power station at Stonebridge Park, pre-figuring the later MGR trains. 92115 is heading north with the empties through Headstone Lane in the late 1950s. Ideally this was how mineral working should have been, and offered the only hope to make it profitable; fast high capacity trains with mechanised loading/unloading. The sheer scale and thereby the ruinous expense of converting BR's vast domestic coal operations all the way down to the level of the local coal merchant meant it could never be much more than a hope and an aspiration. **Photograph John Wiseman.**

9Fs engaged on short run iron ore trains did less than half the annual mileage of the home - grown 28XX 2-8-0s but these were taking coal trains from South Wales to London, Shrewsbury, the North West and so on. By the late 1950s when there were many more 2-10-0s and they had more of this 'general' traffic (Banbury, especially, had a rewarding traffic flow in this sense) the 9Fs eclipsed the still numerically far superior 28XXs. Yet the coal and iron ore, slow and ponderous, was there, so that's what the 9Fs did.

On the Eastern, with longer runs, mileages were higher (approaching 30,000 a year) from the first while the LMR was not far behind. If the early designs of BR had come even part way to fruition, very much more of the coal traffic would have been mechanised, the London congestion eased and locomotives would manage much higher daily mileages. The LM's 'ghost train' of bogie hoppers, feeding the bunkers of the Stonebridge Park power station, which in turn fed the Watford electric lines in an intensive 'merry go road' fashion, was the way in which BR would have preferred to deliver all its coal and would have allowed much higher mileages. The highest annual mileage seems to have been 92087's 48,467, for it had the advantage of the intensive GC freight service – the celebrated 'runners'. Over the whole system as the great part of the fleet came into service the average annual mileages rarely rose above about 35,000.

Given the right circumstances it was possible, if not to revolutionise traffic, then to markedly improve its working. Built at least in part with a fast freight artery in mind, the Great Central presented a chance for the operators to do something with freight after the fashion of the Liverpool Street-Norwich passenger service, re-cast and transformed by the coming of the Britannias. The 'windcutters' or 'runners' of various trains but mainly coal, saw accelerated schedules, 50mph loose coupled between Annesley and Woodford. There was strict adherence to the schedules, aided by the high availability of the 9Fs and the relative paucity of passenger working. This saw mileages rise well above those elsewhere. Atkins has calculated

Where the tablet exchange apparatus was fitted to a 9F on the S&D it was mounted on the leading end of the tender on the left-hand side. The arm itself wasn't always visible but the mounting bracket was – to avoid fouling the loading gauge the arm was placed in position only when about to be used. Witness 92006 on 9 September 1961, leaving Bath Green Park with the 7.43am (SO) Bradford-Bournemouth West.

that the two return trips a day from Annesley to Woodford with a third one at least got underway within 24 hours promised an annual mileage of up to 70,000 though 92087's 48,000-plus, mentioned above, seems to have been the best actually achieved.

Availability of well above 80% has been claimed for the 9Fs and this indeed would have made 70,000 miles per annum a possibility. But like mileage, availability can be a slippery concept... It might be quoted, for instance, minus time in, or awaiting works! Main line diesels rarely consistently achieved more than 80%, allowing for all contingencies, and in later days the Brush Type 4s, over 500 of them, only managed to average around 75%. Of course being available, and actually being used, are two different issues. A locomotive travelling to shed to turn and water before the next turn was 'available'. Locomotives were very often used, in effect, as expensive taxis to get the men to and from their booking on/off points – a practice continued with the diesels. The awkward fact remained that quite a few diagrams were inherently low when it came to productivity.

Typical late scene; filthy, knocked about and chalked numbers/shed codes. Crosti conversion 92024 (its Card shows it at 12A Kingmoor by this time, though the 8H Birkenhead plate might have been pinched) stands next to Birkenhead's 92101 at Leeds Holbeck on 23 June 1967.

Quite a picture! At Cricklewood shed on 28 April 1956 we have 92065, destined for air pumps and transfer to Tyne Dock, alongside one of the Crostis, 92027. The need to modify the Crostis, of course, was why the Tyne Dock engines were operating conventionally on the Midland, standing in at Wellingborough while the Crostis underwent modification. Toton had 92065 for a while before the NER finally prised it from the LMR's grasp, hence the 18A shed plate. Photograph Hugh Ramsey, Initial Photographics.

The last year or two of iron ore working is played out in the North East, as one of Tyne Dock air pump 9Fs comes into Consett at Carrhouse West, by the steelworks. British Steel Corporation tracks glint in the light in the foreground, September 1964. Photograph M. Dunnett.

The Official View, 92000 at Crewe with the obligatory whited-out background. Considerations of a 'political' nature came into play when the distribution of all the BR Standards was determined. Each class, whether large or small, was usually allocated over several Regions which, for various reasons, could not help but 'blunt' the impact of the new engines.

THE RECORD

For obvious reasons, the works histories of the 9Fs, as derived from the Engine History Cards, are not as thoroughly complete as some classes. For a start some began going to the happy hunting ground when only six years old (EVENING STAR was just 'five' at withdrawal). This was only the black nadir of a chaotic, crazy business, one moreover that was to be repeated in some of its grisly elements with the 'new' diesels a decade later. The trouble is that many of them had not even had a General before the collapse in record keeping that came with the early 1960s. But with delving at the National Railway Museum Library and the Public Record Office a useful picture has emerged, one that will pass muster, I'm sure, with other Irwell Press locomotive volumes. For the record, the original material at the National Archives (PRO) were the BR 9215 Record Cards and BR9637 Forms and at the NRM York the 'ERO 3666' Engine History Cards.

Health warnings are always necessary; it must be borne in mind that the Engine History Cards tell a story – a fascinating one – but not a cast-iron gold-plated one of the sort of accuracy that sparks anxious debate in some circles. Works habitually 'fiddled' odd days at either end of an engine's visit, for accounting reasons and in truth it is daft to quote mileages down to the odd mile for some of it, on some jobs, was nominal and some of it (when sheds pinched other shed's engines for instance) simply went unrecorded. As I think we've said before, the way mileage was calculated could be somewhat *laissaiz-faire,* and ex-railwaymen usually have a laugh when exact figures are quoted to within a mile! They could be up to 20% out at least, and almost always on the low side. For example, when engines were used on ballast jobs, a standard mileage was entered irrespective of what they actually did and how far they went. The point is, however, that the Engine History Cards *tell a story over time* and (this is the secret) *can be compared like for like.* Happy engine picking.

Mileage figures are generally 'since previous General or intermediate repair'.

The later entries for 'Works' also include dates, where available, derived from *The Railway Observer.* Withdrawal, storage and scrapping information is taken from P.B. Hands series *What Happened to Steam.* First boiler and first tender information taken from *The British Railways Standard 9F 2-10-0* by Philip Atkins published by Irwell Press 1993. All shed allocations and reallocation dates are 'period ending'.

By the time the 9Fs made works visits the overhaul codes seemed more or less common to all Regions; the following is what evolved:

GO   General Overhaul*
HI   Heavy Intermediate
HC   Heavy Casual
LI   Light Intermediate
LC   Light Casual**
NC   Non Classified
ADJ   Adjustment***
RECT   see ADJ

> **PRODUCTION SNAPSHOT 1954**
> **From The Railway Observer**
> At Crewe on 24th January new 2-10-0s were completed to 92004, which was painted, whilst 92005 was complete outside No.9 Shop, 92006, 92007 and 92008 were well advanced with boilers on, 92009, 92010 and 92011 were laid down and frames set up for 92012 and 92013 in the Heavy Machine Shop. 92000-92003 were still working from Crewe, presumably running in, the first engine having left the works on 7th January. The Order No. is 487 and they have tender type BR1G Nos.949/953 onwards.

Possibly the earliest working view of 92000, still clean before delivery to the Western Region, in the period when it was 'temporarily retained by the LMR'. This was doubtless a trial period intended to reveal teething difficulties, something which, in the event, was only manifest once the engines got to South Wales.

EO 'Engine Order'#
CB 'Change of Boiler'
(**UNSCHED** as in the case of 92006, for instance, must mean 'unsheduled', and might mean anything
*equivalent to Heavy General
**usually a response to some damage or unlooked-for defect
*** 'Adjustment' seems to have been analogous to the LMR **RECT** which simply meant 'rectification'. Both typically took place a day or two after a major repair – that is, tightening up bits that had come loose and loosening bits that were too tight. If the part was difficult to get at the task might range as far as opening up a piece of boiler cladding. This would not warrant taking the engine inside if the weather was fine and the job would be done in the Works yard. #'Engine Order', under which some jobs seem to have been ordered out of the normal run of things.

PRODUCTION SNAPSHOT 1956
From The Railway Observer
On 8th July, new construction of 2-10-0s at Crewe was: 92099 (Tender Type BR1G – 1309) in the Paint Shop, work commenced on 92100-92104 in the Erecting Shop, frames and cylinders for 92105-92107 in No.9 Shop, and those for 92108 and 92109 together with the frames for 92110 and 92111 in the Heavy Machine Shop.

PRODUCTION SNAPSHOT 1957
From The Railway Observer
On 20th March 92128 was ready for painting at Crewe. Inside No.10 Shop were 92129 (boiler on), 92130 and 92131 (wheeled) and 92132 and 92133 (frames, motion and cylinders). No.92134 (frames and cylinders in No.9 Shop) is the last of order 493 for 38 engines. In the Heavy Machine Shop work is well in hand on the first engines of order 494 (43 2-10-0s, 92135-92177) but production is being retarded by shortage of materials. Crostis 92024, 92027 and 92029 were having their preheaters retubed and new blast chambers and chimneys fitted, 92023 was in for a casual (collison damage).

PRODUCTION SNAPSHOT 1958
From The Railway Observer
Swindon. On 28th September, D801 VANGUARD was complete, D802 almost finished and D803-D806 in progress. 92198 was completed and painted; 92199 (frames, cylinders, wheels and motion) and 92200 and 92201 (frames set up were under construction).

PRODUCTION SNAPSHOT 1956
From The Railway Observer
On the occasion of the London Branch visit to Swindon on 12th August, new construction in 'A' Shop consisted of 92089 (frames, motion and cylinders) and 92090 and 92091 (frames and cylinders).

PRODUCTION SNAPSHOT 1957
From The Railway Observer
On 3rd November new construction at Swindon included 92178 (double chimney) on steaming trials, 92180 (single chimney) outside complete, 92181 boiler on, 92182 frames and cylinders.

PRODUCTION SNAPSHOT 1958
From The Railway Observer
Crewe. On 9th November steam construction was drawing rapidly to a close. 92246 was in the Paint Shop (tender BR1G 1557), 92247 complete outside the Erecting Shop, 92248 almost complete, 92249 had its boiler mounted and the frames and cylinders of 92250 were in the Erecting Shop.

Below. 92001 in the Crewe Paint Shop yard. Original single chimney, three sand fillers on this starboard side. Photograph B.K.B. Green, Initial Photographics.

Bottom right. A rather grimier 92001, now with double chimney, at its home shed, Ebbw Junction outside Newport about 1961. It was the small differences, as much as anything else, that led WR crews to set their faces a'gin the Standards. One feature would have been the 'missing lamp irons' – the (G)WR engines had a row of irons on the right-hand running plate for 'spare' lamps but on the 9Fs, or any other Standards, there was none. Lamps instead were stowed on the tender front. The engine has been left in full forward gear – not good; WR ATC brake valve on vacuum ejector at join of smokebox and boiler. Photograph J. Davenport, Initial Photographics.

92000

To traffic 5/1/54

Works
20/10/54-5/11/54**U**	Swindon
3/5/56-10/5/56**U**	Swindon
1/8/56-8/8/56**U**	Swindon
10/10/56-18/12/56**LC**	Swindon
11/8/59-3/60**GO**	Swindon
12/62	Gorton

Tenders
BR1G no.949 from new
BR1G no.1513 from 92206

Boiler
no.1128 from new

Sheds
Ebbw Jct 30/1/54
Bath Green Park 17/6/61
Banbury 7/10/61
Old Oak Common 24/3/62
Tyseley 14/7/62
Bristol Barrow Road 15/12/62
Gloucester Horton Road 7/3/65

Condemned 2/7/65, stored at 85B Gloucester Horton Road 7-10/65, cut up at Birds, Long Marston 11/65.

92001

To traffic 12/1/54

Works
28/9/57-14/10/57**LC**	Swindon
28/9/59-20/4/60**HI**	Swindon
17/2/61-10/3/61**LC**	Caerphilly
27/5-28/8/64**HI[CB]**	Crewe
3/5/65-4/6/65**LC**	Crewe Attention to boiler

Annual mileage
1960 16,929
1961 23,308
1963 11,302
Mileage at 30/12/62 131,671

Sheds
Ebbw Jct. 30/1/54
Bath Green Park 17/6/61
Cardiff Canton 4/11/61
Bath Green Park 14/7/62
Oxford 6/10/62
Tyseley 17/11/62
Wakefield 5/11/66

Tender
BR1G no.950 from new

Boiler
no.1129 from new

Condemned 17/1/67, stored at 56A Wakefield 1-4/67, cut up at Cox and Danks, Wadsley Bridge 5/67.

92002

To traffic 16/1/54

Works
25/1/57-21/5/57**LC**   Swindon
11/11/58-20/1/59**LC**   Swindon
20/7/60-1/12/60**GO**   Swindon
2/62   Darlington
13/9/63-23/10/63**HC**   Crewe
25/3/64-14/5/64**C**   Crewe

Annual mileage
1960 4,567
1961 21,493
1963 8,162
Mileage at 7/7/62 118,989

Sheds
Ebbw Jct. 30/1/54
Tyseley 4/5/63
Banbury 18/7/64
Tyseley 7/11/64
Saltley 12/11/66
Birkenhead 3/12/66

Tender
BR1G no.951 from new

Boilers
no.1130 from new
no.1947 1/12/60

Condemned 11/11/67, stored at 8C Speke Jct. 11/67-3/68, cut up at Campbells, Airdrie 4/68.

92003

To traffic 25/1/54

Works
29/10/54-16/11/54**LC**   Swindon
14/5/57-31/7/57**LC**   Swindon
11/58*   Swindon
7/10/59-31/10/59**U**   Ebbw Jct.
7/9/60-10/1/61**GO**   Swindon
25/6/62-6/7/62**LC**   Caerphilly
11/63   Swindon
*minor collision damage

Annual mileage
1963 16,789
Mileage at 31/12/62 129,893

Sheds
Ebbw Jct. 30/1/54
Cardiff Canton 1/11/58
Cardiff East Dock 8/9/62

Tender
BR1G no.952 from new

Boilers
no.1131 from new
no.1946 10/1/61

Condemned 26/3/65, stored at 88A Cardiff East Dock 3-6/65, cut up at Cashmores, Newport 7/65.

Below. 92001 climbing towards Devonshire Tunnel with the 7.40 (SO) Bradford-Bournemouth, 14 July 1962. Photograph Ivo Peters, courtesy Julian Peters.

Double chimney 92002 at where else but Ebbw Junction. It was in a sense asking for trouble, with the furore over the Britannias yet to fade, to send the first ten (actually the first eight, which made even less sense) to the Western Region, where the new engines, subject to suspicion from the first (they were driven from the 'wrong' side after all) were a mere drop amid a sea of the Region's very own 2-8-0s and eight-coupled tanks. Photograph J. Davenport, Initial Photographics.

92002 awaiting brake testing at Swindon in May 1954, following the unfortunate collision at Ebbw Junction. Photograph Hugh Ballantyne.

92003 at the time of the 'Paint Shop Presentation'. The logical step of course was to allocate the first thirty or so to the LM, preferably as close to Crewe as possible. Perhaps the natural, understandable urge was to put them on something eye-catchingly formidable; the Ebbw Vale workings were certainly that.

Minor collision damage on 92003, at Swindon shed at the end of 1958, awaiting attention in the nearby works.

92004

To traffic 30/1/54

Works

3/11/54-17/1/55**U**	Swindon
16/3/55-25/3/55**U**	Swindon
30/10/56-18/2/57**HC**	Swindon
11/10/57-25/10/57**LC***	Caerphilly
18/3/59-7/9/59**HI**	Swindon
3/1/62-27/1/62**LC**	Eastleigh 'cylinders re-bored, right linered up'
5/11/64-23/12/64**C**	Crewe
10-11/66	Crewe

*minor collision damage

Annual mileage
1960 25,128
1961 15,129
1963 16,789
Mileage at 7/7/62 129,893

Sheds
Ebbw Jct. 30/1/54
Cardiff Canton 3/10/59
Southall 27/2/60
Old Oak Common 5/11/60
Bristol Barrow Road 28/1/61
Banbury 30/3/63
Carlisle Kingmoor 9/10/66
Carnforth 27/1/68

Tender
BR1G no.953 from new

Boiler
no.1132 from new

Condemned 23/3/68, stored at 10A Carnforth 3-6/68, cut up at Cashmores, Newport 7/68.

92005

To traffic 5/2/54

Works

24/7/57-14/10/57**LC**	Swindon
11/59	Bromsgrove*
15/12/59-20/5/60**HI**	Swindon
9/65	Crewe

*are no suggestions as to what this might indicate!

Sheds
Ebbw Jct. 11/2/54
Cardiff Canton 1/11/58
Ebbw Jct. 20/5/61
York 8/9/63

Tender
BR1G no.954 from new

Boiler
no.1133 from new

Condemned 30/8/65 [Condemned on shed at 5B Crewe South LMR], stored at 5B Crewe South 10-11/65, cut up at Wards, Beighton, Sheffield 12/65.

Below. 92004 at the end of its life, at Carnforth in 1968 and almost certainly already condemned. 'Long live steam' on the smoke deflectors, 'The Flying Scotsman' on the smokebox door, numberplate pinched or removed for safekeeping, shed plate hacked off leaving part of it in place, 10A daubed on the smokebox door and connecting rod gone, odd but common dent in smokebox deflector hand rail. Note curious hybrid collection of lamp irons and compare, say, with 92005 next. Photograph J. Davenport, Initial Photographics.

Another of the original Western 9Fs to find their way to the outer reaches of BR by the middle 1960s. Double chimney 92005 is at Woodford Halse on 25 August 1964, sporting the same distorted deflector hand rail as others of its fellows about this time. It is a York engine by now, though it has yet to get the 50A plate. Still with WR lamp irons at the front. The second tender emblem lurks beneath that grime. Photograph Peter Groom.

92005 passing Barnwood Junction and the ex-MR shed, Gloucester, 7 July 1962. STAR chalked, somewhat uninspiringly, on smoke deflector. Photograph Norman Preedy.

92006

To traffic 10/2/54

Works

9/11/57-13/12/57**LC**	Swindon
23/2/60-21/9/60**GO**	Swindon
	Double chimney
11/9/64-23/1/65**UNSCHED**	Crewe
6/8/65-2/10/65**INTER**	Crewe

Sheds
Ebbw Jct. 27/2/54
Bath Green Park 15/7/61
Ebbw Jct. 7/10/61
York 8/9/63
Wakefield 4/11/66

Tender
BR1G no.955 from new

Boilers
no.1134 from new
no.1908 21/9/60

Condemned 10/4/67, stored at 56A Wakefield 4-10/67, cut up at Drapers, Hull 11/67.

92007

To traffic 18/2/54

Works

31/12/56-12/4/57**LC**	Swindon
4/5/59-8/10/59**HI**	Swindon

Sheds
Ebbw Jct. 27/2/54
Bristol Barrow Road 31/12/60
Gloucester Horton Road 7/3/65
Cardiff East Dock 11/7/65
Severn Tunnel Jct. 8/8/65
Gloucester Horton Road 7/11/65

Tender
BR1G no.956 from new

Boiler
no.1135 from new

Condemned 31/12/65, stored at 85B Gloucester Horton Road 12/65-1/66, cut up at Cashmores, Newport 2/66.

92008

To traffic 1/3/54

Works

8/3/54-15/3/54**NC (Rect)**	Crewe 81
1/6/54-17/6/54**NC[Mod]**	Crewe 4,731
23/8/54-1/9/54**LC**	Crewe 10,026 Frames
12/11/57-6/12/57**LI**	Crewe 92,907 R5900 provision of safety links
11/10/60-5/11/60**GO**	Crewe
10/10/63-15/11/63**LC**	Crewe
14/2/64-13/3/64**LC**	Crewe
9/10/64-27/11/64**LC**	Crewe
13/5/65-27/5/65**LC**	Crewe

Annual mileage
1954 18,977
1955 25,226
1956 19,872
1957 31,187
1958 28,698
1959 35,419
1960 20,014

Sheds
Wellingborough 27/3/54
Saltley 13/6/57
Rowsley 16/11/59
Toton 27/1/62
Rowsley 27/2/62
Saltley 23/6/62
Rowsley 11/7/63
Kirkby-in-Ashfield 2/5/64
Speke Jct. 19/11/64
Warrington Dallam 12/8/67

Tenders
BR1G No.957 from new
BR1F No.1160 at Annesley 5/9/64 from 92095

Boilers
no.1136 from new
no.1908 5/11/60

Condemned 5/10/67, stored at 8C Speke Jct. 10/67-6/68, cut up at Buttigiegs, Newport 8/68.

92006 in fine fettle, at Swindon works at an unknown date; it would seem to be September 1960, when it got its double chimney. Photograph J. Davenport, Initial Photographics.

92006 out on the road on the Somerset & Dorset, at Masbury, in the summer of 1961, with Bath Green Park 82F shed plate. The mounting bracket for the tablet exchange arm is visible behind the base of the hand rail at the tender front. Photograph Prorail UK (Durrant), The Transport Treasury.

92008 fresh out of the Paint Shop at Crewe, 14 March 1954. Diverted from the WR's allocation, along with 92009, it carries the WR ATC conduit along the base of the running plate, though whether the detector shoe and so on was fitted is not known. The answer is probably yes it has, for the WR ATC brake valve is in place on the vacuum ejector. Note the dual purpose lamp irons fitted for 92008's unexpected diversion to the LMR. Did this mean it was expected to proceed to the WR in due course? (It never did.) Photograph B.K.B. Green, The Transport Treasury.

92008, new, in Willesden roundhouse on 20 June 1954, the beret-clad fitter intent on what is going on below. A fitter, fireman or steamraiser, he is putting on one of the live steam injectors. He had to open the water control valve using a handle in the cab, then open the steam valve alongside until it 'picked up' – that is, the flow of water ceased and the injector 'sang'. Photograph A.R. Carpenter, The Transport Treasury.

Above. 92008 at home in the new modern shed at 16E Kirkby in Ashfield. Only latterly, when it had begun not to matter, were allocations of these wonderful modern engines concentrated at particular sheds and in particular coal fields, where their power and reliability could be utilised to the maximum.

Below. 92009 on passenger work, coming into Leeds City (41267 on right) at an unknown date. It can be assumed that it is summer – 1958 at a guess. Photograph The Transport Treasury.

92009

To traffic 12/3/54

Works

12/5/54-28/5/54**NC**	Crewe 3,802
25/1/55-1/2/55 **NC[EO]**	Derby 18,827 Brake fitting
25/7/55-12/8/55**NC**	Crewe 35,588 Boiler
1/5/57-5/6/57**LI**	Crewe 75,696 R5900 provision of safety links
13/3/59-16/4/59**GO**	Crewe 56,166
30/1/61-10/3/61**HC**	Crewe 58,146
19/2/63-16/3/63**LC**	Crewe
18/7/63-24/8/63**LC**	Crewe
5/3/65-3/4/65**HI**	Crewe Boiler overhaul
6/4/66-21/5/66**HC**	Crewe Boiler change

Annual mileage
1954 20,703
1955 23,512
1956 23,428
1957 26,891
1958 31,630
1959 37,462
1960 25,918

Sheds
Wellingborough 27/3/54
Saltley 13/6/57
Burton 11/9/57
Saltley 2/3/58
Annesley 26/10/58
Saltley 19/11/58
Rowsley 16/11/59
Saltley 23/6/62
Westhouses 2/7/62
Rowsley 7/10/63
Kettering 2/5/64
Carlisle Kingmoor 14/6/64
Carnforth 27/1/68

Tenders
BR1G no.958 from new
BR1C no.1168 from 92079 19/5/56

Boilers
no.1137 from new
no.1901 16/4/59

Condemned 23/3/68, stored at 10A Carnforth 3-6/68, cut up at Cashmores Newport 7/68.

92009, the second one diverted to the LMR, with WR ATC conduit and the dual purpose lamp irons, at Cricklewood off a coal working, 8 May 1955. Photograph A.W. Battson, The Transport Treasury.

92009 still on the Midland somewhere but now working from Rowsley (17C) shed. Observe how the LM lamps fit, the WR 'side' irons going unused. The engine now has a BR1C tender; it got this from the Lickey Banker in mid-1956, a few years before going to Rowsley. Half a dozen 9Fs came to Rowsley from Saltley in 1959, with six BR Standard Class 5s, coincidentally, coming from Derby at the same time. The 9Fs increased to fourteen by the time of the shed's closure in 1964 and they worked widely, from Liverpool and Birmingham jobs to banking turns, depending on the traffic conditions and the motive power available. They also strayed on to the 'Londons' which were BR Class 5 diagrams. Photograph Peter Coster.

92010

To traffic 13/5/54

Shops
5/10/54-2/12/54**LC**	Crewe 9,301
8/57	Briquette tube feeder
11/6/58-17/7/58**LI**	Crewe 90,583
25/3/59-10/4/59 **LC[EO]**	Rugby 33,111
11/3/61-5/5/61**GO**	Crewe 112,714
5/63	Crewe
Mileage at 31/12/57 80,677	

Annual mileage
1958 31,482
1959 40,622
1960 43,309

Sheds
March 22/5/54
Annesley 27/1/57
Wellingborough 9/3/63
Leicester Midland 22/6/63
Newton Heath 2/5/64
Carlisle Kingmoor 27/6/64

Tenders
BR1F no.959 from new
BR1F no.1163 from 92074 7/5/58
BR1F no.962 17/3/61

Boilers
no.1138 from new
no.1424 5/5/61

Condemned 2/4/66, stored at 12A Kingmoor 4-5/66, cut up at Arnott Young, Carmyle 6/66.

92011

To traffic 19/5/54

Works
10/9/57-9/11/57**GO**	Darlington 75,818
	Briquette tube feeder
14/10/58-16/12/58**LC[EO]**	Crewe 37,108
15/12/59-29/1/60**LC[EO]**	Crewe 75,423
7/65	Crewe
Mileage at 31/12/57 93,383	

Annual mileage
1958 32,903
1959 36,611
1960 33,742

Sheds
March 22/5/54
New England 25/9/55
Annesley 19/5/57
Birkenhead 7/8/65

Tender
BR1F no.960 from new

Boiler
no.1139 from new

Condemned 11/11/67, stored at 8A Edge Hill 11-12/67, cut up at Campbells, Airdrie 1/68.

BR tended, overwhelmingly, to allocate locomotives to the Regions in blocks of five. So it was that 92010-92014, with the 7 ton 5,700 gallon flat-sided BR1F tenders, were for the Eastern Region. 92010, work-stained but magnificent with that big tender, stands at March on 22 May 1955. Photograph J. Robertson, The Transport Treasury.

A 'runner'. 92010 leaves Barnston tunnel (on the GC north of Loughborough) with one of the celebrated Annesley-Woodford fast freights on 4 September 1959. In 1957 it had gone to Annesley – still an Eastern Region shed – but passed, with the shed, to the LMR in the following year. Photograph Peter Groom.

92011, by now an Annesley engine, at Crewe Works on 9 November 1958. All five of the 92010-92014 batch with the distinctive flat-sided BR1F tenders (marked by this largely straight top edge) went to March for specialised or at least a certain heavy type of traffic, just as the WR ones. They could only work between Whitemoor and Temple Mills via Ely and thence to Stratford shed, on a variety of Class 'H' coal trains. The coal came via the Joint Line and was destined in the main for power stations such as Brimsdown in the flourishing Lea Valley. Photograph A.W. Battson.

92012

To traffic 31/5/54

Works
3/3/55-16/4/55**LC** Crewe
7/6/57-1/8/57**GO**   Darlington
13/1/58-14/1/58**NC**   Darlington
27/10/58-22/11/58**LI**   Crewe 117,490

B8245 Continuous blowdown valve and added washout plugs
E3329 modified piston for continuous blowdown valve
R8600 provision of chain safety device
19/12/60-10/2/61**HC**   Crewe 88,069
29/10/62-13/11/62**GO**   Crewe
5/64   Crewe
19/10/65-4/12/65**HI**   Crewe
Mileage at 31/12/57 88,429

Annual mileage
1958 32,884
1959 43,866
1960 40,380

Sheds
March 31/5/54
New England 25/9/55
Annesley 26/5/57
Rowsley 3/8/63
Kettering 2/5/64
Carlisle Kingmoor 27/6/64

Tenders
BR1F no.961 from new
BR1F no.1162 from 92073 2/9/58

Boilers
no.1140 from new
no.1876 1/8/57

Condemned 28/10/67, stored at 12A Kingmoor 10/67-1/68, cut up at McWilliams, Shettleston 2/68.

92013

To traffic 23/4/54

Works
22/4/55-26/5/55**LC**   Darlington 17,004
8/57   Briquette tube
                            feeder
23/6/58-19/9/58**GO**   Crewe 78,823
R8245 continuous blowdown valve and additional
washout plugs
20/4/59-5/6/59 **NC[EO]**   28,753
9/9/61-23/10/61**GO**   Crewe 106,746
11/63   Crewe
4-6/65   Crewe
Mileage at 31/12/57 70,945

Annual mileage
1958 19,903
1959 41,021
1960 32,553

Sheds
March 24/4/54
Rugby Testing Station 23/4/54
March 28/10/54
Annesley 27/1/57
Woodford Halse 3/10/59
Annesley 24/10/59
Banbury 12/6/65
Saltley 10/9/66

Tenders
BR1F no.962 from new
BR1F no.1183 29/9/60 from 92094

Boilers
no.1141 from new
no.1410 23/10/61

Condemned 1/10/66, stored at 2E Saltley 9/66-4/67, cut up at Cohens, Kettering 5/67.

92012 at what looks like March. This first ER complement of five all eventually went to Annesley to work the 'runners'. Throughout their time on the ER, they went almost exclusively to Crewe for overhaul. Photograph R. Butterfield, Initial Photographics.

92012 with a down empty 'runner' clanking through the mortal remains of Carrington station, on the Great Central line north of Nottingham in 1962. Mansfield Road Tunnel in the background. The station is being demolished in a desultory sort of way (observe the left-most bridge upright with its precarious capstones!) though the box still seems to be in use. Photograph Prorail UK (Durrant), The Transport Treasury.

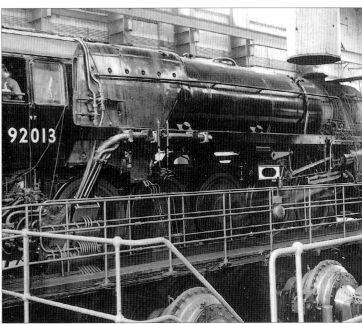

92013 was one of the three 'practically new' 9Fs selected for Plant and road tests in 1954-55, finally reported in *Bulletin No.13* in 1959. It was the work with 92013 that resulted in adjustments to the blast, driving up the power output. The others were 92015 (Plant tests only) to determine what to do about the throttle troubles at Ebbw Junction and the third was 92050.

92014

To traffic 23/5/54

Works
1/3/57-27/3/57**LC**	Darlington
28/5/57**NC**	Stratford Briquette water tube feeder
23/10/57-10/12/57**GO**	Doncaster
29/9/58-18/10/58**LC**	Crewe 35,972 PV liners

R8245 continuous blowdown valve and added washout plugs
E3329 modified piston for continuous blowdown valve
22/1/59-21/2/59**LC**	Crewe 45,947
16/8/60-10/9/60**LC**	Gorton 93,947
10/1/62-10/2/62**LC**	Gorton
5/3/62-24/3/62**Return**	Gorton
25/7/63-13/9/63**GO**	Crewe

Mileage at 31/12/57 71,077

Annual mileage
1958 43,798
1959 33,495
1960 20,296

Sheds
March 18/5/54
Willesden 19/5/54 [Exhibition]
March 6/6/54
Stratford 8/8/54
March 21/1/56
Annesley 16/2/57
Saltley 7/4/60
Toton 16/9/60
Cricklewood 4/7/61
Annesley 7/10/61
Birkenhead 23/5/65

Tenders
BR1F no.963 from new
BR1F no.1119 at Annesley 17/3/64 from 92030
BR1C no.1323 from 92113

Boiler
No.1142 from new

Condemned 9/10/67, stored at 8C Speke Jct. 10/67-3/68, cut up at Buttigiegs, Newport 3-8/68.

92015

To traffic 25/9/54

Works
9/10/57-9/11/57**LI**	Crewe 76,939
2/11/59-5/12/59**GO**	Crewe 53,661
30/1/63-28/2/63**LC**	Gorton
4/1/65-6/2/65**HI**	Crewe

Annual mileage
1954 4,540*
1955 25,479
1956 27,322
1957 23,784
1958 27,550
1959 24,344
1960 33,631
*includes Rugby
Testing Station

Sheds
Wellingborough 9/10/54
Rugby (loan)
Wellingborough 18/11/54
Saltley 21/12/57
Newton Heath 12/7/58
Bolton 16/9/62
Newton Heath 22/12/62
Carlisle Kingmoor 27/6/64

Tender
BR1C no.964 from new

Boilers
no.1143 from new
no.1907 5/12/59

Condemned 29/4/67, stored at 12A Kingmoor 5-10/67, cut up at McWilliams Shettleston 11/67.

A new 92014; the mirror finish with light powdering of soot on top of the boiler indicates it is only recently returned from the Exhibition of Rolling Stock held at Willesden 25 May-4 June 1954, in connection with the International Railway Congress. The actual date is 15 June 1954 and 92014 has charge of a Whitemoor-Temple Mills coal train near Newport, Essex; view is from Weddington Road bridge about three quarters of a mile south of Newport station. As yet without shed plate, though the 'SC' plate was a confounded nuisance when it came to fitting the shed plate – that's why they largely disappeared, 'lost' at sheds. Spare lamp on tender front. Photograph D.M.C. Hepburne-Scott, Rail Archive Stephenson.

A very different 92014, dirty and slightly knocked about, at Stratford shed in September 1956. It is still without the 31B March shed plate! Photograph A.G. Ellis, The Transport Treasury.

Gowhole, Derbyshire, June 1961. Two crew members pass the time of day as Newton Heath's 92016 completes its turn ready for the run home. These extensive sidings, with a holding capacity of nigh on a thousand wagons, lay some eight miles beyond the Pennine divide at Peak Forest and Midland Division trains from Rowsley were remarshalled for destinations on the Western and Central Divisions and vice versa. The empty mineral wagons beyond the engines are in the throat of the Up Sidings and further away are the yard offices and the old local control room. Together with those at Rowsley and Chaddesden, its duties were taken over by the Derby District Control Office in 1948. The number of locos visible (note the 8F and 4F in the Down Sidings) are an indication of the intensity of freight working at this relatively little-known location. Photograph Dr A.H. Roscoe, The Transport Treasury.

92016

To traffic 7/10/54

Works

2/12/57-28/12/57**LI**	Crewe 88,511 R5900 provision of safety links
10/11/60-16/12/60**HC**	Crewe 69,666
27/10/61-5/12/61**GO**	Crewe
29/5/64-23/7/64**LC**	Crewe
15/3/66-16/3/66**LI**	Crewe

Annual mileage
1954 6,388
1955 28,701
1956 28,806
1957 24,851
1958 30,382
1959 24,625
1960 14,548

Sheds
Wellingborough 9/10/54
Saltley 2/12/57
Newton Heath 12/7/58
Bolton 10/9/62
Newton Heath 22/12/62
Carnforth 17/6/67

Tender
BR1C no.965 from new

Boiler
no.1144 from new

Condemned 21/10/67, stored at 10A Carnforth 10/67, cut up at McWilliams, Shettleston 4/68.

92017

To traffic 13/10/54

Works

3/2/56-6/3/56 **LC[EO]**	Crewe 31,237
25/3/58-25/4/58**LI**	Crewe 86,193
R5900 provision of safety links	
E3329 modified piston for continuous blowdown valve	
19/4/60-19/5/60**GO**	Crewe 51,394
14/11/61-12/12/61**HC**	Crewe
18/3/65-25/4/65**LI**	Crewe
26/5/66-21/6/66**LC**	Crewe

Annual mileage
1954 4,954
1955 25,583
1956 24,478
1957 24,175
1958 25,991
1959 25,399
1960 27,907

Sheds
Wellingborough 6/11/54
Saltley 2/12/57
Newton Heath 12/7/58
Bolton 10/9/62
Newton Heath 22/12/62
Carlisle Kingmoor 27/6/64

Tender
BR1C no.966 from new

Boiler
no.1145 from new

Condemned 23/12/67, stored at 12A Kingmoor 12/67-3/68, cut up at Arnott Young, Parkgate and Rawmarsh 4/68.

Meat and Drink for a 9F; 92017 on a Blackpool-Manchester Victoria train passing Farington Curve Junction. There is no date but it's a safe bet that this is a summer Saturday. Photograph J. Davenport, Initial Photographics.

92018

To traffic 21/10/54

Works
17/4/56-19/5/56**LC**   Crewe 35,735
3/6/58-24/6/58**LI**   Crewe 89,744
E3329 modified piston for continuous blowdown valve
R5900 provision of safety links
4/5/60-10/6/60**HC**   Crewe 51,971
21/12/60-21/1/61**LC**   Crewe 69,693
24/11/61-30/12/61**GO**   Crewe
11/6/65-17/9/65**LI**   Crewe

Annual mileage
1954 5,882
1955 26,609
1956 19,510
1957 27,331
1958 28,500
1959 29,081
1960 22,524

Sheds
Wellingborough 6/11/54
Cricklewood 2/12/57
Wellingborough 16/12/57
Rowsley 20/3/62
Kirkby-in-Ashfield 2/5/64
Newton Heath 26/9/64
Carlisle Kingmoor 6/8/66

Tenders
BR1C no.967 from new
BR1C no.1148 6/8/65 from 92116

Boiler
no.1146 from new

**Condemned 22/4/67, stored at 12A Kingmoor 4-7/67,
cut up at Motherwell Machinery and Scrap Co., Wishaw 8/67.**

92019

To traffic 25/10/54

Works
26/9/57-26/10/57**HI**   Crewe
24/10/58-6/11/58   Crewe Tubes
13/5/60-16/6/60**GO**   Crewe
3/9/62-9/11/62**LC**   Gorton
19/10/64-5/12/64**HI**   Crewe

Sheds
Wellingborough 6/11/54
Cricklewood 2/12/57
Wellingborough 16/12/57
Toton 27/1/62
Wellingborough 10/3/62
Rowsley 20/3/62
Wellingborough 2/4/62
Kettering 13/1/64
Carlisle Kingmoor 12/7/64

Tender
BR1C no.968 from new

Boiler
no.1147 from new

**Condemned 10/6/67, stored at 12A Kingmoor
6-12/67, cut up at Motherwell Machinery
and Scrap Co., Wishaw 1/68**

Location unrecorded but 'Somewhere in the North West' would surely cover it, with 92018 and an 8F hurrying for home with a PW working about 1965; typical run-down station of the time and latter-day re-configuration of lamp irons. The top one at the front is now mid-smokebox to avoid electrocuting the fireman and the middle buffer beam one has shifted rightwards (as we look at it).

Cricklewood shed yard, 25 June 1960. For modellers, the 9Fs offer a chance of freedom even for those not expert in the dark arts of weathering. You can start with a fairly respectable black, as here, covered in some more or less delicate lime stains from a water charged exhaust, as here and, if not satisfied, then pile on almost anything! Photograph Peter Groom.

92019 with a lovely mixed freight, at Beattock in 1964 – and a 9F in Scotland for a change! The 9Fs were by now allocated to Kingmoor, so were penetrating north of the border every day but for some years the English 9Fs (as they all were) had been almost unheard of beyond Carlisle. The train shows just how 'mixed' a mixed freight could be – mineral wagon followed by van, followed by a flat and another flat bearing a Land Rover mounted like a First World War tank, opens, a Presflo, pipes and what could even be oil or milk. Dare to model it! The Moffat branch and headshunt are on the right; in fact, the branch had only recently closed to goods, though the passenger service had ceased ten years before. Although there are 'fitted' wagons at the front, the train is running as Class 8, no doubt due to the weight. That train would take some holding coming down the bank. The repositioned lamp irons maintained the correct display for a Class 8 goods, i.e. one above the other (almost). Photograph Prorail UK (Durrant), The Transport Treasury.

Duller times. 92019 in its last full year of life, standing in the up loop at Blea Moor waiting for a passenger train to head south, 4 July 1966. The train is the Long Meg-Widnes anhydrite working, one of the many cases where men from sheds which did not have 9Fs nonetheless worked them on a regular basis. It was Lower Darwen men who worked this train from Blea Moor, to Blackburn, and who also brought the empties as far as Blea Moor. Train is Class 6, partially 'fitted'. Photograph Paul Cotterell

Down and out at Kingmoor, one of the 'ever-shrinking pools' of BR steam. This is 10 September 1966 and the 9F is receiving attention; the blastpipe and other parts are out and the front running plate panel looks like it has been off recently to give access to the cylinders and valves. It never got AWS and retained the old style footsteps at the front to the end. Photograph J. Davenport, Initial Photographics.

Boiler for a Crosti with underslung preheater. Work began on the locos at Crewe at least as early as January 1955 and by 20 February the frames and cylinders for the first, 92020, had been set up in the Erecting Shop (though this is the Boiler Mounting Shop, where the preheaters were attached to the boilers) and the boiler with preheater was ready for attachment. Without the usual chalk or stencil marks, there is no real way of knowing which one this is; you'd assume 92020 but there is another boiler/preheater 'set' behind so we are already a way into the process. The chalked 'No.4' on the smokebox is perhaps a clue to the boiler's destination. Note the exhaust outlet from the preheater (the oblong opening at the rear) and feed clacks. In the view of the left-hand side (below) the big pipe connection under the sling takes the left-hand exhaust to the blast nozzles. Note in these pictures the 'lid' with its smokebox-style 'dart' over the conventional chimney – the only existing views, it would seem, of this odd feature.

THE CROSTI 9Fs

Odd as it may seem, the post-war period saw an acute shortage of coal in Britain. It is hard to imagine the impact of this now, when coal hardly merits a second thought for most of us, but in those years it was the lifeblood of the economy and all other activities, in the end, flowed from it. We are largely remote now from the various energy sources that affect our lives, having only to strike a switch but back then, and indeed throughout the 1950s and beyond, coal was vital, and an everyday presence. Buckets of the shiny stuff were carted through every home, every day. And every winter, housewives shook their heads at the latest increase in its price.

So if BR were but the housewife writ large, a hefty saving on coal for an undertaking like the newly nationalised railway was hugely desirable – BR consumed some 14 million tons a year of the high quality 'large' coal, the supply of which was already becoming less certain. When projects end in failure we all happily condemn them and though the Crosti boiler 9Fs failed of the hopes held for them, *in the circumstances of the time*, BR would have been irresponsible *not* to have explored their use, so promising was the prize – no less than a 20% saving in coal, a fuel, moreover, that was rising in price alarmingly, even as its quality fell.

That some of the 9Fs should run with the Italian Franco-Crosti system was foreseen from the first and its promotion owed much to P.M. Kalla-Bishop, the British Empire Representative for Franco-Crosti and, incidentally, for some time London and Southern Area Secretary of the Stephenson Locomotive Society. He it was, who was 'largely instrumental in getting this experimental boiler built in this country'.

The Franco-Crosti system was one of 'contraflow' in which the exhaust gases, normally passing through the boiler tubes to then be exhausted through the chimney to the atmosphere, are instead diverted *back* through small 'preheaters' slung below and/or either side of the main boiler. They are then finally exhausted to atmosphere through sideslung blastpipes/chimneys nearer to the cab. This 'contraflow' was neatly explained in the railway press in August 1955. The hot gases and cold water flowed in opposite directions through the system. This enabled the maximum amount of heat to be extracted from the gases, tending 'as it does to equalise the temperature gradient between gases and water at all stages'. What this means is that (see the diagram) the coldest water is heated by the cooling ('coldest') gases at the far (that is, the second or final smokebox) end of the preheater. The hottest water, around the firebox, is accordingly being heated by the hottest gases. Straight off the grate, as it were.

> **PRODUCTION SNAPSHOT 1954**
> **From The Railway Observer**
> At Crewe on 20th February, new construction of Cl. 9F 2-10-0s was as follows: 92046 and 92047 running in, 92048 in the Paint Shop, and 92049 (No.20 of order E489) complete in the Erecting Shop. Work had commenced on the Crosti boilered 2-10-0s. The frames and cylinders were set up in the Erecting Shop for 92020, and the boiler, BR Type 9, No.1148, with the small Crosti boiler attached to the underside, was ready to be placed on the frames. In the Heavy Machine Shop, the frames and cylinders were set up for 92021, and the frames for 92022 and 92023. One unattached Crosti boiler was noted in the Erecting Shops, and seven more were lying in the Scrap Shed. The main shell of a Crosti boiler was seen recently marked Type BR9A. The same boiler was later observed to have had the BR9A cancelled out and BR12 added.

One of the German Crostis, rebuilt from a Class 50 2-10-0, at Schwerte Works in 1958/59. It is clear how much 'tighter' everything was on the BR design. Loading gauge constraints in Britain of course were close in the extreme. All the better to show the BR design for the notable piece of work it was. Photograph Phyllis Rampton Narrow Gauge Railway Trust, G.S. Moore Collection, courtesy Allan C. Baker.

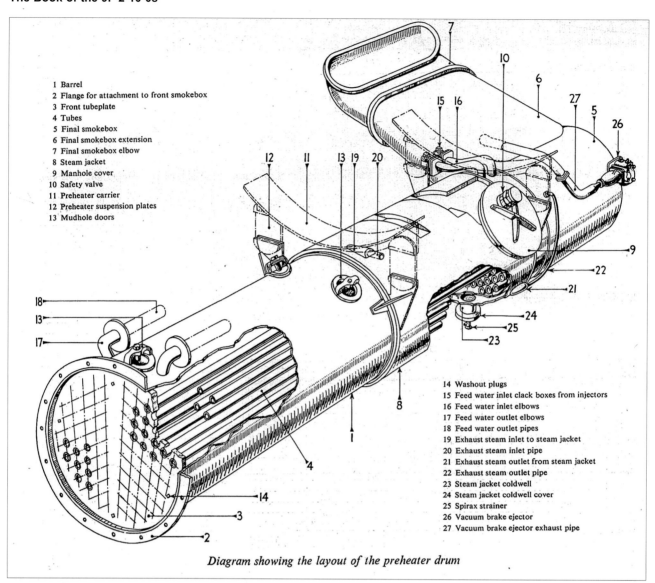

1 Barrel
2 Flange for attachment to front smokebox
3 Front tubeplate
4 Tubes
5 Final smokebox
6 Final smokebox extension
7 Final smokebox elbow
8 Steam jacket
9 Manhole cover
10 Safety valve
11 Preheater carrier
12 Preheater suspension plates
13 Mudhole doors

14 Washout plugs
15 Feed water inlet clack boxes from injectors
16 Feed water inlet elbows
17 Feed water outlet elbows
18 Feed water outlet pipes
19 Exhaust steam inlet to steam jacket
20 Exhaust steam inlet pipe
21 Exhaust steam outlet from steam jacket
22 Exhaust steam outlet pipe
23 Steam jacket coldwell
24 Steam jacket coldwell cover
25 Spirax strainer
26 Vacuum brake ejector
27 Vacuum brake ejector exhaust pipe

Diagram showing the layout of the preheater drum

A preheater getting its cladding. *The Railway Gazette* contemporary account lists the outside manufacturers involved in the Crostis' construction. A number of components were customarily supplied from outside, such as bearings, superheater elements and so on; the preheaters, welded drums of ninety 2¼ steel tubes 19ft 3in between tubeplates, were manufactured by Babcock & Wilcox. Prominent is the manhole cover with its hole for the safety valve, to be set at 275psi just in case! We are looking at the 'front' where the final smokebox will later be attached – this view can be usefully aligned with the diagram. The two pipes on the top were where the feed clacks would go.

'No.4' from below showing the substantial bracket by which the preheater was attached to the smokebox at the front. Inside the loops of the sling is the regulator operating housing.

The water thus heated in the preheater raised the temperature of the boiler feed water to high levels, barely below that in the main boiler. This should have effected an economy in the amount of coal necessary to steam the boiler. The secret of course, as in all these technical advances, was that, throughout the lifetime of a locomotive and/or the modifications, the savings made in fuel should not be outweighed by the extra costs of installation/maintenance. The last truly worthwhile fundamental technical advance in Britain is said to have been the superheater, many years before, and though feedwater heating was desirable in principle it had never really caught on in this country. This was despite the fact of its universal employment in North America for well over a generation and its extensive use in Europe. Was the Crosti preheater just another feedwater heater, albeit a sophisticated one?

While the exchange, cost for savings, seems to have been a clearly positive one in Italy, it turned out to be not nearly so clear in Britain. Some Italian 2-6-2s had been converted in the 1940s; the coal savings were found to be in excess of 20%, a remarkable outcome and one well worth pursuing. After the Second World War the Germans too, tried the Franco-Crosti arrangement, later employing more extensively the true 'Crosti' as opposed to the 'Franco-Crosti'. The Crosti had only *one* preheater, slung centrally below the boiler. This was the fashion of mounting adopted by BR so, strictly speaking, it was the 'Crosti' not the 'Franco-Crosti'.

Cox repeats the contemporary 'contraflow' description from *Trains Illustrated*, *The Railway Gazette* and others (after all, he almost certainly penned it for the press in the first place) in his book *British Railways Standard Steam Locomotives*. As he

(cont. page 63)

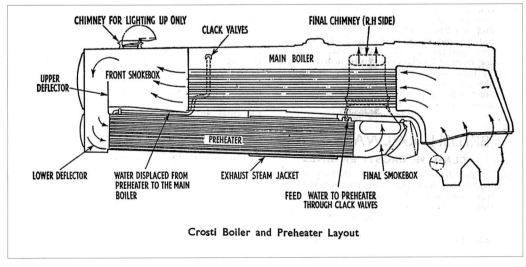

Crosti Boiler and Preheater Layout

This, presumably, is destined to become 92024, that is, the fifth one, in No.9 Shop prior to transfer into 10 Shop – the 'Erecting Shop South'. It was customary to erect locos up to this stage in 9 Shop. The seating bracket for the preheater is visible between the cylinders. In fact there would be a stretcher here anyway, for it was a weak point for any outside cylinder engine. The view shows well the arrangement on the Standards of placing the hornplates central to the frame plates, allowing a better distribution of the piston forces. The Crosti project was *not* a fiasco, as is sometimes suggested. It was justified in the light of the times and although it was extraordinarily clever engineering design to get the preheater in to such a restricted space, it was even cleverer than that – the thing was *designed* to be converted back to conventional operation with the minimum of work, should the experiment fail...

Crostis lined up at Crewe, three of them in No.10 Shop, on the New Work Belt. All sorts of details visible; a 'container' of lubricators, springs waiting to go on, the welded ashpan and rocking grate slung under the firebox, top half of another ashpan/grate on the floor and so on. Front sand boxes had to be placed where they were because the preheater prevented them being placed in the normal position. Note different arrangement of steam pipes; the cylinders were different to the normal 9Fs which is why, on rebuilding, they got the large casing over the steam pipes alongside the smokebox. A chalked number later in this sequence of photographs reveals that this is in fact 92020.

Left. The Crosti firebox. The strange cradle supported either a rivet gun or a tube expander – the latter in this case, by the look.

Below. Lowering on to the frames, the preheater painted a thick anti-corrosive black gloss. By 15 May 1955 the Crosti Lot, E488, was well advanced, with 92020-92023 in the Paint Shop, 92024 complete in 10 Shop and 92025 and 92026 approaching completion. 92027 was ready to receive its boiler while the last two, 92028 and 92029, were still little more than frames and cylinders. On the floor are slidebars and springs and, towards the rear, reversing shaft and lifting arm. Note dents in preheater lagging – they must have tried getting it in earlier!

Getting there. 'Unclothed' like this, it's possible to appreciate the position of the front sandbox and the long delivery pipe to the front wheels – this box was largely invisible when the engines were running. Note the extraordinarily long front sandpipe is without any brackets.

Boiler in place. Rear and left-hand sand box feeding the rear of the middle flangeless wheels also fitted, but not yet the third sand box feeding the front of the intermediate pair.

It's getting tight in there... Middle (more properly 'intermediate') sand box in place on the left-hand side, feeding to the front of the middle (intermediate) flangeless wheel.

says there, the Italian system boldly sought increased efficiency 'by modification to what was already the most efficient part of any steam locomotive, namely the boiler'. The whole of Cox's book is of course a joy to anyone with an interest in the BR Standards and in his Crosti notes his learning and sense of humour shine through even more than usual. The inventor of the new system had been Dr (*Dott.Ing.*) Piero Crosti of Milan, 'a small man of boundless energy with an infectious enthusiasm'. Close collaboration was made with him throughout the evolution of the design. So much so that the Crosti 9F was surely the only BR locomotive first worked out as a design in Milan! Cox was on holiday about this time (it would be 1950-51) and took the opportunity (we've all done this, in some degree or other) to look over the Franco-Crostis working from a Venice shed, leaving his wife to explore St Mark's Square and the canals. The good Mrs Cox must have had more time to herself that holiday for her husband also took time out for various footplate runs. In Milan he 'pursued further discussions with the volatile master himself on his homeground'. One hugely positive outcome of this meeting was Cox's determination never to see a British engine without a chimney. In any case, it turned out, 'the good doctor' recommended for BR a conventionally

sited chimney for lighting up purposes. Once the locomotive was ready to move the chimney would be closed off by a plate, secured by a dart. This was done from outside, and steps and handrail were provided on the smokebox.

The design was passed to Brighton where an arrangement was prepared in 1951; this was amended three or four times to give the BR Crosti 9F of 1955. A detailed agreement was drawn up between BR and the Societa Anonima Locomotive a Vapore Franco which set out payments to be made to the Italian firm based on coal savings made during an agreed testing procedure.

The fact that money depended on the outcome of the tests doubtless meant, as in the case of the other 'good doctor' (the one from Austria) that subsequent correspondence would be somewhat burdensome. Quite how burdensome is only hinted at by Cox – his understated description, 'voluminous correspondence and records' seems to say it all. The results on the Rugby Testing Plant, comparing Crosti 92023 with the conventional 92050, were disappointing in the extreme, more so of course for the Italians. Perhaps it was inevitable. Reed in *Loco Profile 33* is perhaps more dismissive than most. Contemporary accounts of the Franco-Crosti system, he writes, tended to over-elaborate,

making of it rather more than it was. The term 'preheater' was in any case a fancy one for a feed water heater (a big one, grant you) using exhaust gas. To accommodate the preheater the Crosti 9F boiler had to be smaller than its conventional brethren, and it had to be pitched higher. In fact, so extensive were the alterations, to firebox and other features, that the Crostis were barely standard in all sorts of ways. Reed seems to deplore the Crosti practice of including the surface area of the preheater as supplementary to the evaporative heating surface of the boiler, 'a notion not entertained by feedwater heater manufacturers since the pre-1914 days of Baldwin flexible boilers on the Atcheson Topeka & Santa Fe'.

Reed also considered that BR was over-concerned with the question of payment which, dependent on performance, might have rendered up a maximum royalty of £800 per engine. As it was, both sides agreed on the scrupulous fairness of the Rugby tests, at which Italian observers were present. The two 9Fs were tested at speeds of 20, 30, 40 and 50 mph to determine the average coal consumption in lbs/drawbar horsepower hour. A saving of 18% would earn the £800; then a sliding scale came into effect and if savings fell below 12%, there was nothing. The Crosti was found to produce consistently lower drawbar

A chalked number at last reveals the Crosti to be 92020, now with much of the 'superstructure' in place, including cab. If it was in the Paint Shop by 15 May, this would be only a week or so before. On the conventional engines the reversing shaft was angled down but on the Crostis it had to be mounted higher; hence, the reversing shaft was parallel and visible above the framing.

horsepower and the saving in pounds of coal minimal or non-existent. The preheater did not produce the expected increase in overall boiler efficiency.

The Italians were understandably non-plussed at this outcome. Unable to comprehend what was (for them) an inexplicable and calamitous result, they called in Andre Chapelon, the Great Man himself, for a post-mortem but it was some two years before he could present his report. He carried out, as you'd expect, an assiduous investigation 'replete with the most erudite calculations and formulae' as Cox puts it. This could make no difference of course. By 1957 the Crosti question was thoroughly dead and buried. In was in this period that Chapelon was invited to Cricklewood shed to inspect a Crosti brought up for the purpose. Amid all the 'erudite calculations and formulae' almost the only reason for the Crostis' failure to shine, that Chapelon could come up with, was that the preheater might have been badly scaled. This Cox found 'difficult to accept' since softened water had been used and the loco was more or less brand new. The basic point seems to have been that the percentage improvements possible with relatively elderly Italian locomotives running without feed water heaters or exhaust steam injectors were simply not there to be had with a much more modern, already highly efficient design like the 9F. BR even ran supplementary tests but the savings found did not match either the royalty agreement threshold or, more disappointingly, the extra costs of maintenance.

There was worse. Once the Crostis were working for a while corrosion, it turned out, was severe. Sulphuric acid formed in the preheater (the chemistry is daunting and sparked a small debate in the railway press) and badly corroded the preheater tubes and its smokebox, as well as the side-mounted chimney. Under the 'first' smokebox – that is, the conventional smokebox standing in as the lighting up smokebox, was a 'blast elbow' (in what is sometimes termed the 'intermediate' smokebox) directing the gases down into the preheater and this was sometimes eaten by the acid 'like moth holes'. P Ransome Wallis (who blamed the high sulphur Belgian coal used at Wellingborough) reported that one or two experiments were made in which the discharge from the continuous blowdown was diverted to the 'intermediate' smokebox. 'An alkaline powder' (from Italy) was dropped in the tender tank so the blowdown discharge served as an alkaline antidote to sulphuric acid. It didn't work. Apparently the problem was not one of high sulphur coal; it was unfortunately intrinsic to the Crosti system. Sulphuric acid corrosion occurred when attempts were made to extract maximum heat from exhaust gas. The acid acted by 'dewing' on the metal tubes, at a certain temperature. In a conventional boiler the water is too hot but the lower temperature in the preheater allowed the 'dewing' to occur inside the tubes. It was the *difference* in temperature between the gas inside the tubes and the water around it that was critical. The Germans found the same problem while the Italians denied its existence. Though they did have that powder...

From the very first crews and shed staff were deeply unhappy with the Crostis. Crews found them hard to get steaming properly and shed staff moaned at the extra tube and smokebox cleaning (the 'final' smokebox was not self cleaning). Worst of all were conditions on the footplate, which could be enveloped

Much of the equipment and pipework (some remains to be attached); live steam injector prominent lower left, exhaust steam injector behind it. Only the Crostis had exhaust injectors, which was a bit tough on 'the good doctor', for it was this device that, more than anything, nullified his hoped-for results. The conventional 9Fs had two Swindon-type live steam injectors. When the Crostis were rebuilt they kept this exhaust injector. Shows construction of step at base of cab and the inset hand rail – see later.

THE CROSTI CAB

1. Large ejector steam valve
2. Steam chest pressure
3. Vacuum
4. Water gauges
5. Bracket for gauge oil lamp (night shift)
6. Low water alarm to blow the whistle
   – peculiar to the Crostis
7. Boiler pressure
8. Manifold shut off
9. Continuous blowdown
10. Steam brake lubricators
11. Rod/lever for rocking grate
12. Rocking grate mechanism, worked
    by said rod/lever
13. Damper controls
14. Exhaust injector overflow
15. Steam to tender brakes
16. Water to injectors
17. Vacuum pipe
18. Steam feed to tender brakes
19. Vacuum reservoir (chamber)
20. Washout plug
21. Vacuum chamber release
22. Sanders
23. Reverser
24. Vacuum brake
25. Jet
26. Regulator
27. Whistle
28. Steam brake
Note no AWS or steam heat

in smoke, while the front window rapidly became sooted over.

Ransome Wallis summarised the tale much later, in 1959, noting among other things that when Chapelon had talked to crews years before at Cricklewood their 'only' complaint had been the entry of smoke and ash into the footplate. There had also been steaming problems early on, resolved by amendments to the nozzle/chimney arrangement. When 92023 was at the Rugby Test Plant, Brighton had to work up a design for the new fittings and they were consigned post-haste to Rugby by the first available train. The rest then had to be altered at Crewe.

The steaming problem was owed, it seems, to the inordinately long path the gases had to travel; by the time they reached the 'final' smokebox under the boiler, they had journeyed some 36 feet, as well as effecting a U-turn. The gases were thus reduced in velocity by the time they were finally exhausted, the 'drag' effect of which was felt back in the firebox. Now Ransome Wallis was a doctor not an engineer but made a brave shot at rendering it intelligible to the rest of

us. Doubtless my simplification wouldn't quite survive a slide rule but here goes. The effect of the 'drag' was to reduce the 'brightness' of the fire at maximum steaming rate. If the engine was thrashed in response, with the coaling per hour rate increased, steam pressure actually *fell* for there was not enough air in the firebox for perfect combustion. Such maximum working was not, anyway, common and the maximum steaming rate of 29,000lb/hour was the same as that of a conventional 9F. 'Theoretically' on the Crosti 9F, maintenance costs and coal consumption were reduced by the 'self limiting' action through the long 36 feet of tubes. The re-arranged nozzle/blastpipe arrangement however, while improving the steaming, had the lamentable effect of increasing coal consumption even beyond that of a conventional 9F; this on a machine which, it was hoped, would be a fifth *better* off with respect to coal consumption! Ransome Wallis recorded that a Crosti on a round trip Wellingborough to Brent and back again burnt *a ton* more than the other 9Fs. You could forgive BR for thinking that maybe there should have been a

The right-hand, sideslung chimney side. Underneath the blast nozzles are two feed water clacks for the preheater barrel fed by the injectors. They are behind (and obscured by) the grease separator (the part connected by prominent piping front and aft) for the exhaust injector. The lagged pipe on the main boiler (there was also one the other side) carried the hot water (only slightly less hot than the water already in the boiler) from the preheater. The single clack on the boiler rear of the lagged one is the live steam injector feed direct to the main boiler. Note disposition of two sand boxes on this right-hand side, next to each other forward of the sideslung chimney.

Above. **Crostis taking shape at Crewe. This would seem to be 92020 again.**

clause that the Italians should pay *them*.

Other grumbles had as much to do with unfamiliarity as anything else, it was surmised, and obviously the smoke in the cab had to be solved, with some urgency. When all ten were back at Crewe for modification to the blast pipe/nozzles at the end of 1955 opportunity was taken to add a smoke deflector which entirely obscured the sideslung chimney. This solved the footplate smoke problems and indeed in 1959 Ransome Wallis pronounced the cab *cleaner* than many other steam locomotives.

There was a plan to move the Crostis away from Wellingborough (blamed for a hidebound attitude, Atkins records) to Annesley and Woodford (recently acquired from the Eastern Region) for the fast GC line goods, equipping them with mechanical stokers at the same time. This notion sank without trace after a while, no doubt to intense relief on the GC.

By 1958 it was all over. *The Railway Observer* reported thus: *The Crosti 2-10-0s are having some experimental alterations made to the boilers. On 22nd June 92024 was on the South shed at Crewe with the preheater blanked off from the main* boiler and the exhaust chimney on the right-side removed. 92022 was also being converted in the Erecting Shop. The latter, it turned out, was not actually being altered and was observed leaving Crewe 'intact' on 18 July 'partly repainted with the old type BR emblem blacked out' – this shows on the Engine Card.

The first Crosti to be converted back to conventional operation, with the *removal* of the preheater, was 92026 in September 1959. By then all the others were in store at Wellingborough and it took three years for the rest to be plucked from rust and decay to be converted to an 8F version of the 9F. There is some confusion though; they still carried 9F on the cab sides! The preheaters were dumped in 'the Melts' – the scrap shed – at Crewe for some years before finally disappearing.

It was odd that about the time of the British Crostis' demise the Germans rebuilt a further two dozen 2-10-0s on the principle. Despite chrome steel tubes in the preheater and other devices they met an early end in the 1960s. The very last roll of the Crosti dice seems to have come in Spain and was reported in *Trains Illustrated* in 1962. The resulting *grotesque* was RENFE 2-8-0 140.2438. The 'good doctor' was, obviously, no less than indefatigable and 'in collaboration with M. Andre Chapelon' had arrived at an arrangement in which the gases travelled front to back in the preheater, exiting thereby through the conventional chimney on top of the smokebox after an even more extended travel through the tubes. After describing the new version Ransome Wallis wrote 'No results of this interesting experiment have so far been made available by the RENFE'.

A scintillating brand new 92024 – observe the perfect reflection of the works plate in the footplating!

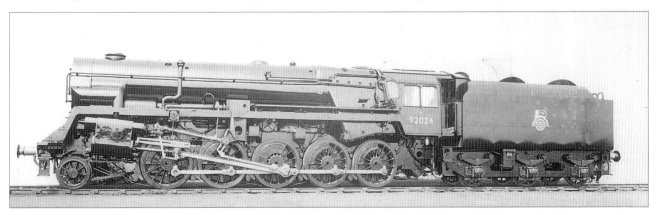

Both sides of 92024, freshly new and cleaner than it will ever be again. A peculiar feature of a peculiar beast were the hand rails and steps on the right-hand side. To permit access to the part of the platform on the right-hand side between the cab and the sideslung chimney, a long step was fitted at the bottom of the cab and flush handrails (sunk in a groove in the cab) along the bottom of the windows. There was also a grab iron at the cab front, around the angle of the front window. All clearly visible here, they enabled access to this otherwise isolated part of the running plate. Not all these features seemed to have survived, in this original form at least, on all examples after conversion to conventional operation. Note also hand hold at the 'false' chimney and the smoke box step so it could be 'sealed off'.

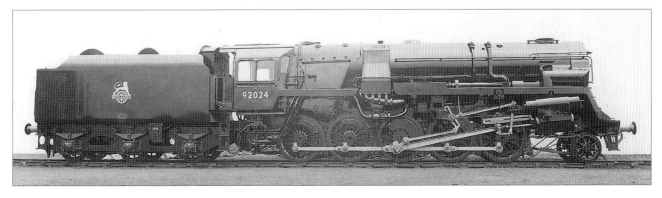

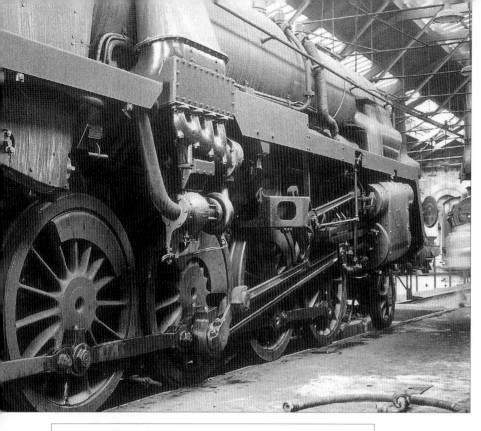

92028 in one of the Toton roundhouses, 24 July 1955. The big downswinging pipe below the blast nozzles is the injector supply to the preheater in the depths beyond; observe the delicacy of the little gravy boat item at the bottom! Only a couple of weeks in service, the layers of filth have yet to build up. Beyond is MR 4F 0-6-0 43988. Photograph R. Wilson, The Transport Treasury.

92020

To traffic 18/5/55

Works
19/7/55-20/9/55**NC**	Crewe 166
17/11/55-18/11/55**NC**	Crewe 4,403
23/11/55-28/11/55**NC**	Crewe 3,937
13/3/56-5/4/56**LC**	Crewe 10,879
5/10/56-1/11/56**LC**	Crewe 21,747 Pre-heater R5900 provision of safety links
25/6/57-3/8/57**HC**	Crewe 37,225
6/8/58-11/9/58**LI**	Crewe 61,479 E3329 modified piston for continuous blowdown valve
24/9/58-29/9/58**NC**	Crewe 608 Tubes
27/3/61-7/6/61 **HC**	Crewe 8,560 R9294 conversion to normal operating boiler
8/1/63-7/2/63**LC**	Crewe
25/7/63-17/8/63**LC**	Crewe
10/1/66-26/2/66**LI**	Crewe

Annual mileage
1955 7,044
1956 19,509
1957 22,521
1958 20,811
1959   120

Sheds
Wellingborough 21/5/55
Kirkby-in-Ashfield 2/11/63
Speke Jct. 4/10/64
Birkenhead 23/1/65

Tenders
BR1B no.969 from new
BR1C no.1141 26/11/59 from 92052
BR1C no.1349 at Saltley 30/7/64 from 92139

Boiler
no.1148 from new

Condemned 21/10/67, stored at 8C Speke Jct.10/67-3/68, cut up at Buttigiegs, Newport 4-8/68.

92021

To traffic 18/5/55

Works
4/11/55-28/11/55**LC**	Crewe 8,450
23/3/56-1/5/56**LC**	Crewe 15,756
28/8/56-27/9/56**LC**	Crewe 21,221 R5900 provision of safety links
7/8/57-24/8/57**LC**	Crewe 39,633
10/9/58-8/10/58**HI**	Crewe 61,990 E3329 modified piston for continuous blowdown valve
26/4/60-7/6/60**LC**	Crewe 6,611 R9294 conversion to normal operating boiler
19/11/60-9/2/61**LC**	Derby 71,146
15/6/62-29/9/62**GO**	Crewe
24/6/65-12/8/65**LI**	Crewe

Annual mileage
1955 10,788
1956 18,003
1957 18,784
1958 21,020
1959   266
1960 20,531

Sheds
Wellingborough 21/5/55
Kettering 13/1/64
Carlisle Kingmoor 12/7/64
Birkenhead 24/7/65

Tenders
BR1B no.970 from new
BR1G no.1551 ex-92233 2/65

Boiler
no.1149 from new

Condemned 11/11/67, stored at 8C Speke Jct. 11-12/67, cut up at Campbells, Airdrie 1/68.

92020 stored at Wellingborough, 26 December 1960. It had been one of the earliest to be put out of use, in April 1959 and was not converted till June 1961, making it one of the longest abandoned of the Crostis. Apparently it had originally been intended to try the Crostis on the Western Region; now that would have been the final nail in the Standards' coffin, so far as that Region was concerned! The right-hand cylinder cover sits above the buffer beam. Photograph Peter Groom.

92020 at Crewe at an unknown date, made ready on the steam cleaning pits for entry to the Works with all removable bits stencilled up so that they come back to the rightful owner. 92020 is AWS fitted by now – note battery box under cab and vacuum reservoir alongside, and pipe running on the lower edge of the running plate. Electrification flashes removed, presumably in anticipation of a repaint. Second tender emblem, obviously – all would have got them on conversion. Note new position of vacuum brake ejector, now in conventional site on smokebox/boiler join. It used to be much further back – it had to be near the blastpipe for the exhaust. Photograph B.K.B. Green Collection, Initial Photographics.

Reinvigorated, 92020 as an 8F, with a freight on the LNW Up Slow at Kensal Green. Hurrying north light on the Down Slow is 2-6-4T 42470, doubtless heading for Willesden shed. The freight from the Midlands to London and the south was vast and the MR main line was always busy, so some of it ran Market Harborough to Northampton and the LNW. So it was that locos off Midland Division sheds were frequently to be found at Willesden. Photograph Prorail UK (Durrant) The Transport Treasury.

Bletchley shed about 1963 and by now 92020 has that thoroughly disreputable look. It is still a Wellingborough engine (it looks like the foundry used the Crewe South 5B shedplate as a pattern!) and it was not transferred away until the end of 1963. A good view of later pattern footstep between the frames (there wasn't any step on the originals or, for a while, on the conversions) and the BR AWS. Photograph The Transport Treasury.

92021 with an up coal train near Plumtree, the side chimney blasting away happily for the moment without benefit of the deflector plates.

Poor old 92021 stored at Wellingborough, suffering in the rain. Photograph Norman Preedy Archive.

A converted 92021. The reversing shaft stayed in the original position, higher than the conventional 9Fs; it was there because of the presence of the preheater, and required a longer lifting link. 92021 was converted in June 1960. Photograph Peter Coster.

Customary condition for 92021. No location or date is given but this would be Cricklewood, in the shed yard with the Carriage & Wagon premises behind. The two features on the boiler behind the smokebox are, firstly, the former clack where the lagged feed water pipe went in during Crosti working days; secondly, the white stained one in front is a washing out hand hole where the hose was attached. Photograph J.G. Walmsley, The Transport Treasury.

92022

To traffic 18/5/55

Works

16/1/56-9/2/56**LC**	Crewe 9,789
22/3/57-17/4/57**LC**	Crewe 37,397 Pre-heater; New chimney and specially treated pre-heater tubes; R5900 provision of safety links
12/6/58-4/7/58**HI**	Crewe 59,995 Partial repaint; E3329 modified piston for continuous blowdown valve
3/4/62-20/6/62**HC**	Crewe R9294 conversion to normal operating boiler
10/5/65-16/6/65**HI**	Crewe

Annual mileage
1955 9,789
1956 23,561
1957 17,922
1958 21,397
1959 12,005

Sheds
Wellingborough 21/5/55
Rowsley 18/7/63
Kettering 2/5/64
Newton Heath 27/6/64
Speke Jct. 5/2/66
Birkenhead 25/2/67

Tenders
BR1B no.971 from new
BR1C no.1171 from 92082

Boiler
no.1150 from new

Condemned 11/11/67, stored at 8C Speke Jct. 11/67-3/68, cut up at Campbells, Airdrie 4/68.

Below. 92022 at Wellingborough. There is no date but it seems to be the period before 92022 went into store. Some work is going on, to judge from the wooden trestle and if it was already in store someone would have pinched that lamp by now. And something's happened to the detail of the running plate at the front... Photograph J. Davenport, Initial Photographics

92023

To traffic 20/5/55

5/1/56-1/2/56	Crewe 8,675 Special exam
25/9/56-17/10/56**LC**	Crewe 23,176 R5900 provision of safety links
10/1/57-2/2/57	Crewe 27,574 Experiment
11/3/57-30/3/57**LC**	Crewe 28,490 Collision damage
5/9/57-28/9/57**LC**	Crewe 37,834 Blast chamber plates
5/9/58-29/9/58**HI**	Crewe 59,586 E3329 modified piston for continuous blowdown valve
19/6/61-27/9/61**HC**	Crewe 10,140 R9294 conversion to normal operating boiler
16/9/63-26/10/63**LC**	Crewe
5/5/65-2/6/65**LI**	Crewe
25/11/65-1/1/66**LC**	Crewe

Annual mileage
1955 18,675
1956 18,145
1957 18,010
1958 22,483
1959 2,407

Sheds
Rugby Testing Station 21/5/55
Carlisle Kingmoor 26/11/55*
Wellingborough 11/12/55
Kettering 29/7/63
Carlisle Kingmoor 17/5/64
Birkenhead 10/7/65
*Scottish Region loan

Tenders
BR1B no.972 from new
BR1C no.1334 24/10/60 from 92124
BR1G no.1537 from 92226

Boiler
no.1151 from new

Condemned 11/11/67, stored at 8C Speke Jct. 11/67-3/68, cut up at Campbells, Airdrie 4/68.

Out in the cabbage patch. 92022 comes south on the Up Goods line north of Ampthill on the Midland main line, 20 September 1955. Out here the goods lines were permissive block and the coal trains could be parked head to tail on occasions. If something went seriously wrong delays could be such that fires would have to be thrown out! Along with 92028 in 1957, 92022 was equipped with 'new chimney and specially treated pre-heater tubes'; this was doubtless a response to the sulphuric acid corrosion problems but it was too late to affect the fate of the Crostis. Photograph The Transport Treasury.

92022 at Derby, en route to Crewe for conversion, 1 April 1962. Photograph Norman Preedy Archive.

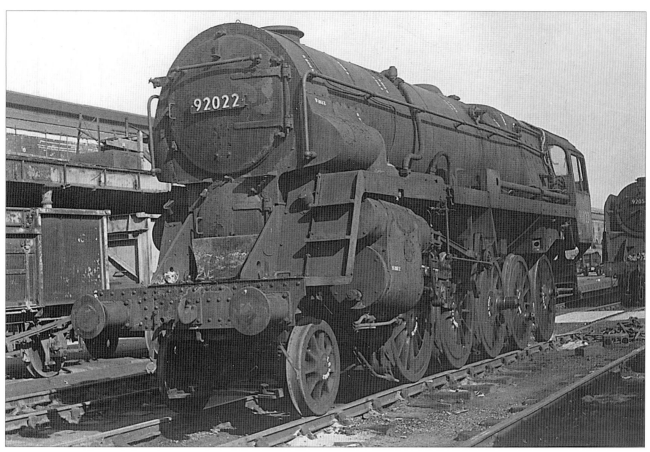

92022 at Crewe on 8 April 1962. It was the last Crosti to undergo conversion, in July 1962 after being in store *since May 1959*. This was the longest period in store for a Crosti – near enough three years. It is unclear what the plate or board is doing between the frames. Photograph P. Hutchinson.

92022 on Shap with an up coal train while working from Newton Heath shed, 27 August 1965. The absence of smoke deflectors certainly didn't seem to affect smoke clearance on the conversions. By this late time the engine has the 'top' lamp iron lowered to a site alongside the numberplate on the smokebox in accordance with safety considerations in the new electric age. Like many 9Fs it has missed the AWS boat by now and will never be so fitted.

92024

To traffic 6/6/55

Works

30/12/55-4/2/56**LC**	Crewe 9,981 Smoke deflector fitted to rear chimney
10/4/56-9/5/56**LC**	Crewe 14,055
7/3/57-10/4/57**HC**	Crewe 36,090 New blast chamber plates and chimney fitted; Pre-heater retubed
1/5/58-14/6/58**HI**	Crewe 61,538 Pre-heater blanked off; Exhaust chimney removed; E3329 modified piston for continuous blowdown valve
12/12/58-21/1/59**LC**	Crewe 10,299
29/12/59-20/2/60**HC**	Crewe 26,456 R9294 conversion to normal operating boiler
13/10/61-16/11/61**GO**	Crewe
27/8/63-20/9/63**LC**	Crewe
6/12/63-15/1/64**LC**	Crewe
2/9/64-14/10/64**HC**	Crewe
26/5/65-25/6/65**LI**	Crewe

Annual mileage
1955 9,981
1956 21,767
1957 23,646
1958 16,443
1959 16,157
1960 27,010

Sheds
Wellingborough 21/5/55
Kettering 13/1/64
Carlisle Kingmoor 17/5/64
Birkenhead 24/7/65

Tenders
BR1B no.973 from new
BR1G no.1560 from 92249
BR1F no.1157 9/12/65 from 92090

Boilers
no.1152 from new
no.1903 16/11/61

Condemned 11/11/67, stored at 8C Speke Jct. 11/67-4/68, cut up at Campbells, Airdrie 5/68.

92025

To traffic 17/6/55

Works

6/6/55-7/7/55**LI**	Crewe 28
2/12/55-29/12/55**LC**	Crewe 10,932
27/8/56-15/10/56**LC**	Crewe 27,472 Pre-heater; R5900 provision of safety links
19/9/57-19/10/57**LC**	Crewe 47,786 Blast chamber plates
10/2/60-8/4/60**LI**	Crewe 67,481R9294 conversion to normal operating boiler
20/10/61-16/1/62**GO**	Crewe
22/4/65-4/6/65**LI**	Crewe

Annual mileage
1955 10,962
1956 19,784
1957 21,361
1958 15,376
1959 2
1960 17,054

Sheds
Wellingborough 21/5/55
Kettering 13/1/64
Annesley 13/4/64
Speke Jct. 1/11/64
Birkenhead 25/2/67

Tender
BR1B no.974 from new

Boiler
no.1153 from new

Condemned 11/11/67, stored at 8C Speke Jct. 11/67-3/68, cut up at Campbells, Airdrie 4/68.

Below. **Perfect portrait of a Crosti, 92023 at Toton shed, 7 September 1958. This 'starboard' side view shows the unfamiliar hand rails and steps necessary for the Crostis, on the cab and immediately in front of it and on the smokebox, where steps and a grab rail were required to seal off the 'lighting up' chimney. The smoke deflector plate obscured the sand box fillers that side, and a hinged plate was provided so that they could be got at, though it remained an awkward operation. When the Crostis were rebuilt into conventional form the drawback of awkward access disappeared. 92023 went into store in April 1959 and was converted in September 1961. Photograph Peter Groom.**

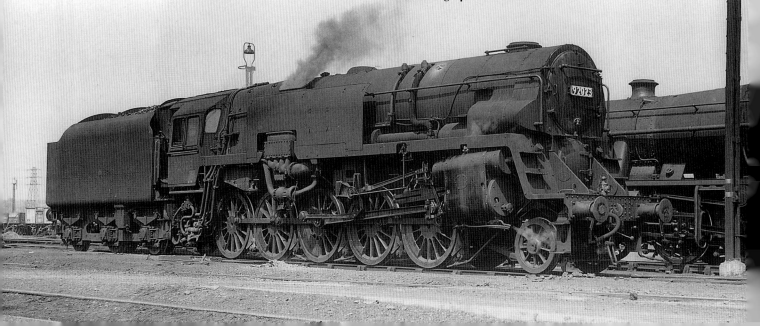

92024, converted from Crosti working early in 1960, at Nottingham shed on 2 May 1960. Photograph Peter Groom, The Transport Treasury.

Late days, 1964-1965 and another 9F without AWS; smokebox lamp iron and buffer beam irons rearranged, wide front step. This is Beattock Summit and 92024 has down empties – some Scottish collieries got empties from England. It is not clear if the engine in the distance is the banker just come off or whether it is in the loop waiting for a path back down the hill. Probably a 9F (even if it was really an 8F – or not) was allowed ten empties unassisted. The carriage in the siding formed the 'Siege', a train that ran from Summit to Beattock on Saturdays to allow railwaymen's wives and sweethearts (but not both) to go shopping in Moffat. It ran until 1966. Photograph T.G. Hepburn, Rail Archive Stephenson.

92024 at Birkenhead shed in July 1965 is in its last weeks as a 12A Kingmoor engine – Birkenhead was in fact to be its next home, from the end of the month, and it may have already 'arrived' there. It has acquired a BR1G tender. 92107 stands beyond. Photograph I. Laidlaw, The Transport Treasury.

92024, now bearing the 8H plate of Birkenhead, runs light through Chester General along with 45149 and 92014, 16 September 1965. Converted in February 1960, 92024 only spent four or five months in store. Photograph B.W.L. Brooksbank, Initial Photographics.

92026

To traffic 17/6/55

Works

15/11/55-30/12/55**LC**	Crewe 9,677 Smoke deflector fitted to rear chimney
4/1/57-30/1/57**LC**	Crewe 35,087 Blast chambers; R5900 provision of safety links
14/8/57-11/9/57**LC**	Crewe 48,300 Blast chambers
28/2/58-2/4/58**HI**	Crewe 58,533 E3329 modified piston for continuous blowdown valve
15/6/59-11/9/59**LC**	Crewe 22,885 R9294 conversion to normal operating boiler
17/10/60-18/11/60**LC**	Crewe 51,646
22/6/62-6/10/62**GO**	Crewe
9/2/66-26/3/66**LC**	Crewe

Annual mileage
1955 9,696
1956 25,299
1957 21,864
1958 20,548
1959 13,776
1960 21,931

Sheds
Wellingborough 21/5/55
Saltley 10/3/61
Wellingborough 25/4/61
Kettering 29/7/63
Kirkby-in-Ashfield 28/10/63
Newton Heath 4/10/64
Birkenhead 22/5/65

Tender
BR1B no.975 from new

Boiler
no.1154 from new

Condemned 11/11/67, stored at 8C Speke Jct 11/67-3/68, cut up at Campbells Airdrie 4/68.

92027

To traffic 25/6/55

Works

18/11/55-3/12/55**NC**	Crewe 9,854
27/2/56-16/3/56**LC**	Crewe 15,155
21/2/57-22/3/57**HC**	Crewe 38,334 Blast chambers and chimney fitted; pre-heaters retubed R5900 provision of safety links
7/1/58-8/2/58**LI**	Crewe 58,263
28/8/60-15/10/60**LC**	Crewe 33,281 R9294 conversion to normal operating boiler
30/8/62-27/10/62**GO**	Crewe
29/4/65-31/5/65**LC**	Crewe

Annual mileage
1955 11,741
1956 22,688
1957 23,725
1958 25,798
1959 7,515
1960 5,304

Sheds
Wellingborough 16/7/55
Kettering 13/1/64
Annesley 13/4/64
Speke Jct. 1/11/64

Tender
BR1B no.976 from new

Boiler
no.1155 from new

Condemned 5/8/67, stored at 8C Speke Jct.8-12/67, cut up at Buttigiegs, Newport 12/67.

Cleaning out the smokebox of 92025 at Wellingborough, 4 May 1958. The centre portion of the deflector plate inside the 'first' smokebox, which directed the gases down into the preheater, was hinged so that it could be lowered to form the platform seen here. This was an aid to shovelling out the char. 92025 was converted in April 1960 after a year in store. Photograph B. Hilton, The Transport Treasury.

92026 on the NER main line, heading for York – Wellingborough had a number of jobs this far north. The Boilersmith at Leicester had experience of the Crostis and was regarded as a specialist – he was often called out to other sheds who didn't like to interfere with these strange beasts. Photograph The Transport Treasury.

92026 was converted in September 1959, going to Crewe (as the first conversion) more or less without having to be stored. This is Cricklewood shed, on 15 June 1963 – it's possible to match the lumps of coal with the picture of 92021 earlier on! Photograph Peter Groom.

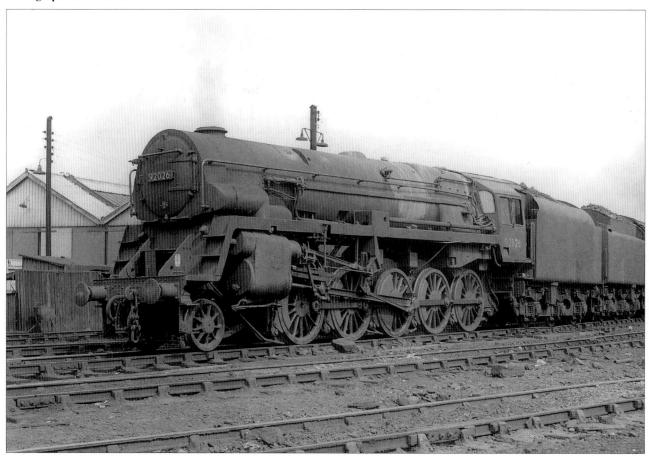

A commendably tidy 92026 at Crewe Works, with altered lamp irons at the front and 92026 still stencilled on its new cab window. The 8H Birkenhead shed plate makes this picture 1965 or after; the occasion is probably 92026's visit in 1966 which is recorded as a Light Casual. It looks as though the engine got more attention than that might imply... Photograph J. Davenport, Initial Photographics.

92027 in original condition and only a month or two old, at Cricklewood shed on 17 August 1955. After storage of over a year, 92027 was converted in October 1960.

92027 at home at Wellingborough, 13 September 1957. At other sheds the Crostis were viewed with deep suspicion; there was never time to master the rather different techniques necessary to make steam well ('the fire was never bright enough') and though the deflector plate cured the smoke problem, their reputation never recovered from those early days of swirling smoke and ash in the cabs. Photograph J. Davenport, Initial Photographics.

Nozzles and blast chamber on 92027. The blast chamber was mounted on a substantial bracket attached to the main frame; sliding bearings allowed for expansion of the preheater. That rectangular plate could be unbolted to remove carbon deposits inside. The lower part with spout was the grease separator for the exhaust injector. Photograph Prorail UK (Durrant), The Transport Treasury.

92028

To traffic 6/7/55

Works

14/12/55-8/2/56**LC**	Crewe
16/4/57-16/5/57**LC**	Crewe Blast chambers; New chimney and specially treated pre-heater tubes
18/10/57-9/11/57**LC**	Crewe Tender frames
25/6/58-12/8/58**HI**	Crewe
2/9/59-3/12/59**LC**	Crewe Crosti pre-heater by passed R9294 conversion to normal operating boiler
16/1/62-20/2/62**GO**	Crewe
3/4/64-14/5/64**LC**	Crewe
10/9/64-7/10/64**LC**	Eastleigh*

Sheds

Wellingborough 16/7/55
Kettering 2/12/60
Saltley 8/10/62
Birkenhead 30/11/63
Saltley 18/4/64
Banbury 6/3/65
Saltley 10/7/65

Tender

BR1B no.977 from new

Boiler

no.1156 from new
* 'now has boiler no.1153'

Condemned 22/10/66, stored at 2E Saltley 10-12/66, cut up at Cashmores, Great Bridge 1/67.

92029

To traffic 8/7/55

Works

19/7/55-20/9/55**NC**	Crewe
23/1/56-23/2/56**LC**	Crewe Smoke deflector fitted to rear chimney
1/3/57-30/3/57**LC**	Crewe Pre-heater retubed; New blast chamber and chimney
2/2/59-25/2/59**LC**	Crewe Tender
3/6/60-6/8/60**HC**	Crewe R9294 conversion to normal operating boiler
6/6/62-16/8/62**GO**	Crewe
18/8/65-30/9/65	Crewe Attention to tyres

Sheds

Wellingborough 16/7/55
Kettering 12/12/60
Saltley 8/10/62
Birkenhead 30/11/63
Saltley 18/4/64
Croes Newydd 28/5/66
Saltley 6/8/66
Birkenhead 31/12/66

Tender

BR1B no.978 from new

Boiler

no.1157 from new

Condemned 11/11/67, stored at 8C Speke Jct. 11/67-1/68, cut up at Campbells, Airdrie 2/68.

Derby shed, 12 February 1956; after brief storage at Wellingborough 92028 was converted at the end of 1959. In the notes, for simplicity, we talk of two smokeboxes on the Crostis, the conventional one in the usual place (the 'first' box, used for lighting up) and the second, or 'final' box out of sight at the end of the preheater under the boiler. But strictly speaking there is a third one, behind that little door at the front below the big smokebox door. It didn't act as a conventional smokebox for there was no exhaust or blastpipe, just the deflector plates or 'blast elbow'. Yet it still had to be opened up and cleaned out every now and then and sometimes it is termed the 'intermediate' smokebox. You can appreciate the (understandably) somewhat jaundiced view of the shed men confronted by this bewildering array of boxes – three instead of one!

Awaiting conversion, 92029 sits mournfully at Wellingborough during its year in store, June 1959 to June 1960. It emerged in conventional form in August 1960. Photograph B. Richardson, The Transport Treasury.

Back to Normal

The conventional 9Fs resume with a magnificent 92030 on the Great Central, passing Rushcliffe Halt with an up Woodford-Annesley coal train. 92030, as the first of the 9Fs on the GN (the ground had already been laid, as the text mentions, with a WD 2-10-0 from Scotland) was the one involved in the braking trials, infamously overshooting the appointed stopping place at Huntingdon by more than half a mile. The deposits on the cylinder casing sometimes seen on the 9Fs indicate leakage (when it was not seated properly) from the cylinder anti-vacuum valve. Photograph T.G. Hepburn, Rail Archive Stephenson.

92030

To traffic 3/11/54

Works
13/6/57-19/6/57**NC**	Darlington
26/6/57-26/7/57**NC**	Stratford
17/1/58-20/2/58**LI**	Darlington 94,843
3/3/58**ADJ**	Darlington
17/4/59-14/5/59**LC**	Crewe 46,355 R8245 continuous blowdown valve and additional washout plugs
15/12/60-20/12/60**NC**	Derby
26/6/61-11/8/61**GO**	Crewe 104,168
7/2/62-16/3/62 **HC**	Crewe
10/4/64-20/5/64**HC**	Crewe
20/8/65-30/9/65**HC**	Crewe Blastpipe

Mileage at 31/12/57 93,618

Annual mileage
1958 35,775
1959 36,830
1960 21,120

Sheds
New England 13/11/54
Annesley 15/6/57
Banbury 20/6/65
Tyseley 8/10/66
Wakefield 6/11/66

Tenders
BR1F no.1119 from new
BR1F no.963 21/3/64 from 92014

Boilers
no.1410 from new
no.1420 12/8/61

Condemned 27/2/67, stored at 56A Wakefield 2-7/67, cut up at Arnott Young, Parkgate and Rawmarsh 7/67.

92031

To traffic 11/11/54

Works
12/1/55-26/2/55**LC**	Crewe 2,694
24/6/55-14/7/55**LC**	Darlington 14,113
30/5/57**NC**	Stratford Briquette tube feeder
7/7/58-27/8/58**LI**	Crewe 97,085 R8245 continuous blowdown valve and additional washout plugs
28/4/61-31/5/61**GO**	Crewe 107,801
16/11/61-29/11/61**NC(Rect)**	Crewe
31/12/63-31/1/64**HI**	Crewe
6/2/64-19/2/64**NC(Rect)**	Crewe

Mileage at 31/12/57 78,556

Annual mileage
1958 35,641
1959 43,221
1960 37,537

Sheds
March 11/11/54
New England 6/3/55
Annesley 19/5/57
Westhouses 28/6/65
Newton Heath 18/7/65

Tender
BR1F no.1120 from new

Boilers
no.1411 from new
no.1433 31/5/61

Condemned 7/1/67, stored at 9E Trafford Park 1-4/67, cut up at Wards, Killamarsh 5/67.

An up GC 'runner' behind 92030, drifting down the grade at Newton towards Rugby on 20 June 1964. Rearranged lamp irons and later style of frontstep. Photograph M. Mitchell.

92032

To traffic 17/11/54

Works

8/57	Briquette tube feeder
18/3/58-18/4/58**LI**	Crewe 95,711
27/1/59-13/2/59**LC[EO]**	Rugby 35,577
29/7/59-18/9/59**LC[EO]**	Crewe 55,228
20/5/60-6/8/60**GO**	Crewe 83,063
13/6/61-7/8/61**LC[EO]**	Crewe 46,051
2/64	Crewe
4/65	Crewe
1/66	Crewe
Mileage at 31/12/57 88,833	

Annual mileage
1958 40,125
1959 30,959
1960 44,830

Sheds
March 'incorrectly' 19/11/54*
New England 21/11/54
Annesley 26/5/57
Kirkby-in-Ashfield 3/7/65
Birkenhead 24/7/65
*The locomotive was 'forwarded' to
New England straight away, more or
less. See also 92033

Tenders
BR1F no.1121 from new
BR1F no.1178 8/6/60 from 92088
BR1F no.1132 from 92043

Boilers
no.1412 from new
no.1145 6/8/60

**Condemned 15/4/67, stored at Birkenhead 3-4/67 and Crewe
South 4-9/67, cut up at Cashmores, Great Bridge 10/67.**

92033

To traffic 19/11/54

Works

19/7/55-21/7/55**NC**	Stratford
24/5/57-29/5/57**NC**	Darlington
12/8/57**NC**	Stratford Briquette tube feeder
6/5/58-30/5/58**LI**	Crewe 94,277 E3329 modified piston for continuous blowdown valve
6/2/59-20/2/59**LC[EO]**	Rugby 29,854
4/8/60-3/9/60**GO**	Crewe 76,015
6/1/61-1/2/61**LC**	Crewe 8,871
11/5/61-6/6/61**LC**	Crewe 21,292
26/4/62-25/5/62**LC**	Crewe
24/1/63-28/2/63**LC**	Crewe E4983 AWS
9/65	Tyres, firebox also V and P
Mileage at 31/12/57 85,811	

Annual mileage
1958 34,801
1959 36,742
1960 21,912

Sheds
March 19/11/54*
New England 21/11/54
Annesley 9/6/57
Banbury 20/6/65
Northampton 17/7/65
*This was 'incorrect' and the
locomotive actually went straight
to New England after reception
at Doncaster. See also 92032

Tenders
BR1F no.1122 from new
BR1F no.959 from 92096 at Annesley 23/5/61

Boilers
no.1413 from new
no.1147 3/9/60

**Condemned 18/9/65, stored at 5B Crewe South 9-11/65,
cut up at Wards, Killamarsh 12/65.**

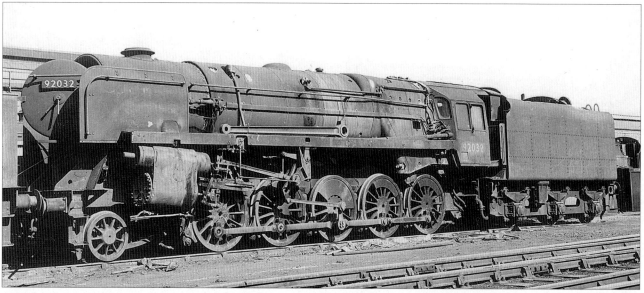

92032 at Crewe Works about 1963-1964. It has been sent there in some disarray, with connecting rods secured to the running plate and access already made for the pistons/valves. On 'opening them up' the shed probably found something it didn't like. 93032 was the second 9F for the GN and was notable for going first to March 'in error'. Photograph J. Davenport, Initial Photographics.

92033 with an up 'runner' of empties, on a remarkable local 'mini-gradient', at Bulwell North Junction on the GC, 1961. 92033 too had been inadvertently allotted to March but unlike 92032 did not actually go there; instead it was diverted in time via Doncaster. Photograph John Henton, courtesy John Edgington.

92034

To traffic 2/12/54

Works
5/57   Darlington
10/59   Darlington AWS
9/60   Darlington
6/62   Darlington
Mileage at 31/12/57 78,763

Sheds
New England 25/12/54
Frodingham 4/1/59
New England 19/4/59
Immingham 16/6/63

Tenders
BR1F no.1123 from new
BR1F no.1394 1/9/61 from 92184
BR1F no.1123 1/10/61 from 92184
BR1F no.1127 5/62 from 92038

Boiler
no.1414 from new

Condemned 31/5/64, stored at 40B Immingham 5-7/65, cut up at Wards, Killamarsh 8/65.

92035

To traffic 3/12/54

Works
12/59   AWS
7/60   Darlington
4-5/63   Crewe

Sheds
New England 25/12/54
Frodingham 4/1/59
New England 19/4/59
Immingham 16/6/63

Tender
BR1F no.1124 from new

Boiler
no.1415 from new

Condemned 6/2/66, stored at 40B Immingham 2-3/66, cut up at Wards, Killamarsh 4/66.

92034 brand new at Crewe Works, 28 November 1954, chocked at opposite 'corners' as it were. Perhaps the tender handbrake was not yet functioning. Photograph R.J. Buckley, Initial Photographics.

On an up fast freight (it might have been a V2 job at another time) passing Stoke box (its roof barely visible behind the train, beyond the colour light signal) on 26 August 1959. Photograph Peter Groom.

92035 at Hatfield, 14 April 1962.

92036

To traffic 2/12/54

Works
7/5/55-23/5/55**LC***	Darlington
2/4/57-8/4/57**NC**	Darlington
26/3/58-2/5/58**LC**	Darlington
17/11/59-27/11/59**NC**	Darlington
27/1/60-17/3/60**LC**	Darlington
1/3/61-22/4/61**GO**	Darlington
15/5/61-19/5/61**ADJ**	Darlington

*minor collision damage – first 9F to visit Darlington

Sheds
New England 2/12/54
Doncaster 23/9/62
Colwick 22/6/63
New England 3/11/63
Colwick 5/1/64
New England 20/6/64

Tenders
BR1F no.1125 from new
BR1F no.1397 from 92187

Boiler
no.1417 from new

Condemned 6/12/64, stored at 34E New England 11/64-4/65, cut up at Cohens, Kettering 5/65.

92037

To traffic 8/12/54

2/58	Darlington
10/59	AWS

Sheds
New England 25/12/54
Immingham 16/6/63

Tenders
BR1F no.1126 from new
BR1F no.1128 14/11/55 from 92039

Boiler
no.1418 from new

Condemned 21/2/65, stored at 40B Immingham 2-5/65, cut up at Drapers Hull 6/65.

92037 outside No.10 Shop at Crewe, in primer and awaiting the completion of various details. Just at the junction of smokebox and boiler the vacuum ejector awaits its exhaust pipe into the smokebox and chimney, for instance. Engines were always steamed before final painting. Photograph A.W. Battson, The Transport Treasury.

92037 now fully painted and ready for running in and then delivery to the Eastern Region. It was to be one of the first to get AWS (habitually called 'ATC' on the Engine History Cards), at Darlington in 1959.

Spending the great part of its life at New England, 92037 has the then new plate of 34E in June 1958. It is standing in Doncaster shed, then in process of re-roofing. Photograph John Robertson, The Transport Treasury.

92038

To traffic 14/12/54

Works
5/2/58-28/3/58**LI**	Darlington
12/1/60-20/1/60**NC**	Darlington AWS
28/4/60-30/6/60**GO**	Darlington
19/11/62-4/1/63**LC**	Crewe

Sheds
New England 14/12/54
Immingham 16/6/63
New England 20/6/64
Langwith Jct. 3/1/65

Tenders
BR1F no.1127 from new
BR1F no.1123 from 92034

Boiler
no.1419 from new

Condemned 11/4/65, stored at 41J Langwith Jct. 4-6/65, cut up at Cashmores, Great Bridge 7/65.

92039

To traffic 17/12/54

Works
9/2/57-15/2/57**NC**	Darlington
12/9/57-19/10/57**LI**	Darlington
6/5/59-13/5/59**NC**	Darlington
17/8/59-26/8/59**NC**	Darlington
21/12/60-4/2/61**GO**	Darlington E/DA/L/82 footsteps between frames in front of smokebox
24/7/61	Doncaster Weighing

Sheds
New England 17/12/54
Immingham 1/2/59
New England 17/9/61
Doncaster 23/9/62
Colwick 22/6/63
Immingham 30/11/63
Doncaster 20/6/64
Langwith Jct. 19/6/65

Tenders
BR1F no.1128 from new
BR1F no.1126 14/11/55 from 92037

Boiler
no.1416 from new

Condemned 17/10/65, stored at 41J Langwith Jct. 10-12/65, cut up at Wards, Killamarsh 1/66

92038 on the GN at Wymondley, in 1961. The AWS vacuum reservoir is visible below the cab. Photograph Prorail UK (Durrant), The Transport Treasury.

92039 at New England; the shed had a reputation for cleanliness that was worse, if that could be so, even than Gateshead; its poor old 9Fs and WDs thus stood no chance. This would be prior to February 1958, when the New England '35' District was done away with. Photograph J. Davenport, Initial Photographics.

92040

To traffic 23/12/54

Works
13/12/57-31/1/58**LI**   Darlington
2/12/59-8/12/59**NC**   Darlington
25/4/60-4/6/60**GO**   Darlington
14/10/60-17/12/60**LC**   Darlington AWS

Sheds
New England 23/12/54
Colwick 9/6/63
Barrow Hill 12/9/64
Langwith Jct. 9/1/65

Tender
BR1F no.1129 from new

Boiler
no.1421 from new

Condemned 8/8/65, stored at 41J Langwith Jct. 8-10/65, cut up at Drapers, Hull 11/65.

92041

To traffic 31/12/54

Works
28/2/58-3/4/58**LI**   Darlington
14/12/59-23/12/59**NC**   Darlington AWS
20/7/60-18/10/60**GO**   Darlington
29/11/62-16/2/63**HI**   Crewe

Sheds
New England 31/12/54
Colwick 9/6/63
Barrow Hill 12/9/64
Langwith Jct. 9/1/65

Tender
BR1F no.1130 from new

Boiler
no.1422 from new

Condemned 29/8/65, stored at 41J Langwith Jct. 8-10/65, cut up at Wards, Beighton, Sheffield 11/65.

92040 passing Huntingdon North with an up coal train, 23 July 1959. Coal came up like this, to Ferme Park and was then tripped back down to many of the stations passed on route. Apparently there were trials on the GN around this time with 2-10-0s on vacuum fitted coal trains but they proved 'premature'. Photograph D.C. Ovenden.

92040 out on a freight job, near Hadley Wood in the early 1960s. The GN, especially since the handover of the GC to the LMR, *was* the Eastern Region's freight traffic. The bulk of ER revenue came from freight and of this, GN Freight Assistant R.T. Munns wrote in *Trains Illustrated* in August 1958, 56% of the merchandise, 75% of the minerals and no less than 91% of the coal which made up the ER's income originated on the GN. There were more than 850 express freights, of which livestock was but one category (as here) originating on the GN every week. Photograph J.G. Walmsley, The Transport Treasury.

Hertford North on 20 May 1960, and 92041 has a train of Presflo wagons – a suitably heavy bulk load for a suitably filthy 9F. The Hertford Loop was of course one of the great assets of the GN route for the diverting of trains in a variety of circumstances. Photograph P.J. Coster.

92041 on the turntable at Hornsey, 18 May 1957; the footbridge behind leads to the station seen at the left. On the buffer beam is the red tail light put on for the 9F's run light from the yards a little to the south (left); it has just come on to the table and will turn 'right' way for the return north. Photograph J. Robertson, The Transport Treasury.

92042

To traffic 12/1/55

Works

14/4/58-20/5/58**LI**	Darlington
22/12/58-20/1/59**LC**	Darlington
24/5/60-8/7/60**GO**	Darlington AWS
3/1/63-9/2/63**LI**	Crewe

Sheds

New England 12/1/55
Colwick 9/6/63
Langwith Jct.10/1/65
Colwick 6/11/65

Tenders

BR1F no.1131 from new
BR1F no.1394 from 92184

Boiler

no.1423 from new

Condemned 19/12/65, stored at 40E Colwick 12/65-3/66, cut up at Wards, Beighton, Sheffield, 4/66.

92043

To traffic 18/1/55

Works

16/6/56**LC**	shed
18/6/57-19/6/57**NC**	Stratford
5/5/58-3/6/58**LI**	Crewe 85,996 E3329 modified piston for continuous blowdown valve
24/2/59-6/3/59**LC**	Rugby 36,893
25/7/60-13/8/60**LC**	Gorton 87,306
4/1/61-10/2/61**GO**	Crewe 98,807
16/3/61-27/3/61**NC[EO]**	Crewe 3,128
21/11/62-18/1/63**HC**	Crewe E4983 AWS
8/2/63-27/3/63**HC[CB]**	Crewe

Annual mileage

1958 36,916
1959 42,236
1960 26,888

Sheds

March 18/1/55
Annesley 10/2/57
Burton 3/1/66
Carlisle Kingmoor 30/1/66

Tenders

BR1F no.1132 from new
BR1F no.1178 from 92032

Boilers

no.1424 from new
no.1412 10/2/61

Condemned 30/7/66, stored at 12A Kingmoor 7-9/66, cut up at Campbells, Airdrie 10/66.
BR9215 card reports "Sold to Campbells A. 13/9/66, despatched 7/10/66"

One of New England's finest, 92042 at Darlington shed in the 1950s. Photograph J. Davenport, Initial Photographics.

Typical 9F memory. Originally a GE line engine, 92043 had been at Annesley when the LMR took over and it then disappeared northwards to find itself at Kingmoor by 1966. Here it is in that year at Ribblehead. Photograph Prorail UK (Durrant), The Transport Treasury.

92044

To traffic 29/1/55

Works
18/3/55-29/4/55**LC**	Crewe
10/10/55-12/10/55**NC**	Stratford
22/10/56-26/11/56**LC**	Darlington
21/8/58-26/9/58**GO**	Darlington
1/5/61-3/6/61**GO**	Darlington
21/2/63-4/4/63**HC**	Crewe

Sheds
March 29/1/55
New England 16/6/57
Doncaster 23/9/62
Colwick 22/6/63
Barrow Hill 12/9/64
Langwith Jct. 9/1/65

Tender
BR1F no.1133 from new

Boiler
no.1425 from new

Condemned 11/4/65, stored at 41J Langwith Jct. 4-6/65, cut up at Cashmores, Great Bridge 7/65.

92045

To traffic 9/2/55

Works
10/8/57-27/9/57**HC[EO]**	Crewe 51,153 R5900 provision of safety links
12/12/58-13/1/59**LI**	Crewe 72,480
24/2/60-7/4/60**LC[EO]**	Crewe 18,906
4-5/62	Crewe
10/62	Gorton
20/10/64-4/12/64**LC**	Eastleigh

Annual mileage
1955 24,381
1956 18,129
1957 14,686
1958 15,384
1959 17,589
1960 17,492

Sheds
Wellingborough 26/2/55
Toton 25/2/56
Bidston 19/5/56
Birkenhead 9/2/63

Tender
BR1C no.1134 from new

Boilers
no.1426 from new
no.1951 4/62

Condemned 16/9/67, stored at 8C Speke Jct. 9/67-1/68, cut up at Wards, Beighton, Sheffield 2/68.

92044 north of Finsbury Park, inching home with coal on 30 May 1960. This is well south of Ferme Park and the destination is something of mystery; it might be coal for Kings Cross shed because the only options were East Goods Yard and Kings Cross Goods Yard, neither of which were well known for dealing with coal. As late as this, former PO wooden wagons are still to be seen. By this time domestic coal for London was very much on the wane, though gas works and power station intakes had risen enormously. A notable development was the opening of Palace Gates automated depot for domestic coal in 1958; this saw three trains a week, each of eighteen 21 ton bottom hopper wagons ('which will ultimately be brake fitted'). They carried the proud legend 'Charringtons' which for Londoners meant either coal or beer. Photograph Peter Groom.

With 92045, deliveries reverted to the Midland and here she is at Cricklewood on 30 April 1955. Reversion too, to the BR1C tender. Photograph A.G. Ellis, The Transport Treasury.

92046

To traffic 11/2/55

Works

3/11/56-28/12/56**LC**	Crewe 40,644 R5900 provision of safety links
24/4/57-8/6/57**LC[EO]**	Crewe 44,808 Firebox restayed
12/6/57-11/7/57**LC[EO]**	Crewe 44,903
10/2/59-26/3/59**LI**	Crewe 73,590
13/2/61-30/3/61**LC**	Crewe 36,274
6/64	Crewe

Annual mileage
1955 23,087
1956 17,678
1957 13,272
1958 17,049
1959 15,860
1960 20,602

Sheds
Wellingborough 26/2/55
Toton 25/2/56
Bidston 19/5/56
Birkenhead 9/2/63

Tender
BR1C no.1135 from new

Boiler
no.1427 from new

Condemned 21/10/67, stored at 8C Speke Jct. 10/67-3/68, cut up at Buttigiegs, Newport 4-8/68.

92047

To traffic 18/2/55

Works

28/6/55-2/7/55**LC[EO]**	Crewe 13,460 Firebox fracture
3/10/56-10/11/56**LC[EO]**	Crewe 31,496 R5900 provision of safety links
28/3/57-8/5/57**LC[EO]**	Crewe 37,398 Firebox stayed
26/7/57-31/8/57**HI**	Crewe 41,018
14/10/57-14/11/57**LC[EO]**	Crewe 2,164
29/1/58-22/3/58**LC[EO]**	Crewe 6,001 Boiler attention
9/9/59-6/11/59**GO**	Crewe 30,351
20/2/61-12/4/61**HC**	Crewe 27,805
12/64	Crewe

Annual mileage
1955 18,805
1956 14,410
1957 12,351
1958 14,804
1959 14,045
1960 22,346

Sheds
Wellingborough 26/2/55
Bidston 13/8/55
Birkenhead 9/2/63

Tender
BR1C no.1136 from new

Boilers
no.1428 from new
no.1137 6/11/59

Condemned 11/11/67, stored at 8C Speke Jct. 11/67-3/68, cut up at Campbells, Airdrie 4/68.

92047 was another of the 1955 batch sent to Wellingborough, and like several others soon went here, to Bidston shed, for iron ore working. The work, later transferring to Birkenhead, was for a John Summers Co. steel works at Shotton, using new bogie hopper wagons belonging to the firm. It had first turned up ('an interesting development' as it was described at the time) during the 1955 ASLEF strike but after colliding with buffers it had to retire hurt to Crewe Works. Photograph A. Scarsbrook, Initial Photographics.

92048

To traffic 26/2/55

Works

25/9/57-24/10/57**LI**	Crewe 68,058
19/8/59-19/9/59**LC**	Crewe 52,670
1/12/60-13/1/61**GO**	Crewe 86,778
12/3/62-14/4/62**LC**	Gorton
8/11/62-11/12/62**LC**	Crewe
4/5/66-11/6/66**LI**	Crewe

Annual mileage
1955 21,591
1956 24,214
1957 29,471
1958 32,707
1959 23,895
1960 23,009

Sheds
Wellingborough 26/2/55
Toton 30/1/56
Saltley 10/6/57
Rowsley 16/11/59
Toton 2/5/64
Warrington 28/3/65
Birkenhead 15/5/65

Tenders
BR1C no.1137 from new
BR1C no.1341 at Rowsley 2/5/60 from 92131
BR1C no.1140 25/11/60 from 92051

Boiler
no.1429 from new

Condemned 16/9/67, stored at 8H Birkenhead 9-10/67 and Speke Jct. 10/67-1/68, cut up at Wards, Beighton, Sheffield 2/68.

92049

To traffic 10/3/55

Works

17/10/57-16/11/57**LI**	Crewe 67,890 R5900 provision of safety links
19/4/61-19/5/61**GO**	Crewe 88,338
13/8/62-5/9/62**LC**	Gorton
9/1/63-26/1/63**NC**	Crewe E4983 AWS
2/6/65-31/7/65**LI**	Crewe

Annual mileage
1955 19,309
1956 25,424
1957 27,510
1958 30,798
1959 27,185
1960 21,379

Sheds
Wellingborough 18/3/55
Toton 30/1/56
Saltley 10/6/57
Rowsley 16/11/59
Toton 2/5/64
Warrington 13/3/65
Birkenhead 19/2/66

Tender
BR1C no.1138 from new

Boilers
no.1420 from new
no.1467 19/5/61

Condemned 11/11/67, stored at 12A Kingmoor 5/68, cut up at Campbells, Airdrie 6/68.

More of the heavy stuff. 92048, by now a Birkenhead engine, on 'oil' empties from Leeds to Stanlow at Ellesmere Port, leaving Neville Hill yard on Saturday 29 April 1967. In 1966 the BRB had announced that a new oil terminal in Leeds was to be built, the forerunner of several to be located inland, where oil was being consumed. Several oil companies would sign up to each terminal, thus sharing the costs of the expensive equipment and services. The 9F has late front lamp irons, second type of step. No barrier wagon(s) behind tender, which was allowable in certain circumstances – if the tanks were empty, for instance, or carried heavy oil and not volatiles. Photograph Gavin Morrison.

92048, a regular on the Stanlow-Leeds oil trains, departing Neville Hill yard on Friday 16 June 1967. The silver tanks denote low flashpoint contents, hence the barrier wagons; black tanks carried the relatively safe heavy oil. Work on the terminal had begun in October the previous year on a 32 acre site at Hunslet East and was expected to be complete in August 1967. It was a very elaborate storage facility and with pumps delivering 250 tons an hour a typical train would be turned round in two hours. These trains were all of course destined to be dealt with at the new terminal but it was not intended that it be served by something so demonstrably from another age as a BR 9F in full glorious grime – though they might have come in useful for steam heating the storage tanks! In fact 9Fs were banned from the Hunslet branch so the possibility would never arise. These were Birkenhead jobs and in any event that shed closed within weeks of the intended full opening of the terminal. Photograph Gavin Morrison.

92048 on the same train of empties back from Leeds on the same day, passing the now-closed to steam shed at Mirfield and running through the celebrated 'Speed Signalling' of the district. A good run of barrier wagons this time, ahead of those silver tanks. Photograph Gavin Morrison.

92050

To traffic 19/8/55

Works
6/2/57-1/3/57**LC**	Crewe
18/11/57-14/12/57**derailment**	Crewe
26/3/58-17/4/58**LC**	Crewe
15/1/60-13/2/60**LC**	Crewe
4/4/62-19/4/62**LC**	Gorton
13/9/62-19/10/62**GO**	Crewe
7/6/65-9/8/65**LC**	Crewe

Sheds
Toton 10/9/55
Rugby Testing Station 10/9/55
Carlisle Kingmoor 26/11/55*
Toton 31/12/55
Rugby Testing Station 23/3/57
Toton 2/5/57
Saltley 4/11/59
Rowsley 16/11/59
Kirkby-in-Ashfield 2/5/64
Newton Heath 4/10/64
Speke Jct. 5/2/66
Warrington 12/8/67
*Scottish Region loan

Tenders
BR1C no.1139 from new
BR1C no.1329 from 92119

Boiler
no.1430 from new

Condemned 30/9/67, stored at 8B Warrington 9/67-1/68, cut up at Buttigiegs Newport 2/68.

92051

To traffic 22/8/55

Works
6/11/58-29/11/58**LI**	Crewe
15/5/61-24/6/61**GO**	Crewe
7/12/64-17/1/65**LI**	Crewe

Sheds
Toton 22/8/55
Wellingborough 21/11/55
Toton 4/12/55
Saltley 10/6/57
Rowsley 16/11/59
Kirkby-in-Ashfield 2/5/64
Newton Heath 4/10/64
Carlisle Kingmoor 4/12/65

Tenders
BR1C no.1140 from new
BR1C no.1341 at Rowsley 25/11/60 from 92048

Boilers
no.1431 from new
no.1944 24/6/61

Condemned 22/10/67, stored at 12A Kingmoor 10/67-2/68, cut up at Motherwell Machinery and Scrap Co., Wishaw 2/68.

A heavy coal train at Stenson Junction, bound for Drakelow power station. Supplying the CEGB was far from straightforward, for not every station had the same requirements. Some could be fed from one or two collieries while others needed special 'fines', which might come from all over the place. This particular 9F had the unusual distinction of going on loan to the Scottish Region at the end of 1955, the circumstances of which are unclear. Photograph R.J. Buckley, Initial Photographics.

More of the hard stuff. An up Long Meg (Appleby) to Widnes anhydrite train near Hellifield behind 92051, Tuesday 13 June 1967. The train became something of an institution in the last days of steam on the Settle & Carlisle, dragging the mineral south to the nameless processes of Widnes (it was used in the production of sulphuric acid). The curious involvement of Lower Darwen crews has already been mentioned. Photograph Gavin Morrison.

92052

To traffic 26/8/55

Works
19/6/58-4/7/58	Derby shed Tubes
4/4/60-6/5/60**HC**	Crewe
9/11/60-13/12/60**LC**	Crewe
7/9/62-10/10/62**GO**	Crewe
30/3/66-18/5/66**LI**	Crewe

Sheds
Toton 26/8/55
Wellingborough 17/3/58
Saltley 17/6/61
Toton 24/6/61
Annesley 7/10/61
Rowsley 31/3/62
Toton 14/7/62
Rowsley 11/7/63
Toton 15/7/63
Wellingborough 11/8/63
Kirkby-in-Ashfield 26/10/63
Newton Heath 10/10/64
Carlisle Kingmoor 17/6/67

Tenders
BR1C no.1141 from new
BR1B no.969 at Wellingborough 26/11/59 from 92020

Boiler
no.1432 from new

Condemned 12/8/67, stored at 12A Kingmoor 8-12/67, cut up at McWilliams, Shettleston 1/68.

92053

To traffic 17/9/55

Works
25/10/55-8/11/55**LC**	Crewe
6/2/59-7/3/59**LI**	Crewe
25/1/61-24/3/61**GO**	Crewe
1/9/61-22/9/61 **NC[Rect]**	Crewe
18/6/62-21/6/62 **NC[Rect]**	Crewe
7/1/63-21/1/63**NC**	Crewe
10/2/64-20/3/64**HC**	Crewe
15/10/64-4/12/64**LC**	Eastleigh

Sheds
Toton 8/10/55
Burton 5/10/57
Saltley 22/3/58
Wellingborough 21/11/59
Toton 22/9/62
Warrington 13/3/65

Tender
BR1C no.1142 from new

Boiler
no.1433 from new

Condemned 19/2/66, stored at 8B Warrington 2-7/66, cut up at W.George, Station Steel, Wath 7-12/66.

92052 at home at Toton on 27 September 1955, one month old but with the carbonate deposits building up nicely as hot water runs from the safety valves and the clacks. This is the annoying stuff round the base of your taps at home. Photograph Peter Groom.

92052 in proper 9F condition, at Matlock Bath, maybe, on 24 August 1963; it appears to be at a stand, while a car whizzes by. Those carbonate deposits continue apace, alternating and mixing with the grime.

92054

To traffic 21/9/55

Works

28/7/58-19/8/58	Derby shed 66,245 Tubes
4/2/59-28/2/59**LI**	Crewe 80,004
	R5900 provision of safety links
23/5/61-16/6/61**LC**	Gorton 72,988
30/3/62-30/5/62**GO**	Crewe
3/7/65-1/8/65**HI**	Crewe

Annual mileage
1955 5,897
1956 25,298
1957 25,553
1958 20,262
1959 33,728
1960 32,258

Sheds
Toton 8/10/55
Wellingborough 17/3/58
Leicester Midland 24/9/62
Westhouses 3/12/62
Speke Jct. 13/6/64

Tender
BR1C no.1143 from new

Boiler
no.1434 from new

Condemned 4/5/68, stored at 9D Newton Heath 5-6/68, cut up at Arnott Young, Parkgate and Rawmarsh 6/68.

92055

To traffic 22/9/55

Works

23/8/58-2/9/58**NC[EO]**	shed 79,511
22/3/60-13/5/60**GO**	Crewe 128,391R5900 provision of safety links E3329 modified piston for continual blowdown valve
12/64	Crewe

Annual mileage
1955 7,521
1956 27,880
1957 27,645
1958 27,092
1959 32,838
1960 30,081

Sheds
Toton 8/10/55
Wellingborough 22/3/58
Toton 24/9/60
Bidston 25/3/61
Toton 29/4/61
Rowsley 17/3/62
Toton 14/4/62
Wellingborough 7/7/62
Toton 22/9/62
Warrington 13/3/65
Speke Jct. 7/10/67

Tenders
BR1C no.1144 from new
BR1C no.1316 26/5/62 from 92106

Boilers
no.1435 from new
no.1428 13/5/60

Condemned 23/12/67, stored at 8C Speke Jct. 12/67-3/68, cut up at Wards, Killamarsh 4/68.

Lovely mix of wagons and loads behind 92054, south of Tebay; Tebay Down Loop goes off to the left beyond the bridge over the River Lune. The 9F was ex-works Crewe in May 1962 and is running in. A Wellingborough engine hereabouts would have been a rare treat indeed for the locals. Photograph T.G. Hepburn, Rail Archive Stephenson.

Darker times awaited 92054, as they did for all the 9Fs of course; at home at Speke Junction, 28 February 1965. Condemned in 1968 a few months before The End, 92054 was stored at Newton Heath for a few weeks before cutting up. Photograph Ian G. Holt.

92055 at Wellingborough shed, its 15A home, around 1958-59. By now the 'look' of Wellingborough was rather different, with the 0-8-0s and Garratts long gone, the 4Fs and 8Fs reduced in number and V2s and other GC line exotica turning up for repairs. Everywhere you looked, however, there were 9Fs. Photograph J. Davenport, Initial Photographics.

Inevitably 92055 found itself in the North West; a good view of the Stanier-style BR1C tender north of Standish Junction in 1963. Photograph Dr A.H. Roscoe, The Transport Treasury.

92056

To traffic 14/10/55

Works

2/6/58-5/6/58**LC[EO]**	Crewe 68,603
	R5900 provision of safety links
17/8/60-29/9/60**GO**	Crewe 133,481
1/11/60-15/11/60**NC[Rect EO]**	Crewe
11/12/61-19/1/62**LC**	Gorton
30/7/63-28/8/63**LC**	Crewe
25/8/64-29/9/64**LC**	Eastleigh

Annual mileage
1955 5,603
1956 26,728
1957 24,866
1958 28,714
1959 34,884
1960 19,012
1961 30,845
1962 22,483
1963 17,783

Sheds
Toton 5/11/55
Wellingborough 17/3/58
Toton 20/9/60
Saltley 27/3/62
Wellingborough 6/5/62
Rowsley 17/9/62
Kirkby-in-Ashfield 2/5/64
Newton Heath 24/10/64
Carlisle Kingmoor 6/8/66

Tender
BR1C no.1145 from new

Boilers
no.1436 from new
no.1684 29/9/60

Condemned 11/11/67, stored at 12A Kingmoor 11/67-1/68, cut up at Motherwell Machinery and Scrap Co., Wishaw 2/68.

92057

To traffic 11/10/55

Works
31/3/59-4/5/59**LI** Crewe 93,573

Annual mileage
1955 5,770
1956 29,503
1957 28,046
1958 24,960
1959 26,689
1960 23,145

Sheds
Toton 5/11/55
Westhouses 30/1/60
Cricklewood 7/5/60
Annesley 14/10/61
Toton 13/4/63
Saltley 12/10/63
Birkenhead 18/4/64

Tenders
BR1C no.1146 from new
BR1C no.1175 2/1/61 from 92086
BR1F no.1177 9/1/62 from 92092

Boiler
no.1437 from new

Condemned 2/10/65, stored at 8H Birkenhead 9-12/65, cut up at Wards, Beighton, Sheffield 12/65.

Approaching Wellingborough with an up working on 16 April 1956, 92056 makes its presence felt. Almost all wagons are wooden. Photograph Peter Groom.

92058

To traffic 13/10/55

Works

25/6/58-2/8/58**LI**	Crewe 73,425
	R5900 provision of safety links
16/5/60-24/6/60**HC[EO]**	Crewe 62,618
10/10/62-14/11/62**GO**	Crewe
6/6/66-30/7/66**HI**	Crewe

Annual mileage
1955 4,226
1956 29,215
1957 27,306
1958 25,244
1959 38,701
1960 32,434

Sheds
Toton 5/11/55
Wellingborough 17/3/58
Toton 20/9/60
Westhouses 7/7/62
Leicester [Midland] 19/4/64
Warrington 28/3/65
Speke Jct. 3/6/67
Carlisle Kingmoor 12/8/67

Tender
BR1C no.1147 from new

Boiler
no.1438 from new

Condemned 4/11/67, stored at 12A Kingmoor 10/67-1/68, cut up at McWilliams, Shettleston 2/68.

92059

To traffic 20/10/55

Works

11/10/58-22/10/58**NC[EO]**	shed 82,205
20/4/60-25/6/60**LC**	Crewe 126,288
	R5900 provision
	of safety links
9/10/61-25/10/61**LC[EO]**	Derby 163,122

Annual mileage
1955 5,317
1956 28,003
1957 28,342
1958 26,158
1959 30,445
1960 23,575

Sheds
Toton 5/11/55
Wellingborough 22/3/58
Toton 24/9/60
Warrington 13/3/65
Birkenhead 15/5/65

Tender
BR1C no.1148 from new

Boiler
no.1439 from new

Condemned 17/9/66, stored at 8H Birkenhead 9-10/66 and 8B Warrington 11/66-1/67, cut up at Drapers, Hull 1/67

Toton's 92057 at Wellingborough in the later 1950s. It was very much a Midland line engine but was never actually allocated to Wellingborough. Photograph J. Davenport, Initial Photographics.

92058 at Leicester shed; she is wearing a 15A Wellingborough shed plate which makes the period between March 1958 and September 1960. Photograph J. Davenport, Initial Photographics.

The Consett air pump fitted 9Fs were unique (apart from 92079 on the Lickey perhaps) in spending their lives devoted to one such highly specific purpose. The jobs were spectacular, made more so by the landscape and the uncompromising nature of the line. In April 1964, a pair of 9Fs forge uphill on the 1/54 gradient, heading west between Stanley and Annfield Plain. The line on the left trails in from Oxhill Junction and Morrison Busty Colliery. If this sort of thing grips you, you're urged to take a look at *British Railways Illustrated Summer Special No.8*, from Irwell Press. Photograph A.R. Thompson.

AIR PUMPS: 1

The staff at Wellingborough were doubtless relieved to receive a batch of new 9Fs from Crewe at the end of 1955 to replace Crostis out of action awaiting modification. One or two of the more observant among them might even have noticed the curious gaps cut in the right-hand running plate and the strange brackets fixed there. The Record Cards show 92060-92066 on loan at this time, though other contemporary reports mention just five, 92060-92064.

In March, April and May the following year this batch of 9Fs began the journey to their intended home, Tyne Dock, going to Crewe on the way to have compressed air pumps fitted. They appear to have progressed to Tyne Dock in number sequence, some after further loan at Westhouses or Toton. 92060 was reported to have arrived in the North East, fitted with air pumps, at the end of April though as usual the Engine Cards vary by a few weeks. The local crews had some acclimatising to do, for 92061 was observed 'slipping furiously' on the bank from Tyne Dock Bottom to the engine shed, 'despite banking assistance from a J25 0-6-0'.

The 9Fs were replacing Q7 0-8-0s and O1 2-8-0s on the iron ore trains up the hills to the Consett steel works and the air pumps were necessary to activate the discharge doors on the special hopper wagons. There were two pumps with associated pipework; at about 90lb/in^2 pressure, one pump charged the compressed air engines on the special wagons, keeping the four side discharge doors shut when loading and running (there was also a manual safety device) and the other opened the doors to discharge the ore onto the conveyor at Consett, which led to the furnaces.

The next three air pump fitted 9Fs, to make the total up to the necessary ten, were delivered new (and directly) in June/July 1956 – see 92097-92099.

Loading the hoppers at Tyne Dock; only at the other end did gravity at last became the friend of the whole process, for the iron ore was discharged downwards out of the side doors, consigning the ore to the furnaces. The engine crews regarded the 9Fs highly, considering that they steamed better than the Q7 0-8-0s and O2 2-8-0s they replaced. Photograph P.J. Coster.

92060

To traffic 5/11/55
Westinghouse air compressor fitted

Works
17/1/57-28/1/57**NC**	Gateshead
23/3/59-29/4/59**GO**	Darlington
11/8/60-7/10/60**LC**	Darlington
10/3/61-20/6/61**HC**	Darlington
15/7/63-29/8/63**GO**	Crewe
27/11/64-2/1/65**NC**	Crewe

Sheds
Tyne Dock 5/11/55*
Wellingborough 10/12/55
Tyne Dock 27/3/56
*You always have to be careful with the Engine History Cards.
This is the date to traffic and Tyne Dock is where 92060
should have gone. In reality 92060-92066 were drafted first to
Wellingborough, to cover for the laid-up Crostis. This was
belatedly recognised on the Cards. The engines then went to
Tyne Dock as intended and calm could descend once more in
the Engine History Card office.

Tenders
BR1B no 1149 from new
BR1B no.1307 30/11/60 from 92097

Boiler
no.1440 from new

**Condemned 23/10/66, stored at 52H Tyne Dock 10/66-3/67,
cut up at Drapers Hull 4/67.**

92061

To traffic 12/11/55
Westinghouse air compressor fitted

Works
29/1/57-7/2/57**NC**	Gateshead
14/10/58-7/11/58**LC**	Darlington
21/1/60-10/3/60**GO**	Darlington
31/5/62-14/8/62**GO**	Darlington
15/10/64-14/11/64**NC**	Crewe
18/11/64**LC**	Crewe

Sheds
Tyne Dock 12/11/55*
Wellingborough 31/12/55
Tyne Dock 8/4/56
*See note under 92060

Tenders
BR1B no.1150 from new
BR1B no.1152 25/5/62 from 92063

Boiler
no.1441 from new

**Condemned 4/9/66, stored at 52H Tyne Dock 9-10/66,
cut up at Drapers, Hull 11/66.**

A lovely crisp portrait of 92060 at Tyne Dock Bottom in
1965, beginning its slog up into the hills with the help of
a diesel shunter! Tyne Dock, the river and its cranes and
the iron ore bunker lie in the background. Photograph P.J.
Robinson.

92060 running back with empties, passing Tyne Dock shed, home of the air pump fitted 9Fs, on 19 May 1964. Photograph Peter Groom.

Inside Tyne Dock shed, and 9Fs 92061 and 92062 stand on the straight roads in May 1966. Tyne Dock had been 52H since February 1958, when Sunderland District sheds were rearranged under Gateshead. As luck would have it Tyne Dock could hardly be less suited to the big 9Fs and this four road straight shed (fashioned from a much earlier roundhouse) was the only part that could accommodate them under cover, apart from the Repair Shop alongside. Photograph A.R. Thompson.

92061 and another 9F banking, in Beamish Woods, where the gradient steepened to 1/51; Beamish station lies beyond: *There was a local league football match being played on a field on the top left in which one team managed to score a goal as the dense black smoke from the two 9Fs swept across the pitch. This led to a furious argument which was still going on long after the train had passed.* The year was 1964. Photograph A.R. Thompson.

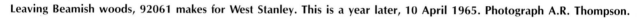

Leaving Beamish woods, 92061 makes for West Stanley. This is a year later, 10 April 1965. Photograph A.R. Thompson.

92062

To traffic 19/11/55
Westinghouse air compressor fitted

Works

12/2/57-14/2/57**NC**	Gateshead Firehole modified
29/7/58-3/10/58**LC**	Darlington Boiler tubes; frames straightened, wheels turned up
10/3/59-21/4/59**LC**	Darlington Boiler retubed
8/12/59-20/1/60**HI**	Darlington 87,200 AWS
16/2/60-7/3/60**adjustment**	Darlington Tubes
22/3/60-1/4/60**NC**	Darlington Tubes
29/4/60-23/6/60**LC**	Darlington Re-tubed
5/4/62-3/8/62**GO**	Darlington
28/8/62-17/9/62**adjustment**	Darlington
9/8/63-3/10/63**LC**	Darlington
28/2/64-2/5/64**HC**	Darlington
Dec.1964	Crewe

Sheds

Tyne Dock 12/11/55*
Wellingborough 31/11/55
Westhouses 25/2/56
Tyne Dock 25/5/56
*See note under 92060

Tenders

BR1B no.1151 from new
BR1B no.1309 25/4/60 from 92099
BR1B no.1151 27/7/60 from 92099

Boilers

no.1442 from new
no.1645 3/8/62

Condemned on shed 26/6/66, stored at 52H Tyne Dock 6-9/66, cut up at Hughes Bolckows Ltd., North Blyth 10/66.

92063

To traffic 25/11/55
Westinghouse air compressor fitted

Works

19/2/57-26/2/57**NC**	Gateshead Firehole modified
12/57	Gateshead
5/1/59-6/2/59**GO**	Darlington 78,500
11/8/60-29/10/60**HI**	Darlington 36,502 AWS
22/5/63-26/6/63**GO**	Darlington
26/8/65-23/10/65**NC**	Crewe
25/11/65**C**	Crewe

Sheds

Tyne Dock 17/11/55*
Wellingborough 10/12/55
Westhouses 18/2/56
Tyne Dock 1/5/56
*See note under 92060

Tenders

BR1B no.1152 from new
BR1B no.1150 25/5/62 from 92061

Boilers

no.1443 from new
no.1425 6/2/59

Condemned 24/11/66, stored at 52H Tyne Dock 11/66-3/67, cut up at Thompsons, Stockton-on-Tees 4/67.

A clean 92062 at rest in Tyne Dock shed yard, early 1960s, showing those pumps. Most of their time stabled was in fact spent in the open, for though Tyne Dock had three roundhouses all were too small for the 2-10-0s. Photograph J. Davenport, Initial Photographics.

South Pelaw, and 92062 drifts downhill with empties for the loading hopper at Tyne Dock. In the distance is the Stella Gill Coking Plant. 'All have now disappeared' writes Alan Thompson; 'all that is left is an official footpath and bridleway, the Consett to Sunderland Walkway using the Consett main line which the 9F is descending'. Photograph J.W. Armstrong Trust.

92062, AWS fitted but with the earlier frontstep arrangement (compare with the view alongside 92061 inside the straight shed). That very straight shed at Tyne Dock is the building in the background. Photograph Peter J. Coster.

Oiling round 92063 on Tyne Dock shed, 25 August 1956. Air reservoir above the Driver's head. Photograph A.G. Forsyth, Initial Photographics.

It will be amusing one day to count the 9Fs specially cleaned – a few when brand new as well as 92014 'dolled up' for the Willesden Exhibition. A handful only, with EVENING STAR the obvious, stand out. Much less known is 92063, done up in Royal fashion for 'The Tyne Docker'. This was the last steam working, on 19 November 1966, sadly banked along the way by a diesel. This is the Consett discharge gantry (bending round to the left); it was at the apex of a triangle so trains could run on, discharge and back on to the second side of the triangle for the engine to take water. The train then continued round the triangle to face Tyne Dock the right way round. Photograph J.W. Armstrong Trust.

92064

To traffic 2/12/55
Westinghouse air compressor fitted

Works

12/9/56-1/10/56**LC**	Gateshead Tyres turned; firehole modified
18/8/59-26/9/59**GO**	Darlington
25/7/61-4/8/61**NC**	Darlington 82,500 AWS
20/11/61-13/1/62**GO**	Darlington
16/11/64-22/12/64**LI**	Crewe
6/6/66-2/7/66**NC**	Crewe

Sheds
Tyne Dock 17/12/55*
Wellingborough 31/12/55
Toton 25/2/56
Tyne Dock 10/5/56
*See note under 92060

Tenders
BR1B no.1153 from new
BR1B no.1155 from 92066

Boilers
no.1444 from new
no.1646 26/9/59

Condemned 24/11/66, stored at 52H Tyne Dock 11/66-3/67, cut up at Thompsons, Stockton-on-Tees 4/67.

92065

To traffic 10/12/55
Westinghouse air compressor fitted

Works

16/8/56-31/8/56**LC**	Gateshead Firehole modified, 'All tyres to be machined'
4/5/59-15/6/59**GO**	Darlington 85,600
13/10/60-15/12/60**LC**	Darlington AWS, wheels turned
7/9/61-4/11/61**GO**	Darlington 70,100
28/5/64-30/9/64**LC**	Crewe

Sheds
Tyne Dock 17/12/55*
Wellingborough 31/12/55
Toton 25/2/56
Tyne Dock 24/5/56
Wakefield 27/11/66
*See note under 92060

Tender
BR1B no.1154 from new

Boilers
No.1445 from new
No.1440 15/6/59
No.1695 4/11/61

Condemned 3/4/67, stored at 56A Wakefield 4-7/67, cut up at Arnott Young, Parkgate and Rawmarsh 8/67.

A good part of the Tyne Dock 9F fleet stabled, coaled and ready for Monday morning, on Sunday 8 September 1963. The Tyne Dock 2-10-0s must have spent the least time under cover of any 2-10-0, apart from maybe 92079. All now with AWS. Photograph A.W. Forsyth, Initial Photographics.

A stunning industrial portrait, and a reminder that the 9Fs did not just work the ore trains. In April 1964 92064 rushes out of Consett Low Yard with the 2.20pm train of steel bar for Tyne Yard, due there at 3.55pm. The slight mist over the steel works only adds to the grandeur of the scene. It would probably all be closed for safety reasons these days. Photograph P.J. Robinson, courtesy A.R. Thompson.

92066

To traffic 15/12/55
Westinghouse air compressor fitted

Works
26/2/57-12/3/57**NC**   Gateshead
14/8/58-11/9/58**LC**   Darlington
13/10/59-26/11/59**GO**   Darlington
10/8/62-22/9/62**HC**   Crewe
8/5/63-13/6/63**HC**   Crewe

Shed
Tyne Dock 17/12/55*
Wellingborough 31/12/55
Toton 25/2/56
Tyne Dock 24/5/56
*See note under 92060

Tender
BR1B no.1155 from new

Boiler
no.1446 from new

Condemned on shed 23/5/65, stored at 52H Tyne Dock 6/65, cut up at Cohens, Cargo Fleet, Middlesbrough 9/65.

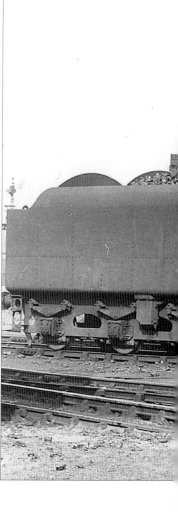

Top right. 92065 in the shed yard at Tyne Dock, 23 May 1965. Way back in the first days of the 9Fs at Tyne Dock 92065 had to be sent to Gateshead for its wheels to be reprofiled, as a result of flats suffered through frequent skidding with the wheels locked. It is not known if this problem persisted, or whether other 9Fs on the Consett trains were affected. Photograph A. Scarsbrook, Initial Photographics.

Below. 92066 in the yard at Tyne Dock, 21 September 1958. No AWS yet. The painted number on the pony wheel is evidence of its Light Casual at Darlington a few weeks before; attention was obviously confined to below the running plate! She still carries the original 54B shed plate, superseded some months before. Photograph The Transport Treasury.

Bottom right. Those big air pumps on 92066, Tyne Dock shed, 19 May 1964. Photograph Peter Groom.

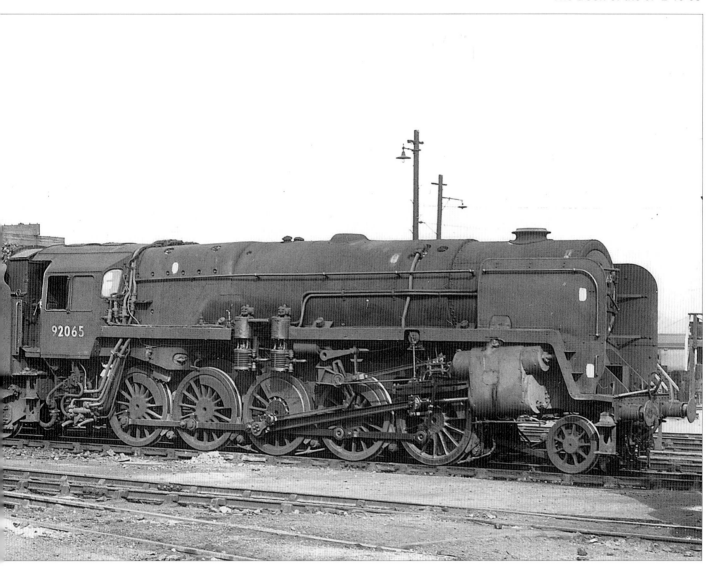

92067

To traffic 20/12/55

Works
23/11/56-29/11/56**NC**	Darlington Firehole modified
6/6/57**NC**	Stratford Briquette tube feeder
15/10/58-12/11/58**LI**	Crewe 86,566 R8245 continuous blowdown valve and additional washout plugs
11/10/61-16/11/61**GO**	Crewe
13/12/63-22/1/64**LC**	Crewe
24/11/64-2/1/65**LC**	Crewe

Mileage at 31/12/57 56,278

Annual mileage
1958 35,647
1959 43,406
1960 33,985

Sheds
Doncaster 20/12/55
Annesley 17/2/57
Banbury 20/6/65
Carlisle Kingmoor 14/10/66

Tender
BR1F no.1156 from new

Boiler
no.1447 from new

Condemned 5/11/66, stored at 12A Kingmoor 10/66-1/67, cut up at McWilliams, Shettleston 2/67.

92068

To traffic 29/12/55

Works
22/10/56-25/10/56**NC**	Darlington Firehole modified
5/9/58-30/9/58**LI**	Crewe 71,234 R8245 continuous blowdown valve and additional washout plugs
25/10/60-25/11/60**LC**	Crewe 83,300
19/6/62-3/8/62**GO**	Crewe
14/11/63-11/12/63**LC**	Crewe

Mileage at 31/12/57 50,145

Annual mileage
1958 34,127
1959 44,020
1960 30,317

Sheds
Doncaster 31/12/55
Annesley 16/3/57
Kirkby-in-Ashfield 2/5/64
Derby 3/1/66

Tenders
BR1F no.1157 from new
BR1F no.1163 2/12/57 from 92074

Boiler
no.1448 from new

Condemned 15/1/66, stored at 12A Kingmoor 12/65-3/66, cut up at Arnott Young, West of Scotland Shipbreaking Co., Troon 4/66.

Back to Normal

From 92067 deliveries went once again to the Eastern Region. The steel industry, centred on Scunthorpe, Rotherham, Sheffield, Staveley and Sheepbridge, was second only to coal on the Eastern Region. It was fed from the coke ovens and ore fields (it comes as a jolt to recall we actually had such deposits once) quarried across Northamptonshire and Lincolnshire, though more and more was coming through Immingham. Steel, coal, raw materials in, finished products out; Doncaster 9Fs worked the lot and 92069 was a batch of ten 92067-92076 (those multiples of five again) which went new to the grand old GN shed over 1955-56. 92069 is some six months old at Doncaster, on 10 June 1956 and the grime is coming along nicely. Photograph B.K.B. Green, Initial Photographics.

92069

To traffic 31/12/55

Works
10/10/56-15/10/56**NC**	Darlington Firehole modified
23/5/57**NC**	Stratford Briquette tube feeder
20/3/58-24/5/58**LI**	Crewe 56,788 R3329 modified piston for continuous blowdown valve
10/2/61-25/3/61**LC**	Crewe 117,556
14/4/61-26/4/61	Crewe Manganese liners bolts
1/2/63-23/3/63**GO**	Crewe E4983 AWS equipment of train control
20/6/66-18/8/66**HI**	Crewe

Mileage at 31/12/57 51,462

Annual mileage
1958 39,865
1959 41,006
1960 40,269

Sheds
Doncaster 31/12/55
Annesley 17/2/57
Birkenhead 23/5/65
Speke Jct. 29/11/67

Tenders
BR1F no.1158 from new
BR1F no.1160 at Annesley, 22/1/61 from 92071
BR1F no.1184, 3/12/63 from 92095
BR1F no.1177, 22/11/65 from 92057
BR1F no.1161, 15/2/66 from 92072

Boiler
no.1449 from new

Condemned 4/5/68, stored at 8C Speke Jct. 5-9/68, cut up at Arnott Young, Parkgate and Rawmarsh 10/68.

92070

To traffic 14/1/56

Works
30/10/56-2/11/56**NC**	Darlington Firehole modified
30/4/57-2/5/57**NC**	Stratford Briquette tube feeder
27/10/58-24/11/58**LI**	Crewe 87,048 R8245 continuous blowdown valve and additional washout plugs
30/1/62-3/3/62**GO**	Crewe

Mileage at 31/12/57 55,562

Annual mileage
1958 34,750
1959 38,348
1960 36,950

Sheds
Doncaster 14/1/56
Annesley 17/2/57
Saltley 7/4/60
Toton 16/9/60
Westhouses 23/6/62
Wellingborough 9/3/63
Leicester Midland 12/5/63
Warrington 28/3/65
Birkenhead 15/5/65

Tenders
BR1F no.1159 from new
BR1C no.1340 13/10/60 from 92130
BR1F no.1158 9/1/62 from 92071 at Annesley

Boiler
no.1450 from new

Condemned 11/11/67, stored at 8H Birkenhead 11-12/67 and Speke Jct. 1/68, cut up at Campbells, Airdrie 2/68.

92071, by now an Annesley engine, has just passed Bulwell Common station on the GC with a motley collection of wagons, 27 June 1957. The whiff of steam on the right is from the staff train to Annesley (the 'Dido'). Men who had worked to Woodford were usually relieved at Bulwell Common and either went home or took the said 'Dido' to Annesley shed. 92071's train has been 'relieved' and is heading down the connection to the GN Leen Valley line. Photograph T.G. Hepburn, Rail Archive Stephenson.

92071

To traffic 21/1/56

Works

28/9/56-4/10/56**NC**	Darlington Firehole modified
21/5/57	Briquette tube feeder
18/12/58-12/1/59**LI**	Crewe 26,810 R8245 continuous blowdown valve and additional washout plugs
3/8/61-31/8/61**LI**	Crewe
4/10/63-20/11/63**GO**	Crewe 102,712
21/12/65-5/2/66**HC**	Crewe

Mileage at 31/12/57 61,973

Annual mileage
1958 26,810
1959 40,844
1960 41,461

Sheds
Doncaster 21/1/56
Annesley 17/2/57
Newton Heath 18/7/65
Carlisle Kingmoor 4/12/65

Tenders
BR1F no.1160 from new
BR1F no.1158 22/1/61 from 92069 at Annesley
BR1C no.1340 9/1/62 from 92070 at Annesley

Boiler
no.1451 from new

Condemned 11/11/67, stored at 12A Kingmoor 11/67-1/68, cut up at Motherwell Machinery and Scrap Co., Wishaw 2/68.

92072

To traffic 1/2/56

Works

19/9/56-22/9/56**NC**	Darlington Firehole modified
19/7/57**NC**	Stratford Briquette feed water tubes
5/8/58-29/8/58**LI**	Crewe 75,362 R8245 continuous blowdown valve and additional washout plugs
18/7/61-23/8/61**GO**	Crewe 121,129
19/9/63-31/10/63**HC**	Crewe

Mileage at 31/12/57 53,186

Annual mileage
1958 39,154
1959 44,890
1960 42,851

Sheds
Doncaster 1/2/56
Annesley 17/2/57
Kikby-in-Ashfield 28/6/65

Tender
BR1F no.1161 from new

Boilers
no.1452 from new
no.1945 23/8/61

Condemned 25/12/65, stored at 16E Kirkby-in-Ashfield 1-5/66, cut up at Wards, Beighton, Sheffield 6/66.

92073

To traffic 9/2/56

Works

10/9/56-13/9/56**NC**	Darlington Firehole modified
5/57	Briquette tube feeder
22/8/58-7/10/58**LI**	Crewe 85,714 E3329 modified piston for continuous blowdown valve and additional washout plugs
18/12/59-4/3/60 **LC[EO]**	53,136
3-4/65	Crewe

Mileage at 31/12/57 59,968

Annual mileage
1958 37,819
1959 41,026
1960 40,459

Sheds
Doncaster 18/2/56
Annesley 24/2/57
Banbury 12/6/65
Birkenhead 17/9/66

Tenders
BR1F no.1162 from new
BR1F no.961 from 92012 2/9/58
BR1F no.1182 17/11/59 from 92093
BR1F no.1179 24/10/60 from 92090

Boiler
no.1453 from new

Condemned 11/11/67, stored at 8H Birkenhead 11-12/67 and Speke Jct. 1/68, cut up at Campbells, Airdrie 2/68.

92074

To traffic 18/2/56

Works
25/8/56-4/9/56**NC**	Darlington Firehole modified
25/7/57**NC**	Stratford Briquette tube feeder
1/10/58-30/10/58**LI**	Crewe 76,472 R8245 continuous
	blowdown valve and additional
	washout plugs
31/5/61-3/7/61**GO**	Crewe 109,633
28/9/64-28/11/64**HC[CB]**	Crewe

Mileage at 31/12/57 49,490

Annual mileage
1958 34,867
1959 43,771
1960 44,947

Sheds
Doncaster 18/2/56
Annesley 24/2/57
Banbury 20/6/65
Saltley 3/1/66
Croes Newydd 28/5/66
Carlisle Kingmoor 31/12/66

Tenders
BR1F no.1163 from new
BR1F no.1157 2/12/57 from 92068
BR1F no.1182 at Annesley 20/11/63 from 92090

Boiler
no.1454 from new

Condemned 15/4/67, stored at 12A Kingmoor 4-10/67, cut up at Motherwell Machinery and Scrap Co., Wishaw 10/67.

92075

To traffic 1/3/56

Works
20/8/56-25/8/56**NC**	Darlington Firehole modified
8/57	Briquette tube feeder
24/9/58-29/10/58**LI**	Crewe 84,598 R8245 continuous
	blowdown valve and additional
	washout plugs
12/10/60-5/1/61**LC**	Crewe 82,170

Mileage at 31/12/57 54,906

Annual mileage
1958 37,194
1959 40,148
1960 34,709

Sheds
Doncaster 24/3/56
Annesley 24/2/57
Toton 20/4/63
Annesley 12/10/63
Kirkby-in-Ashfield 3/7/65
Carlisle Kingmoor 2/4/66

Tender
BR1F no.1164 from new

Boiler
no.1455 from new

Condemned 17/9/66, stored at 12A Kingmoor 9/66-1/67, cut up at Drapers, Hull 2/67.

92077 in its last days, as a Carnforth engine. On 19 August 1967 it beats its way past the little Bell Busk signal box north-west of Skipton on the Midland with a down freight. Photograph Gavin Morrison.

92076

To traffic 6/3/56

Works

29/7/56-10/8/56**NC**	Darlington Firehole modified
7/6/57**NC**	Stratford Briquette tube feeder
30/5/58-2/7/58**LI**	Crewe 67,275 R8245 continuous blowdown valve and additional washout plugs
10/3/59-25/3/59**LC[EO]**	Rugby 34,458
18/2/61-18/3/61**LC**	Gorton 115,737
16/11/61-13/12/61**LC**	Crewe
5/1/62-9/2/62**LC**	Crewe
8/2/63-20/3/63**GO**	Crewe E4983 AWS
8/3/65-1/4/65**LC**	Crewe

Mileage at 31/12/57 51,776

Annual mileage
1958 41,487
1959 44,319
1960 40,389

Sheds
Doncaster 6/3/56
Annesley 24/2/57
Rowsley 21/10/63
Kirkby-in-Ashfield 2/5/64
Newton Heath 4/10/64
Carlisle Kingmoor 9/1/65

Tender
BR1F no.1165 from new

Boiler
no.1456 from new

Condemned 25/2/67, stored at 8C Speke Jct.1-4/67, cut up at McWilliams Shettleston 6/67.

92077

To traffic 13/3/56

Works

3/4/56-23/4/56**NC**	Crewe
4/5/59-1/6/59**LC**	Crewe 75,566 R5900 provision of safety links; E3329 modified piston for continuous blowdown valve
22/6/61-11/8/61**HC[EO]**	Crewe 59,120
22/1/63-23/2/63**GO**	Crewe E4983 AWS
14/3/66-15/4/66**HC**	Crewe

Annual mileage
1956 20,579
1957 29,359
1958 20,076
1959 24,433
1960 26,715

Sheds
Toton 13/3/56
Wellingborough 11/8/63 (loan)
Kirkby-in-Ashfield 24/10/63
Newton Heath 12/7/64
Carnforth 22/4/67

Tenders
BR1C no.1166 from new
BR1C no.1373 1/7/63 from 92154

Boiler
no.1457 from new

Condemned 22/6/68, stored at 10A Carnforth 6-9/68, cut up at Campbells, Airdrie 10/68.

A 9F at Mirfield, after it got AWS in 1963 – note the vacuum reservoir under the cab. The number is helpfully repeated in chalk on the cabside. Photograph *www.vintage-images.co.uk*

92078

To traffic 21/3/56

Works

31/12/56-15/1/57**LC[EO]**	Crewe 22,250 R5900 provision of safety links
16/12/59-16/1/60**LC**	Crewe 96,225
26/1/63	E4983 AWS
2/65	Crewe

Annual mileage
1956 22,188
1957 27,428
1958 23,797
1959 22,976
1960 29,467

Tender
BR1C no.1167 from new

Boiler
no.1458 from new

Sheds
Toton 24/3/56
Warrington 13/3/65

Condemned 6/5/67, stored at 8B Warrington 3-12/67, cut up at Thompsons, Stockton-on-Tees 1/68.

Toton's 92078, perfectly repainted so far as the smokebox is concerned, running past its home shed on 26 August 1956. Photograph B.K.B. Green, Initial Photographics.

THE LICKEY BANKER

British steam locomotives were distinguished by the almost complete absence of the headlight. Just about the only exception that comes to mind is Big Bertha, the 0-10-0 Lickey banker, 58100. It was long in the tooth, however, and the odd decision was taken to replace it with a more or less brand new 9F. Odd because any number of older Class 8 2-8-0s might have done; was a banking job the best use of new power? It's hard to accept that 'Bertha' was even on its last legs. For a single locomotive it enjoyed, almost uniquely, a *spare boiler* and after withdrawal still looked good enough to go on display for an open day at Derby.

Whatever the circumstances, BR decided upon a 9F for the Lickey – maybe because the Lickey was a famous, celebrated bank and it was thought appropriate that a new Standard should adorn it. 92008 had appeared at Bromsgrove in August 1955, to gauge the suitability of a 2-10-0 for the work. It was a success obviously, and in May the following year the venerable 0-10-0 went off to Derby for the last time. In an almost co-ordinated toppling of dear old Bertha, 92079, her chosen successor, was also at Derby, ready to take over the electric headlight. 92079 had also exchanged the BR1C tender with which it should have run, for the inset bunker BR1G one from 92009. The reason was the better lookout running backwards. 92079 was distinguished further by the rectangular cut-out in the bunker, left-hand side, to aid hand coaling at Bromsgrove South. For all the concerns regarding the lamp, it is said banking crews were reluctant to use it because of a conviction that, if the train engine crew knew the 'big 'un' was on, they wouldn't try so hard!

92079

To traffic 29/3/56

Works

7/5/56-12/5/56**NC**	Crewe 2,454 Modified to work on the Lickey incline
16/8/57-28/9/57**LI**	Crewe 32,158 R5900 provision of safety links
27/2/58-29/3/58**LC**	Crewe 10,000 [entered in pencil] Leaky tube plate
15/5/59-4/1/60**HC**	Swindon
1/10/64-28/11/64 **LI[CB]**	Crewe

Annual mileage
1956 18,167
1957 19,774
1963 1,787

Sheds
Toton 21/4/56
Bromsgrove 19/5/56
Birkenhead 12/10/63

Tenders
BR1C no.1168 from new
BR1G no.958, 19/5/56 from 92009, Modified for use on the Lickey Incline

Boiler
no.1459 from new

Condemned 11/11/67, stored at 8C Speke Jct. 11/67-3/68, cut up at Campbells, Airdrie 4/68

Right. 92079 at Bromsgrove with 8405, one of the pannier tanks which had begun to arrive in July 1956. Trains warranted bankers according to their weight and the crews endeavoured to ensure that they all did their jobs up the bank in strict order, so that firemen all had the same amount of work to do. Photograph J. Davenport, Initial Photographics.

Below. Fit for the Prairies or the Veldt, 92079 outside the Crewe Paint Shop, 23 September 1957. The electric generator for the headlight was underneath the cab on the left-hand side, and was driven by a small steam turbine controlled by a valve in the cab. Photograph Peter J. Coster.

92079 at work on the bank. The light was for the big engine to buffer up and in truth it seemed to owe as much to 'custom and practice' as to the realities of everyday working. 'Bertha' had had a lamp, so the 9F had to have one. After all, every other driver in the country was buffering up every kind of locomotive, in difficult conditions, every minute of the day without problems; the Bromsgrove crews didn't use the lamp when it suited them and anyway it was taken off, according to Atkins, about 1960. Photograph The Transport Treasury.

The famous cut-out in the tender to aid hand coaling at Bromsgrove South. As the loco always pointed the same way the cut-out was only needed, of course, on this side. It's a pretty dull day, 20 August 1960 and 92079 (the headlight is gone by now) is working hard on a Bournemouth West-Nottingham train. She is showing the white feather (though this could be deceptive – Ross pop safety valves commonly failed to seat 100 per cent when shut, so a light discharge would ensue whatever the pressure) and has an almost clear chimney. Though it appears effortless, it certainly is not. The train engine, incidentally, was Black Five 44962. The 9F was transferred away towards the end of 1963 for no obvious reason, without any concern, it would seem, for the coaling considerations. It fell prey, apparently, to an inter-Regional edict in which four Western Region 9Fs went to the LMR in exchange for three BR Class Fives and a BR Class 4 4-6-0. At least two more 9Fs followed, 92223 and 92230, the Record showing that their stays overlapped; presumably this is in error, and in fact indicates when one stood in for the other. After its transfer to Birkenhead 92079 became oddly anonymous and it is not known what the locals up there thought of the 'funny 'ole' in the tender. Photograph David Horne, The Transport Treasury.

Back to Normal

92080

To traffic 14/4/56

Works
2/7/58-10/7/58**NC[EO]**   shed
24/5/60-1/7/60**LC**   Crewe 118,640 R5900 provision
                             of safety links
May 1964   Crewe

Annual mileage
1956 20,532
1957 27,914
1958 23,611
1959 34,425
1960 32,073

Sheds
Toton 21/4/56
Wellingborough 22/3/58
Kettering 3/8/63
Newton Heath 27/6/64
Carlisle Kingmoor 13/8/66

Tenders
BR1C no.1169 from new
BR1C no.1372 12/7/64 from 92134

Boiler
no.1460 from new

Condemned 6/5/67, stored at 12A Kingmoor 5-10/67, cut up at McWilliams, Shettleston 11/67.

92081

To traffic 23/4/56

Works
8/9/58-11/10/58**LI**   Crewe 71,336 E3329 modified
                             piston for continuous
                             blowdown valve; R5900
                             provision of safety links
22/2/60-29/4/60**LC**   46,081
6/9/61-17/10/61**GO**   Crewe 91,777

Annual mileage
1956 20,303
1957 28,766
1958 32,070
1959 35,411
1960 25,875

Sheds
Toton 19/5/56
Annesley 13/12/58
Toton 2/5/59
Wellingborough 7/11/59
Kettering 3/8/63
Newton Heath 27/6/64

Tenders
BR1C no.1170 from new
BR1C no.1330 29/2/60 from 92120

Boiler
no.1461 from new

Condemned 12/2/66, stored at 9D Newton Heath 2-6/66, cut up at W.George, Station Steel, Wath 6/66.

92082

To traffic 3/5/56

Works

21/5/58-6/6/58	**LC[EO]**	shed 55,649
P/E 3/10/59		E3491 Provision and fitting of fibreglass boiler insulation mattresses
26/9/60-22/10/60	**LC**	Crewe 115,885
2/11/61-8/12/61	**GO**	Crewe
17/2/64-28/3/64	**HC**	Crewe
19/5/64	**Rect**	Crewe

Annual mileage
1956 19,833
1957 29,789
1958 22,116
1959 27,310
1960 23,913

Sheds
Wellingborough 3/5/56
On loan Toton 27/1/62
Wellingborough 4/3/62
Annesley 7/2/63
Saltley 23/2/63
Birkenhead 30/11/63

Tenders
BR1C no.1171 from new
BR1B no.971 3/10/59 from 92022

Boiler
no.1462 from new

Condemned 11/11/67, stored at 8C Speke Jct. 11/67-3/68, cut up at Campbells, Airdrie 4/68.

The Lickey 9F, 92079, would have stayed at Toton if not diverted to Bromsgrove as part of a series of ten for the Midland lines, and the coal traffic to London. In that way it would have led a very different life, alongside many others, like 92081 at Toton shed in the late 1950s. Photograph J. Davenport, Initial Photographics.

92083

To traffic 11/5/56

Works

21/5/58-10/6/58	**LC[EO]**	shed 54,907
10/8/60-9/9/60	**LC**	Crewe 118,842 E3329 modified piston for continuous blowdown valve; R5900 provision of safety links
19/1/62-24/2/62	**HC**	Crewe
18/7/63-23/8/63	**GO**	Crewe

Annual mileage
1956 19,150
1957 30,264
1958 26,247
1959 28,766
1960 28,712

Sheds
Wellingborough 11/5/56
On loan Annesley 10/11/60
Wellingborough 27/2/61
Annesley 7/2/63
Wellingborough 9/3/63
Kettering 13/1/64
Leicester [Midland] 19/10/64
Annesley 4/1/65
Birkenhead 23/5/65

Tenders
BR1C no.1172 from new
BR1F no.1176 from 92086

Boiler
no.1463 from new

Condemned 18/2/67, stored at 8H Birkenhead 2-7/67, cut up at Drapers, Hull 7/67.

Birkenhead shed, in the mid-1960s. Half the LM 9Fs seem to spend some time here at least and the shed's closure in 1967 and the loss of its 2-10-0s was one of the worst blows to the class. Dear old 92082 looks in fair good shape, though. Photograph J. Davenport, Initial Photographics.

92083 with an up freight on Saxby curve, in the summer of 1958. The M&GN 'link' line (Saxby-Bourne) is over to the right of the loco. Photograph Peter Groom.

92084

To traffic 19/5/56

Works

6/6/58-16/6/58**NC[EO]**	Derby shed
14/10/59-13/11/59**LI**	Crewe 94,024 R5900 provision of safety links
29/3/62-16/5/62**LC**	Gorton
12/7/63-17/9/63**GO**	Crewe
31/3/65-20/4/65**LC**	Crewe

Annual mileage
1956 18,825
1957 27,502
1958 27,296
1959 24,316
1960 36,102

Sheds
Wellingborough 19/5/56
Kettering 13/1/64
Speke Jct. 14/10/64
Birkenhead 23/1/65

Tenders
BR1C no.1173 from new
BR1F no.1142 at Warrington from 92053

Boiler
no.1464 from new

Condemned 11/11/67, stored at 8H Birkenhead 11/67-2/68, cut up at Campbells, Airdrie 3/68.

92085

To traffic 26/5/56

Works

10/6/58-19/6/58 **NC[EO]**	Derby shed Tubes
13/6/60-5/7/60**LC**	Gorton 114,424
24/8/61-29/9/61**GO**	Crewe 141,957 R5900 provision of safety links
7/4/64-20/5/64**HC**	Crewe
24/9/65-16/10/65**LC**	Crewe

Annual mileage
1956 17,944
1957 30,570
1958 28,280
1959 24,073
1960 27,009

Sheds
Wellingborough 26/5/56
Kettering 12/12/60
Saltley 8/10/62
Tyseley 30/11/63
Willesden 19/9/64
Birkenhead 5/12/64

Tenders
BR1C no.1174 from new
BR1F no.1181 at Birkenhead 29/12/66 from 92094

Boilers
no.1465 from new
no.1411 29/9/61

Condemned 24/12/66, stored at Woodham Brothers, Barry 1/67-7/80, cut up 7/80.

92084 at Crewe South some time after January 1965, when it became a Birkenhead (8H) engine. With its connecting rod roped to the running plate it is obviously on its way to works. Condemned in late 1967, it was cut up at Airdrie after storage at Birkenhead shed so this is almost certainly the occasion of its Light Casual at Crewe at the beginning of 1965. Photograph J. Davenport, Initial Photographics.

92086

To traffic 6/6/56

Works

16/6/58-4/7/58**NC[EO]**	Derby Tubes
29/2/60-24/3/60**LC**	Crewe 105,514 E3329 modified piston for continuous blowdown valve; R5900 provision of safety links
16/1/61-17/2/61**LC**	Crewe 132,638
24/6/63-15/8/63**GO**	Crewe

Annual mileage
1956 16,757
1957 31,042
1958 23,046
1959 32,777
1960 28,856

Sheds
Wellingborough 6/6/56
Kettering 13/1/64
Leicester [Midland] 19/10/64
Warrington 28/3/65
Birkenhead 19/6/65

Tenders
BR1C no.1175 from new
BR1C no.1146 at Cricklewood from 92057 2/1/61
BR1C no.1176 2/1/61 from 92087
BR1C no.1172 at Wellingborough from 92083 22/12/61
BR1C no.1169 from 92134 15/1/67

Boilers
no.1466 from new
no.1747 15/8/63

Condemned 11/11/67, stored at 8C Speke Jct. 11/67-3/68, cut up Campbells, Airdrie 4/68.

92087

To traffic 29/8/56

Works

26/6/57**NC**	Stratford Briquette tube feed; water tubes
1/12/58-24/12/58**LI**	Crewe 77,317 R8245 continuous blowdown valve and additional washout plugs
23/1/61-30/3/61**GO**	Crewe 92,948
24/5/61-12/6/61**LC**	Crewe 8,193
5/3/63-5/4/63**LC**	Crewe
13/10/64-4/12/64**LC**	Crewe
10/2/66-23/3/66	Crewe Attention to boiler
Mileage at 31/12/57	46,872

Annual mileage
1958 30,503
1959 43,817
1960 48,467

Sheds
Doncaster 29/8/56
Annesley 24/2/57
Banbury 20/6/65
Northampton 10/7/65
Tyseley 2/10/65
Carnforth 12/11/66

Tenders
BR1F no.1176 from new
BR1C no.1146 3/3/61 from 92086

Boilers
no.1467 from new
no.1436 6/3/61

Condemned 25/2/67, stored at 12A Kingmoor 1-5/67, cut up at McWilliams, Shettleston 6/67.

An up freight between Melton Mowbray (Town) station and Brentingby box, 21 December 1957, behind 92086. There's something more than coal in those (covered) mineral wagons! Photograph Peter Groom.

92087 outside 10 Shop at Crewe Works, after painting in the shop – probably 1963, looking at the Record. The final adjustments are being made before the engine is reunited with the tender, to then proceed to the Vacuum Pits for steam tests. Photograph The Transport Treasury.

92087 was the first of the Swindon 9Fs, of Lot 421, actually transferred from Crewe. These were 92087-92096 for the Eastern Region. At Gloucester Central on 16 July 1966, 92087 by now is a Tyseley engine. Through the course of Regional boundary changes it had gone from the ER to the LMR via, among others, a couple of former GWR engine sheds – a process that was by no means out of the ordinary. Bent deflector hand rail - again! Photograph Norman Preedy.

92088

To traffic 24/10/56

Works

4/1/57-17/1/57**LC**	Darlington 3,896 Collision damage, frames repaired
21/5/57**NC**	Stratford Briquette tube feeder
27/11/58-23/12/58**LI**	Crewe 72,171 R8245 continuous blowdown valve and additional washout plugs
8/3/60-9/4/60**LC**	Crewe 44,936
22/8/61-28/9/61**GO**	Crewe 95,616
12/10/64-16/12/64**HI[CB]**	Crewe

Mileage at 31/12/57 37,364

Annual mileage
1958 34,975
1959 39,826
1960 37,915

Sheds
Doncaster 24/10/56
Annesley 24/2/57
Toton 24/5/63
Annesley 11/8/63
Toton 28/6/65
Birkenhead 18/7/65
Carnforth 29/11/67

Tenders
BR1F no.1178 from new
BR1C no.1121 8/6/60 from 92032

Boilers
no.1469 from new
no.1454 28/9/61

Condemned 27/4/68, stored at 10A Carnforth 5-9/68, cut up at Arnott Young, Dinsdale 10/68.

92089

To traffic 26/9/56

Works

14/6/57**NC**	Stratford Briquette tube feeder
23/12/58-22/1/59**LI**	Crewe 69,142 R8245 continuous blowdown valve and additional washout plugs
4/4/61-3/5/61**LC**	Gorton
31/1/62-10/3/62**GO**	Crewe
22/5/63-15/6/63**LC**	Crewe

Mileage at 31/12/57 44,317

Annual mileage
1958 24,825
1959 39,963
1960 42,535

Sheds
Doncaster 26/9/56
Annesley 3/3/57
Leicester Midland 8/2/63
Speke Jct. 4/10/64
Birkenhead 23/1/65

Tenders
BR1F no.1177 from new
BR1F no.1181 from 92092 at Annesley 9/12/60
BR1F no.1163 at Annesley 17/3/61

Boiler
no.1468 from new

Condemned 18/2/67, stored at 8H Birkenhead 2-7/67, cut up at Drapers Hull 7/67.

92088 at Doncaster shed in 1957. Its 38B code is Annesley, which will become 16D when the GC was lost to the LMR the following year. Photograph J. Davenport, Initial Photographics.

A new Swindon 9F. 92089 at its birthplace, 9 September 1956. The Swindon 9Fs would have run in on the usual turns from Swindon – pick-up goods to Didcot and so on but pictures of them so engaged (*ditto* the Crewe examples) seem not to exist. County 4-6-0 1015 alongside makes an amusing sight parked next to a low sided tender.

92089, location and period unknown but in a magnificent pose. The lack of a shed plate suggests it has just been transferred from one shed to another. Photograph The Transport Treasury.

92090

To traffic 8/11/56

Works

8/4/57-3/5/57**LC**	Darlington 9,287 Superheater header repaired
11/5/57-13/5/57**NC**	Stratford Briquette tube feeder
20/2/59-25/3/59**LI**	Crewe 78,479 R8245 continuous blowdown valve and additional washout plugs
7/11/60-1/12/60**LC**	Gorton 61,764
31/10/62-7/12/62**GO**	Crewe
3/12/63-24/1/64**HC**	Crewe
25/5/64-10/7/64**LC**	Crewe
21/12/65-12/2/66**LI**	Crewe

Mileage at 31/12/57 36,946

Annual mileage
1958 39,445
1959 36,879
1960 30,588

Sheds
Doncaster 8/11/56
Annesley 3/3/57
Birkenhead 23/5/65

Tenders
BR1F no.1179 from new
BR1F no.1182 24/10/60 from 92073
BR1F no.1157 30/11/63 from 92074
BR1G no.1560 from 92024 9/12/65
BR1C no.1311 from 92101 12/4/67

Boiler
no.1470 from new

Condemned 15/5/67, stored at 8H Birkenhead 5-9/67, cut up at Cohens, Kettering 10-12/67.

92091

To traffic 27/11/56

Works

26/6/57**NC**	Stratford Briquette tube feeder
18/1/59-21/2/59**LI**	Crewe 82,451 R8245 continuous blowdown valve and additional washout plugs E3329 modified piston for continuous blowdown valve
2/61	Derby
6/10/61-28/10/61**LC[EO]**	Gorton 94,853
5/65	Crewe

Mileage at 31/12/57 41,258

Annual mileage
1958 40,028
1959 37,556
1960 34,755

Sheds
Doncaster 15/12/56
Annesley 3/3/57
Speke Jct. 31/7/65
Carnforth 11/5/68

Tender
BR1F no.1180 from new

Boiler
no.1471 from new

Condemned 6/68, stored at 10A Carnforth 6-10/68,

92090 at Nottingham Victoria, date unknown, with a southbound coal train. The 9F carries Class 'H' lamps; under the out-and-home scheme introduced by the ER on the Great Central line (the 'runners' as they came to be known) this meant 45 loaded minerals (or 60 goods or 70 empties) at an average speed of 30 mph. In the down direction from Woodford loads were lighter. The big innovation seems to have been the rigid insistence on 'right time' away from Annesley. Photograph The Transport Treasury.

Carrington again (see 92012 earlier page 49) with 92090 on an Annesley-Woodford coal train, 4 May 1965. Some of these trains ran with a fitted 'head' of vans or a parcels van, as here, to increase the braking power. The inflexibility as to departure times (it had probably slipped a bit by now) was deliberate and it was considered to have great psychological and practical value. Not only did it ensure that with punctual departures that pathing was maintained, the crews had an incentive to get away promptly off the shed, otherwise the train was cancelled and they'd have to go home on a less important job. Another principle of the scheme was that out and home workings were under the supervision of single sheds, ensuring good maintenance, and thereby higher mileages. Photograph Malcolm Castledine.

92093 ready to leave Valley Road goods station in Bradford, with the 7.40pm freight to Carlisle on 19 July 1967. A Kingmoor engine by now, it was returning home. Photograph Gavin Morrison.

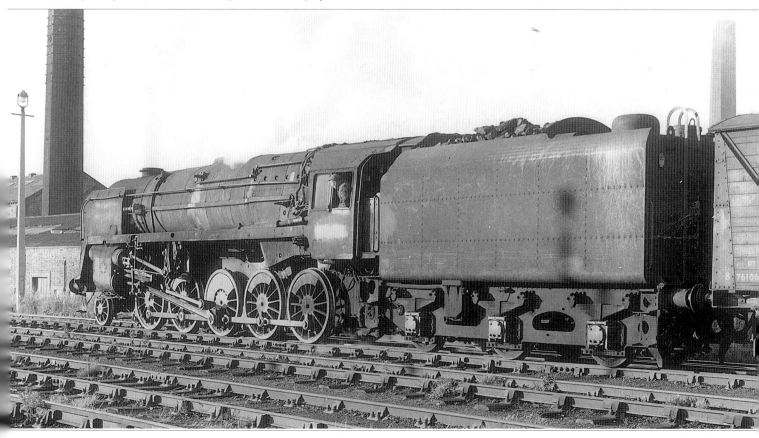

92092

To traffic 13/12/56

Works

21/6/57-22/6/57**NC**	Stratford Briquette tube feeder
30/9/58-1/11/58**LI**	Crewe 72,824 R8245 continuous blowdown valve and additional washout plugs
19/10/60-18/11/60**HC**	Crewe 82,759
6/1/61-24/1/61**LC**	Gorton 84,685
8/2/63-16/3/63**GO**	Crewe E4983 AWS

Mileage at 31/12/57 43,273

Annual mileage
1958 35,342
1959 43,098
1960 35,751

Sheds
Doncaster 13/12/56
Annesley 3/3/57
Birkenhead 23/5/65

Tenders
BR1F no.1181 from new
BR1F no.1177 at Annesley 19/12/60 from 92089
BR1C no.1175 at Annesley 9/1/62 from 92057
BR1C no.1325 from 92115

Boiler
no.1472 from new

Condemned 22/10/66, stored at 8H Birkenhead 10/66-3/67, cut up at Drapers, Hull 4/67.

92093

To traffic 15/1/57

Works

14/5/57**NC**	Stratford Briquette tube feeder
1/10/58-23/10/58**LI**	Crewe 72,035 R8245 continuous blowdown valve and additional washout plugs
24/11/59-2/1/60**LC**	Crewe 42,459
29/4/60-6/6/60**LC**	Crewe 52,883
18/12/61-27/1/62**HC**	Crewe
30/4/63-6/6/63**GO**	Crewe
4/1/65-13/2/65**LC**	Crewe
22/2/66-1/4/66**LI**	Crewe

Mileage at 31/12/57 40,497

Annual mileage
1958 40,082
1959 33,936
1960 38,912

Sheds
Doncaster 15/1/57
Annesley 3/3/57
Kirkby-in-Ashfield 28/6/65
Carlisle Kingmoor 30/1/66

Tenders
BR1F no.1182 from new
BR1F no.961 at Annesley 17/11/59 from 92073

Boilers
no.1473 from new
no.1950 6/6/63

Condemned 2/9/67, stored at 12D Workington 8/67-1/68, cut up at Motherwell, Machinery and Scrap Co., Wishaw 2/68.

The Annesley water was famously awful (around this time it swapped one of its O2 2-8-0s for a Wellingborough 8F to compare the effects on the boiler tubes) and the deposits on one of the shed's finest, 92094, provide ample confirmation. A glorious state to get into, one that the boldest modeller might shrink from. Photograph T.G. Hepburn, Rail Archive Stephenson.

92094

To traffic 4/2/57

Works

1/3/57-15/3/57**NC**	Doncaster Briquette tube feeder
	Equalising type of brake valve
29/6/59-15/8/59**LC**	Crewe 67,380
	E3329 modified piston for continuous
	blowdown valve
	R8245 continuous blowdown valve and
	additional washout plugs
5/10/60-5/11/60**LC**	Crewe 118,276
21/11/61-13/1/62**LC**	Gorton
27/12/62-26/1/63**GO**	Crewe E4983 AWS
10/3/64-23/4/64**LC**	Crewe
1/7/65-20/8/65**HI**	Crewe
19/10/65-6/11/65**LC**	Crewe
4/1/66-12/1/66**Rect**	Crewe

Mileage at 31/12/57 36,665

Annual mileage
1958 24,395
1959 25,892
1960 39,102

Sheds
Doncaster 4/2/57
Annesley 20/4/57
Toton 8/12/58
Annesley 28/4/59
Birkenhead 23/5/65
Speke Jct. 29/4/67

Tenders
BR1F no.1183 from new
BR1C no.962 at Annesley 29/9/60 from 92013
BR1F no.1181 at Annesley 12/4/61
BR1C no.1174 at Birkenhead 29/12/66 from 92085

Boiler
no.1474 from new

Condemned 4/5/68, Stored at 8C Speke Jct 5-8/68, cut up at Arnott Young, Parkgate and Rawmarsh 9/68.

Annesley's 92096, on an up 'runner' to Woodford Halse
Photograph M. Kinder.

92095

To traffic 6/3/57

Works

15/7/57**NC**	Stratford Briquette tube feeder
29/3/58-17/5/58**LC**	Crewe 45,266
5/2/59-23/4/59**LI**	Crewe 76,074
24/6/60-17/9/60**LC[EO]**	Crewe 50,357
9/11/60-7/12/60**LC**	Gorton 58,650
4/62	Crewe

Mileage at 31/12/57 35,383

Annual mileage
1958 36,553
1959 33,462
1960 30,300

Sheds
Annesley 16/3/57
Kirkby-in-Ashfield 3/7/65
Warrington 28/5/66

Tenders
BR1F no.1184 from new
BR1F no.1160 3/12/63 from 92069
BR1G no.957 5/9/64 from 92008

Boiler
no.1475 from new

Condemned 1/10/66, stored at 8B Warrington 9/66-2/67, cut up at Drapers, Hull 4/67.

92096

To traffic 2/4/57

Works

25/5/57**NC**	Stratford Briquette tube feeder
21/10/58-15/11/58**LI**	Crewe 70,256 R8245 continuous blowdown
	valve and additional washout plugs
19/2/59-17/3/59**LC**	Crewe 9,911
30/12/59-30/1/60**LC**	Crewe 36,395
19/7/61-24/8/61**HC**	Crewe 98,278
25/4/62-23/6/62**HC[CB]**	Crewe
17/8/65-4/10/65**HI**	Crewe

Mileage at 31/12/57 35,845

Annual mileage
1958 39,844
1959 30,962
1960 42,212

Sheds
Annesley 2/4/57
Derby 25/12/65
Kingmoor 5/1/66

Tenders
BR1F no.1185 from new
BR1F no.959 on 5/10/60 from 92068
BR1F no.1122 on 3/5/61 from 92033

Boiler
no.1476 from new

Condemned 2/67, stored at 12A Kingmoor 2-5/67, cut up at McWilliams, Shettleston 6/67.

AIR PUMPS:2

92097

To traffic 27/6/56
Westinghouse air compressor fitted

Works

7/3/57-22/3/57**NC**	Gateshead Firehole modified
29/10/59-22/12/59**GO**	Darlington 77,100
27/2/62-28/4/62**GO**	Darlington
18/7/62-20/8/62**LC**	Crewe
11/3/63-18/4/63**GO**	Crewe
22/12/64-5/3/65**LC**	Crewe

Sheds
Tyne Dock 27/6/56

Tenders
BR1B no.1307 from new
BR1B no.1149 30/12/60 from 92060

Boilers
no.1644 from new
no.1446 22/12/59
no.1646 18/4/63

Condemned 23/10/66, stored at 52H Tyne Dock 10/66-2/67, cut up at Drapers, Hull 4/67.

92098

To traffic 4/7/56
Westinghouse air compressor fitted

Works

21/3/57-5/4/57**NC**	Gateshead Firehole modified
1/9/59-22/10/59**HI**	Darlington 77,200 AWS
22/3/62-1/6/62**GO**	Darlington
18/6/62-28/6/62**Adj**	Darlington
30/7/62-17/8/62**Adj**	Darlington
17/8/64-22/10/64**GO**	Crewe
31/10/64**Casual**	Crewe

Sheds
Tyne Dock 4/7/56

Tenders
BR1B no.1308 from new
BR1B no.1155 on 27/3/63
BR1B no.1153 on 28/7/64

Boilers
no.1645 from new
no.1446 1/6/62

Condemned 31/7/66, stored at 52H Tyne Dock 8-9/66, cut up at Drapers Hull 10/66.

An unusual view of an air pump 9F, 92097 at Crewe South shed on 21 April 1963, fresh out of a Heavy Casual at the works. Some items of motion or pipework are clean, presumably the parts that have been attended to. The tender looks like it merely waited out the job! Note the lone 9 above the number, without the 'F'. Photograph R.J. Buckley, Initial Photographics.

92097 in 1965, passing through Beamish Woods with a Type 4 diesel banking at the rear. Photograph A.R. Thompson.

92098 in select company at Gateshead shed; it went, in fact, to Gateshead for minor work in the 1950s and to Darlington thereafter, so it could have found its way to the Newcastle shed in a variety of ways. Photograph P. Edwards, Norman Preedy Archive.

Pontop Crossing, where the Consett line crossed the Sunderland-Newcastle line (Sunderland is to the right) on the level. The box is Pontop Crossing Signal Box. These are empties bound for Tyne Dock, passing a train (or at least a rake) of 'ordinary' hoppers, behind 92098. The wagon fleet (in German style, apparently – and note the bogie covers) was made up of thirty wagons, maintained at Tyne Dock. This gave four trains of eight wagons with two spare but the 9Fs could take nine at once, one more than an O2 2-8-0, so there were then three trains of nine wagons with three spare for maintenance and repair. A compelling feature of the whole operation was the way so little labour was used. At the loading hopper, for instance, P. Ransome Wallis wrote: *...there was little sign that the plant was working, and indeed, apart from a man in a hut with a small control panel in front of him and another man working the "tram" between storage bunkers and hoppers, only the whirring of the conveyer belt gave a hint that the whole really was working. The same*

was true at the iron works. Iron ore doesn't help when it comes to adjudging the success of the 9Fs, though they were intimately associated with it. In Britain iron and steel works grew up on local ironstone and then drew supplies from further off as local lodes gave up. Later we had steel works sited for the purposes of government regional policy, with less regard for the inherent economics. This meant in the 1950s that a number of important steelworks required imported ore from a port – and thus at sea level – which meant one of the heaviest materials known always had to go 'up'. The iron ore runs were often short with turnround figuring relatively large in the timings, so mileage was suppressed. Or so you'd think... Students of 'mileage' might care to examine the relatively high figures of the Tyne Dock engines with the relatively low figures of the Ebbw Junction ones, engaged in such similar work. For the former we have a wondrous photographic record; the latter, unfortunately, next to nothing. Photograph The Transport Treasury.

92099

To traffic 23/7/56
Westinghouse air compressor fitted

Works
4/4/57-16/4/57**NC**	Gateshead Firehole modified
21/7/59-14/9/59**GO**	Darlington 71,000
15/8/61-24/8/61**NC**	Darlington AWS
10/9/62-20/11/62**LC**	Gorton
3/12/62-14/12/62**Rect**	Gorton
7/1/64-15/2/64**UNS**	Crewe
15/2/65-13/3/65**LC**	Crewe

Sheds
Tyne Dock 23/7/56

Tenders
BR1B no.1309 from new
BR1B no.1151 25/4/60 from 92062
BR1B no.1309 27/7/60 from 92062

Boilers
no.1646 from new
no.1445 14/9/59

Condemned 4/9/66, stored at 52H Tyne Dock
9-10/66, cut up at Drapers, Hull 11/66

Above. 92098 with a loaded train near Tyne Dock shed, 19 May 1964. A day's work for a crew was one trip to Consett with a full load and return with the empties; average loads for the 9Fs were 787 tons but that had to be lifted a thousand feet above sea level (i.e. the elevation of the loading hopper at Tyne Dock) round continuous curves. A banker was employed for the first half mile out of Tyne Dock (using what was available – hence the diesel shunter seen earlier behind 92060 on page 114) and then another Tyne Dock 9F (its air pumps not required) over the ten miles or so between South Pelaw and Medomsley. Photograph Peter Groom.

Top right. 92099, with another 9F banking, meet the 1 in 35 gradient leading to Annfield Plain station. Trains could 'stick' here due to the curvature and the grade. This was only one of several 'awkward' spots of course, for apart from the grades, the line twisted continuously through a succession of cuttings and embankments. Photograph A.R. Thompson.

Bottom right. The end draws nigh at Tyne Dock shed, 17 July 1965, the last year of steam on the ore trains. In fact the decline seems to have been a protracted one. Diesels took over the banking at the end of 1964 and in 1965 Type 2s were fitted up with pumps so that they could work the trains – in pairs that is. So ten 9Fs were replaced by ten diesels plus a banking diesel. This was not the rate of exchange that the dieselisation programme was supposed to promulgate. The diesels in tandem did not require bankers, though some older hands at Tyne Dock reckoned a 9F could equally well do the job unaided. Others thought not. The very last ore train, 'The Tyne Docker' seen earlier, ran on 19 November 1966. The Tyne Dock 9Fs seem then to have found employment here and there, and all seem to have been withdrawn from their home shed. One, 92065, was officially transferred to Wakefield at the end of 1966 but was withdrawn soon after and was stored there, still with pumps, for some time. It is not clear if it did any work or not. Photograph The Transport Treasury.

92100

To traffic 30/7/56

Works

4/8/60-24/8/60**LC**	Gorton 108,909
16/8/61-21/9/61**HC[EO]**	Crewe 128,220
13/8/63-16/10/63**GO**	Crewe
9/9/64-24/10/64**LC**	Crewe

Annual mileage
1956 11,739
1957 28,295
1958 31,431
1960 19,926

Sheds
Toton 30/7/56
Leicester Midland 17/3/58
Toton 11/12/59
Westhouses 25/1/60
Wellingborough 9/3/63
Leicester Midland 12/5/63
Birkenhead 10/4/65

Tenders
BR1C no.1310 from new
BR1F no.1386

Boiler
no.1647 from new

Condemned 11/5/67, stored at 8H Birkenhead 5-8/67 and 5B Crewe [South] 9-11/67, cut up at Cohens, Kettering 11/67-1/68.

92101

To traffic 13/8/56

Works

20/8/56-23/8/56**NC[EO]**	Crewe 197 Damage
28/9/60-29/10/60**LC[EO]**	Crewe 115,339
25/9/62-3/11/62**GO**	Crewe

Annual mileage
1956 10,470
1957 28,721
1958 27,065
1959 28,515
1960 26,042

Sheds
Toton 13/8/56
Leicester [Midland] 17/3/58
Wellingborough 4/1/60
Leicester [Midland] 7/4/60
Birkenhead 25/4/65

Tenders
BR1C no.1311 from new
BR1G no.1560 from 92090 12/4/67

Boiler
no.1648 from new

Condemned 10/67, stored at 8C Speke Jct 11/67-3/68, cut up at Buttigiegs, Newport 4-8/68.

Back to Normal

92100 was a Crewe-built engine, and the first of many destined for the Midland Division of the LMR. This is the north end of Derby station, with 92100 on the Down Goods heading north. The box is Engine Sidings No.1, closed in 1969. Photograph The Transport Treasury.

92101, now with BR1G tender, enters Newlay cutting (five miles north of Leeds) on the 12.55pm freight for Carlisle, Monday 12 June 1967. Late lamp iron positions, smokebox plate AWOL; the make up of the train is a delight. Photograph Gavin Morrison.

92102

To traffic 15/8/56

Works
29/3/57-3/5/57**LC[EO]**	Crewe 18,108 Collision damage
27/4/60-27/5/60**LC**	Crewe 104,295
19/2/62-24/3/62**LC**	Gorton
22/8/63-5/10/63**GO**	Crewe
16/4/64-19/5/64**LC**	Crewe
11/5/65-21/5/65**LC**	Crewe

Annual mileage
1956 11,550
1957 25,617
1958 28,733
1959 30,683
1960 28,421

Sheds
Toton 15/8/56
Leicester Midland 17/3/58
Birkenhead 25/4/65

Tender
BR1C no.1312 from new

Boiler
no.1649 from new

Condemned 11/11/67, stored at 8C Speke Jct 11/67-1/68, cut up at Campbells, Airdrie 3/68.

92103

To traffic 18/8/56

Works
20/8/57-14/9/57**LC**	Crewe 27,991 Boiler
21/12/59-9/1/60**LC**	Crewe 92,835
28/5/62-21/7/62**GO**	Crewe
13/8/63-17/9/63**LC**	Crewe

Annual mileage
1956 10,163
1957 26,901
1957 30,806
1958 25,034
1959 26,425

Sheds
Toton 18/8/56
Leicester Midland 17/3/58
Birkenhead 10/4/65

Tenders
BR1C no.1313 from new
BR1C no.1317 off 92045

Boiler
no.1650 from new

Condemned 27/5/67, stored at 8H Birkenhead 6-9/67 and 8C Speke Jct 10/67, cut up at Cohens, Kettering 11/67-6/68.

Thoroughly weathered, to that 'BR Grey' livery, Leicester's 92102 stands at Toton shed in the late 1950s. Photograph J. Davenport, Initial Photographics.

92102, blacker than ever but still a Leicester engine, passes an A3 Pacific on the approach to Wortley Junction, Leeds, Wednesday 3 May 1961. Photograph The Transport Treasury.

92104

To traffic 24/8/56

Works

10/12/56-27/12/56**LC[EO]**	Crewe 7,412 Damage
11/11/57-30/11/57**LC[EO]**	Crewe 32,264 Collision
28/8/60-17/9/60**LC**	Gorton 111,377
25/8/61-30/10/61**HC**	Crewe 137,867
5/4/63-29/5/63**GO**	Crewe
16/6/64-7/8/64**LC**	Crewe

Annual mileage
1956 7,541
1957 26,514
1958 29,535
1959 28,747
1960 28,335

Sheds
Toton 24/8/56
Leicester Midland 17/3/58
Westhouses 7/4/62
Speke Jct 29/11/64
Birkenhead 15/5/65

Tenders
BR1C no.1314 from new
BR1E no.1271 18/8/61from 92150
This tender 1271 first fitted to 71000
from new. Converted to a BR 1C but
carrying 9 tons instead of 10. Renumbered BR1C no.1360 (see 92162)

Boiler
no.1651 from new

**Condemned 25/2/67, stored at 8A Edge Hill
[Liverpool] 4-7/67, cut up at Drapers, Hull 7/67**.

92105

To traffic 7/9/56

Works

26/8/58-9/9/58	Derby shed 50,509 Tubes
9/12/59-2/1/60**LC**	Crewe 84,158
4/1/60-9/1/60**NC**	Crewe
15/2/62-16/3/62**LC**	Crewe
12/7/63-13/9/63**GO**	Crewe

Annual mileage
1956 8,186
1957 26,544
1958 23,186
1959 26,242
1960 33,943

Sheds
Wellingborough 7/9/56
Kettering 28/11/56
Wellingborough 11/3/63
Kettering 13/1/64
Leicester Midland 19/10/64
Birkenhead 10/4/65

Tender
BR1C no.1315 from new

Boiler
no.1652 from new

**Condemned 14/1/67, stored at 8H Birkenhead
1-4/67, cut up at Wards, Killamarsh 5/67.**

92104 climbing towards Irchester with an up freight, 24 December
1959. The double track 'main' line is to the left and the freight
lines have already started away on the more gentle rise of the
Wymington Deviation to Sharnbrook tunnel. Photograph Peter
Groom.

92104 ex-works at Crewe, the work indicated by the odd stencilled numbers scattered about and the 'OK' on the tender frame. The date is 1 October 1961. Photograph A.W. Battson. The Transport Treasury.

Kettering's 92105 on shed at Cricklewood. Each and every weekday it was the fate of the 9Fs to clump up and down the Midland with coal. There were evergreen dreams of fully braked block trains – a 1,000 tons at a time, maybe, whishing along under electric wires. The decline of the coal traffic of course was unsuspected and the last thing you'd expect to see now on the long-electrified Midland would be a train of speeding bogie wagons laden with… coal! Photograph J. Davenport, Initial Photographics.

92106

To traffic 12/9/56

21/10/58-30/10/58**NC[EO]**	Derby shed 50,853 Tubes
15/6/60-8/7/60**LC**	Gorton 100,233
24/9/60-29/10/60**Rect**	Gorton 105,138
31/5/62-13/8/62**LC**	Gorton
30/9/63-23/10/63**GO**	Crewe

Annual mileage
1956 8,279
1957 26,116
1958 21,833
1959 31,326
1960 21,813

Sheds
Wellingborough 12/9/56
Kettering 28/11/56
Leicester Midland 19/10/64
Birkenhead 10/4/65

Tenders
BR1C no.1316 from new
BR1C no.1144 26/5/62 from 92055
BR1C no.1328 from 92118 28/7/67

Boiler
no.1653 from new

Condemned 29/7/67, stored at 8H Birkenhead 7-10/67, cut up at Thompsons, Stockton-on-Tees 12/67.

92107

To traffic 29/9/56

Works
23/6/58-11/7/58 **NC[EO]**	Derby shed Tubes
4/12/59-2/1/60**LC**	Crewe 90,570
6/4/61-12/5/61**LC**	Crewe 129,728
30/5/62-26/6/62**GO**	Crewe
13/2/63-28/2/63**LC**	Crewe
3/2/65-20/3/65**LC**	Crewe
30/11/65-15/1/66**HI[CB]**	Crewe

Annual mileage
1956 7,969
1957 31,079
1958 26,894
1959 24,693
1960 32,733

Sheds
Wellingborough 20/9/56
Saltley 7/12/61
Banbury 30/11/63
Willesden 19/9/64
Birkenhead 5/12/64

Tenders
BR1C no.1317 from new
BR1C no.1134 from 92045

Boiler
no.1654 from new

Condemned 25/2/67, stored at 8H Birkenhead 2-7/67, cut up at Drapers Hull 7/67.

92108

To traffic 12/10/56

Works
18/1/60-19/2/60**LC**	Crewe 93,776
18/6/62-24/8/62**LC**	Gorton
25/2/63-29/3/63**GO**	Crewe

Annual mileage
1956 7,610
1957 28,275
1958 27,863
1959 29,836
1960 31,950

Sheds
Wellingborough 12/10/56
Cricklewood 12/11/56
Wellingborough 13/4/59
Leicester Midland 5/3/60
Wellingborough 7/2/62
Leicester Midland 24/9/62
Birkenhead 10/4/65

Tender
BR1C no.1318 from new

Boiler
no.1655 from new

Condemned 11/11/67, stored at 8C Speke Jct 11/67-1/68, cut up at Campbells, Airdrie 2/68.

92109

To traffic 15/10/56

Works
21/1/59-12/2/59**LI**	Crewe 58,000
28/5/62-6/7/62**LC**	Gorton
16/10/63-18/11/63**GO**	Crewe

Annual mileage
1956 5,515
1957 26,849
1958 24,522
1959 33,940
1960 31,997

Sheds
Toton 15/10/56
Saltley 6/3/57
Wellingbrough 10/6/57
Leicester Midland 5/8/57
Annesley 27/11/63
Leicester Midland 25/4/64
Birkenhead 10/4/65

Tenders
BR1C no.1319 from new
BR1C no.1329 off 92119 at Leicester Midland 22/9/61
BR1C no.1139

Boiler
no.1656 from new

Condemned 11/11/67, stored at 9D Newton Heath 11/67-2/68, cut up at Campbells, Airdrie 3/68.

Leicester ex-Midland shed, north of the station, eventually acquired a useful stud of its own 9Fs, including this one, 92108 on 28 June 1959. The name HANNAH, in chalk on the smoke deflector, is not really a bad one at all! Photograph P. Hutchinson.

92110 with another of those lovely 'consists' (horrible word) bowling along with the 12.55pm Leeds Hunslet-Carlisle goods, entering Radley Cutting on Friday 23 June 1967. Photograph Gavin Morrison.

92110

To traffic 23/10/56

Works

11/4/60-12/5/60**LC**	Gorton 93,936
14/9/60-14/10/60**LC**	Crewe 103,685
24/10/62-21/11/62**GO**	Crewe
19/4/66-26/5/66**HI**	Crewe

Annual mileage
1956 4,574
1957 28,715
1958 27,233
1959 26,170
1960 21,587

Sheds
Toton 23/10/56
Cricklewood 12/11/56
Wellingborough 13/4/59
Leicester Midland 5/3/60
Wellingborough 8/7/62
Leicester Midland 24/9/62
Kirkby-in-Ashfield 21/11/63
Newton Heath 4/10/64
Carlisle Kingmoor 22/5/65

Tenders
BR1C no.1320 from new
BR1C no.1322 on 10/11/61 at Leicester Midland from 92112

Boiler
no.1657 from new

Condemned 30/12/67, stored at 12A Kingmoor 12/67-2/68, cut up at Arnott Young, Parkgate and Rawmarsh 3/68.

92112

To traffic 17/11/56

Works

20/10/58-13/12/58**LC**	Crewe 55,098 Collision
7/12/60-12/12/60**LC**	Wellingborough shed 113,578
16/11/61-22/12/61**LC**	Gorton
13/6/63-3/8/63**GO**	Crewe

Annual mileage
1956 3,089
1957 29,938
1958 22,744
1959 34,249
1960 24,807

Sheds
Cricklewood 17/11/56
Wellingborough 13/4/59
Leicester Midland 5/3/60
Birkenhead 25/4/65

Tender
BR1C no.1322 from new

Boiler
no.1659 from new

Condemned 11/11/67, stored at 12A Kingmoor 11/67-3/68, cut up at Campbells, Airdrie 3/68.

92111

To traffic 6/11/56

Works

21/1/57-13/2/57**LC[EO]**	Crewe 5,087 Damage
29/1/60-27/2/60**LC[EO]**	Crewe 84,511
14/12/60-7/1/61**NC[EO]**	Derby shed 110,947
17/1/62-23/2/62**LC**	Crewe
21/11/63-2/1/64**GO**	Crewe

Annual mileage
1956 4,307
1957 26,327
1958 25,401
1959 27,818
1960 27,123

Sheds
Cricklewood 6/11/56
Wellingborough 13/4/59
Leicester [Midland] 5/3/60
Speke Jct 4/10/64
Birkenhead 23/1/65

Tender
BR1C no.1321 from new

Boiler
no.1658 from new

Condemned 27/10/67, stored at 8H Birkenhead 10-12/67 and 8C Speke Jct 1/68, cut up at Wards, Beighton Sheffield, 2/68.

92113

To traffic 24/11/56

Works

5/1/61-16/2/61**LC**	Gorton 94,358
26/7/63-7/9/63**GO**	Crewe
27/1/65-27/2/65**LC**	Crewe

Annual mileage
1956 2,430
1957 22,962
1958 21,351
1959 21,669
1960 25,910

Sheds
Westhouses 24/11/56
Toton 13/6/60
Bidston 25/3/61
Toton 29/4/61
Rowsley 14/4/62
Toton 10/2/64
Annesley 21/10/64
Westhouses 28/6/65
Birkenhead 15/8/65

Tenders
BR1C no.1323 from new
BR1F no.1119 at Annesley from 92014

Boiler
no.1660 from new

Condemned 7/10/67, stored at 8C Speke Jct 10/67-3/68, cut up at Buttigiegs, Newport 4-8/68.

92112 with up coal, Syston 30 August 1961; down empties stand alongside. The economics of coal working were moving against these traditional trains of small, disparate wagons. Photograph The Transport Treasury.

The perfect 9F and train portrait. Toton's 92116 has down empties at Tapton Junction, Chesterfield. One way to make coal working more economic was to move from the traditional sixteen tonners seen here to the 21 or 24½ ton wagon, the largest practicable on four wheels; their use could mean a reduction in wagons used by 15%, but thousands of older terminals and sidings could not take them. Photograph The Transport Treasury.

92114

To traffic 29/11/56

Works
13/4/60-20/5/60**LC**   Crewe 81,366
13/12/63-23/1/64**GO**   Crewe

Annual mileage
1956 2,143
1957 22,744
1958 24,073
1959 26,733
1960 27,785

Sheds
Westhouses 29/11/56
Toton 13/6/60
Rowsley 9/4/62
Kirkby-in-Ashfield 2/5/64
Newton Heath 26/9/64
Carlisle Kingmoor 22/5/65

Tender
BR1C no.1324 from new

Boiler
no.1661 from new

Condemned 22/7/67, stored at 12A Kingmoor 7/67-1/68, cut up at Campbells, Airdrie 2/68.

92115

To traffic 12/12/56

Works
25/5/60-24/6/60**LC**   Gorton 88,129
26/9/60-12/11/60 **LC[EO]**   Crewe 94,939

Annual mileage
1956   693
1957 23,880
1958 23,250
1959 29,898
1960 20,731

Sheds
Westhouses 12/12/56
Speke Jct. 13/6/64

Tender
BR1C no.1325 from new

Boiler
no.1662 from new

Condemned 19/2/66, stored at 8H Birkenhead 2-5/66, cut up at W.George, Station Steel, Wath 6/66.

92116

To traffic 22/12/56

Works
31/5/63-26/6/63**GO**   Crewe
7/12/64-8/1/65**LC**   Eastleigh

Sheds
Westhouses 29/12/56
Wellingborough 9/3/63
Kettering 15/2/64
Warrington 28/3/65

Tenders
BR1C no.1326 from new
BR1C no.1148 from 92059 3/4/65
BR1C no.967 from 92018 6/8/65

Boiler
no.1663 from new

Condemned 12/11/66, stored at 8B Warrington 11/66-7/67, cut up at Drapers, Hull 7/67.

92117

To traffic 27/12/56

Works
2/6/60-6/7/60**LC**   Crewe
11/9/62-13/10/62**GO**   Crewe
13/11/64-19/12/64**LC**   Crewe
9/11/65-11/12/65**HC**   Crewe

Sheds
Westhouses 27/12/56
Annesley 7/10/61
Rowsley 8/3/62
Wellingborough 2/4/62
Toton 10/2/64
Speke Jct. 4/10/64

Tender
BR1C no.1327 from new

Boiler
no.1664 from new

Condemned 23/12/67, stored at 8C Speke Jct 12/67-3/68, cut up at Wards, Killamarsh 4/68.

92117, light engine at Wakefield Kirkgate in August 1966. The station was still rewarding even as steam on the nearby GN was more or less eliminated. The reason was that Wakefield ex-L&Y shed still flourished, relatively speaking; with so many yards and collieries in the district and the shed so near, there were steam hauled coal trains, empties and light engines all the time. Photographs D.H. Beecroft, The Transport Treasury.

Beyond the deep shadow, 92118 sits in the sunlight at what is almost certainly Carnforth, its last shed, on 9 July 1967. Alongside is some of the shed's stock of spare parts, which would seem to include firebricks. There were experiments early on to provide concrete brick arches on the 9Fs, but it is not known how far this practice spread, if at all. Photograph R. Butterfield, Initial Photographics.

92118

To traffic 28/12/56

Works
2/1962   Swindon
4/1962   Crewe

Sheds
Westhouses 28/12/56
Wellingborough 7/11/59
Saltley 20/1/62
Banbury 18/7/64
Tyseley 7/11/64
Carnforth 12/11/66

Tender
BR1C no.1328 from new

Boiler
no.1665 from new

Condemned 25/5/68, stored at 10A Carnforth 6-7/68, cut up at Wards, Beighton, Sheffield 9/68.

92119

To traffic 12/1/57

Works
9/6/59-1/7/59**LC**   Crewe
25/9/61-27/10/61**HC**   Crewe
21/1/64-21/2/64**GO**   Crewe

Sheds
Westhouses 12/1/57
Cricklewood 5/1/59
Leicester Midland 9/4/59
Warrington 13/3/65
Speke Jct. 3/6/67
Carlisle Kingmoor 9/8/67

Tenders
BR1C no.1329 from new
BR1C no.1319 on 22/9/61 at Leicester Midland from 92109

Boiler
no.1666 from new

Condemned 23/9/67, stored at 12A Kingmoor 9/67-1/68, cut up at Motherwell Machinery and Scrap Co. Wishaw 2/68

More oil. 92118 gets a lead from Type 2 D5175, leaving Skipton on Saturday 30 September 1967 with oil tanks from Heysham. A brake van serves as the 'barrier'. Photograph Gavin Morrison.

92120

To traffic 28/1/57

Works
24/5/60-15/6/60**LC**	Gorton
25/1/61-3/3/61**C**	Crewe
23/3/62-28/4/62**GO**	Crewe
31/12/62-19/1/63**LC**	Crewe

Sheds
Westhouses 28/1/57
Annesley 20/10/58
Westhouses 28/11/58
Saltley 1/12/58
Wellingborough 16/11/59
Leicester Midland 25/3/60
Annesley 10/11/60
Leicester Midland 7/10/61
Birkenhead 25/4/65

Tenders
BR1C no.1330 from new
BR1C no.1170 at Leicester Midland on 23/2/60 from 92081
BR1C no.1344 from 92134

Boiler
no.1667 from new

Condemned 3/7/67, stored at 8H Birkenhead 7-12/67 and 5B Crewe [South] 1/68, cut up at Birds, Long Marston 2/68.

92121

To traffic 8/2/57

Works
18/1/61-21/2/61**LC**	Crewe 112,586
2/8/61-23/8/61 **LC[EO]**	Crewe 123,208
21/2/64-4/4/64**LI**	Crewe

Annual Mileage
1957 25,523
1958 29,010
1959 28,788
1960 28,212

Sheds
Wellingborough 8/2/57
Saltley 4/3/57
Wellingborough 10/6/57
Leicester [Midland] 5/8/57
Birkenhead 10/4/65

Tender
BR1C no.1331 from new

Boiler
no.1668 from new

Condemned 24/7/67, stored at 8H Birkenhead 7-10/67 and 8C Speke Junction 12/67, cut up at Thompsons, Stockton-on-Tees 1/68.

92122

To traffic 18/2/57

Works
20/9/58-9/10/58 **NC[EO]**	Derby shed 49,690 Tubes
18/6/60-9/8/60**LC**	Gorton 105,886
19/11/62-5/1/63**LC**	Crewe E4983 AWS
4/3/64-18/4/64**GO**	Crewe

Annual Mileage
1957 28,184
1958 28,614
1959 36,586
1960 26,191

Sheds
Wellingborough 18/2/57
Leicester [Midland] 25/3/60
Wellingborough 2/7/62
Leicester [Midland] 24/9/62
Birkenhead 10/4/65

Tender
BR1C no.1332 from new

Boiler
no.1669 from new

Condemned 11/11/67, stored at 8H Birkenhead 11/67 and 8C Speke Jct 12/67-1/68, cut up at Campbells, Airdrie 2/68.

In very different condition – this is the 'before' to 92122's 'after' – 92123 is also at Crewe in 1964. On 10 May it was waiting, stencilled up in the usual fashion, for entry with another, unidentified, 9F. Photograph J. Davenport, Initial Photographics.

92122, putting the other inhabitants to shame, at Crewe South. The 9F is at the shed after works attention nearby – the occasion is presumably its works visit in early 1964 – by which time its home shed Leicester had become 15A. Photograph J.G. Walmsley, The Transport Treasury.

92123

To traffic 26/2/57

Works
14/9/58-27/9/58**NC[EO]**	Derby shed 47,777 Tubes
30/8/60-30/9/60**HC[EO]**	Crewe 107,513
12/9/61-12/10/61**LC**	Crewe 137,041
28/11/61-21/12/61**LC**	Crewe
23/7/63-16/8/63**LC**	Crewe
5/64	Crewe
5/8/64-15/8/64**LI**	Crewe
18/3/66-30/4/66**HC(CB)**	Crewe

Annual Mileage
1957 28,733
1958 28,087
1959 33,736
1960 25,700

Sheds
Wellingborough 26/2/57
Leicester [Midland] 25/3/60
Birkenhead 10/4/65

Tender
BR1C no.1333 from new

Boiler
no.1670 from new

Condemned 27/10/67, stored at 8C Speke Jct 11/67-1/68, cut up at Wards, Beighton, Sheffield 2/68.

92124

To traffic 2/3/57

Works
21/5/58-30/5/58**NC[EO]**	Derby
18/12/58-1/1/59**LC**	Crewe 52,453
11/8/60-3/9/60**LC**	Gorton 108,418
13/4/61-11/5/61**HC[EO]**	Crewe 125,312
25/9/63-4/11/63**GO**	Crewe
6/8/65-11/9/65**LC**	Crewe

Annual Mileage
1957 25,671
1958 26,782
1959 37,920
1960 25,668

Sheds
Wellingborough 2/3/57
Kettering 10/2/64
Warrington 28/3/65

Tenders
BR1C no.1334 from new
BR1B no.972 6/9/60 from 92023

Boiler
no.1671 from new

Condemned 3/12/66, stored at 8C Speke Jct 1-3/67, cut up at Wards, Killamarsh 4/67.

92124 climbing towards Irchester on the Midland Goods Lines with an up freight, 24 December 1959. Photograph Peter Groom.

92125

To traffic 9/3/57

Works
13/5/58-2/6/58**NC[EO]**	Crewe 37,075 P and V exam
14/11/58-26/11/58**NC[EO]**	Derby shed 54,269 Tubes
12/9/60-12/10/60**LC**	Crewe 113,881
9/11/61-13/12/61**LC**	Crewe
26/7/63-29/8/63**GO**	Crewe

Annual Mileage
1957 24,487
1958 32,924
1959 36,296
1960 30,065

Sheds
Wellingborough 9/3/57
Kettering 12/12/60
Saltley 7/12/63
Croes Newydd 28/5/66
Carlisle Kingmoor 31/12/66

Tender
BR1C no.1335 from new

Boiler
no.1672 from new

Condemned 30/12/67, stored at 12A Kingmoor 12/67-3/68, cut up at Arnott Young, Parkgate and Rawmarsh 4/68.

92126

To traffic 18/3/57

Works
28/7/58-12/8/58**NC[EO]**	Derby shed 43,780 Tubes
23/9/60-26/10/60**LC**	Gorton 111,988
1/8/62-31/8/62**GO**	Crewe
17/4/64-21/7/64**LC**	Crewe

Annual Mileage
1957 24,913
1958 33,197
1959 32,857
1960 27,207

Sheds
Wellingborough 18/3/57
Kettering 10/2/64
Warrington 13/3/65

Tender
BR1C no.1336 from new

Boiler
no.1673 from new

Condemned 5/8/67, stored at 8B Warrington 8-11/67, cut up at McWilliams, Shettleston 1/68.

Seen from the high ground at the rear of Wellingborough shed (that's No.2 Roundhouse below right) 92126 approaches the station with an up coal train on 28 August 1963. Photograph Peter Groom.

92127

To traffic 29/3/57

Works

11/10/58-22/10/58**NC[EO]**	Derby shed 48,486 Tubes
12/9/60-12/10/60**LC**	Gorton 106,168
29/8/61-4/10/61**LC**	Crewe 134,151
22/3/63-25/4/63**GO**	Crewe

Annual Mileage
1957 24,106
1958 30,849
1959 31,735
1960 27,472

Sheds
Wellingborough 29/3/57
Rowsley 15/7/63
Kirkby-in-Ashfield 2/5/64
Speke Jct 4/10/64
Birkenhead 23/1/65

Tenders
BR1C no.1337 from new
BR1K no.1376 at Birkenhead 30/8/67 from 92166

Boiler
no.1674 from new

Condemned 19/8/67, stored at 8H Birkenhead 9-11/67, cut up at Buttigiegs, Newport 12/67.

92128

To traffic 5/4/57

Works

25/7/60-13/8/60**LC**	Gorton 93,039
27/9/60-3/11/60**NC[EO]**	Gorton 96,104
28/11/62-7/1/63**LC**	Crewe E4983 AWS
20/11/63-3/1/64**HC[CB]**	Crewe

Annual Mileage
1957 22,962
1958 28,341
1959 28,101
1960 22,829

Sheds
Toton 5/4/57
Leicester [Midland] 17/3/58
Saltley 25/6/62
Banbury 18/7/64
Saltley 10/9/66
Carnforth 31/10/66

Tender
BR1C no.1338 from new

Boiler
no.1675 from new

Condemned 11/11/67, stored at 10A Carnforth 11-12/67, cut up at McWilliams, Shettleston 5/68.

With 'the roof off' for some relief, 92127 leaves Asfordby tunnel with a down freight, 12 April 1958. This line later on became the Old Dalby test track. Shows well the uncluttered running plate this side, without the sand fillers. The 9F regulator rodding, being shorter, managed without the intermediate supports of the Britannias. Steam lazily leaks from a safety valve. Photograph Peter Groom.

The familiar Crewe Paint Shop yard again, with a new 92128 in April 1957. The Crab, fairly revolutionary in its own way more than thirty years before, looks more than a little antique alongside the massively boilered 9F.

It took years to eliminate the older, smaller and often wooden wagons and their demise in truth owed as much to declining traffic as the provision of enough new wagons. So even in 1958 92128 could trundle over the crossing at Beeston with this motley lot. Photograph Peter J. Coster.

92129

To traffic 10/4/57

Works
13/12/60-14/3/61**LC**	Derby 107,154
22/2/62-28/3/62**LC**	Crewe
30/1/64-14/3/64**LI**	Crewe

Annual Mileage
1957 22,973
1958 29,188
1959 29,230
1960 25,763

Sheds
Saltley 10/4/57
Toton 10/6/57
Kettering 22/7/59
Toton 1/2/60
Cricklewood 3/5/60
Annesley 7/10/61
Saltley 9/12/61
Banbury 18/7/64
Carlisle Kingmoor 11/9/66

Tender
BR1C no.1339 from new

Boiler
no.1677 from new

Condemned 1/7/67, stored at 12A Kingmoor 6-10/67, cut up at Motherwell Machinery and Scrap Co., Wishaw 11/67.

92130

To traffic 15/4/57

Works
28/10/60-5/12/60**LC**	Crewe 92,830
1/8/63-28/9/63**GO**	Crewe

Annual Mileage
1957 22,917
1958 24,369
1959 26,859
1960 20,321

Sheds
Saltley 15/4/57
Toton 10/6/57
Carlisle Kingmoor 23/5/64

Tenders
BR1C no.1340 from new
BR1F no.1159 off 92070, 14/10/60

Boiler
no.1677 from new

Condemned 14/5/66, stored at 12A Kingmoor 5-10/66, despatched 6/10/66 and cut up at Motherwell Machinery and Scrap Co. Wishaw 11/66.

92129 at Toton shed in 1960, while it was briefly allocated to Cricklewood. This was unusual, for like the GN coal trade, that on the Midland was conducted largely using locomotives based at 'country' sheds, working 'out and home' to London. Photograph J. Davenport, Initial Photographics.

92131

To traffic 25/4/57

Works
10/5/60-21/6/60**LC[EO]**	Crewe 80,006
16/9/60-11/10/60**LC[EO]**	Crewe 83,368
11/10/62-25/10/62**LC**	Gorton
30/9/63-8/11/63**GO**	Crewe
14/5/64-8/7/64**LC**	Crewe

Annual Mileage
1957 22,482
1958 26,977
1959 26,409
1960 12,446

Sheds
Saltley 25/4/57
Toton 10/6/57
Westhouses 25/1/60
Speke Jct. 29/11/64
Birkenhead 15/5/65

Tenders
BR1C no.1341 from new
BR1C no.1137 2/5/60 from 92048

Boiler
no.1678 from new

Condemned 23/9/67, stored at 8H Birkenhead 9-12/67 and 8C Speke Jct. 12/67-1/68, cut up at Wards, Beighton, Sheffield 2/68.

92132

To traffic 29/4/57

Works
20/9/58-10/10/58**NC[EO]**	Derby shed 48,475 Tubes
11/11/59-5/12/59**LC**	Crewe 84,840
15/5/61-20/6/61**HC**	Crewe 126,511
1/8/63-9/10/63**GO**	Crewe
15/12/64-23/1/65**LC**	Crewe

Annual Mileage
1957 25,270
1958 30,281
1959 32,039
1960 30,168

Sheds
Saltley 29/4/57
Wellingborough 21/12/57
Kettering 10/2/64
Annesley 24/2/64
Banbury 20/6/65
Northampton 21/8/65
Banbury 2/10/65
Warrington 13/8/66
Carlisle Kingmoor 7/10/67

Tender
BR1C no.1342 from new

Boiler
no.1679 from new

Condemned 21/10/67, stored at 12A Kingmoor 10/67-1/68, cut up at Motherwell Machinery and Scrap Co. Wishaw 2/68.

Stirring passenger work for a 9F. Toton's 92130 is at Rotherham at an unknown date but possibly in 1958, a year when this 9F seemed particularly busy. This was the one that even found itself on empty stock pilot duties at Euston, after all; certainly it was active on August bank holiday relief traffic in 1958. Photograph The Transport Treasury.

92131 was the second of the series of ten that all went to Saltley and here it is at that very large shed in 1957, more or less new in the couple of months before it moved on to Toton. The 9Fs by now, of course, had been appearing with the second (1957) tender emblem from new. Photograph E.A. Elias, The Transport Treasury.

The onlooker seems to be making sure of the number of 92132, bereft as it was of its smokebox plate at Kingmoor in 1967! It was withdrawn only a couple of weeks after arrival at the Carlisle shed so presumably suffered some defect that prompted the authorities to condemn it. Photograph J. Davenport, Initial Photographics.

92133

To traffic 22/5/57

Works

14/8/58-26/8/58**NC[EO]**	Derby shed 44,782 Tubes
7/9/60-8/10/60**LC**	Crewe 107,939
18/10/60-21/10/60**NC[EO]Rect**	Crewe Alterations to brick arch
7/9/61-9/10/61 **LC[EO]**	Crewe 135,989
25/7/63-28/8/63**GO**	Crewe
12/2/65-30/3/65**LC**	Crewe

Annual Mileage
1957 25,537
1958 31,450
1959 33,500
1960 24,754

Sheds
Saltley 22/5/57
Wellingborough 2/12/57
Leicester [Midland] 10/2/64
Birkenhead 10/4/65

Tender
BR1C no.1343 from new

Boiler
no.1680 from new

Condemned 22/7/67, stored at 8H Birkenhead 7-11/67 and 8C Speke Jct. 12/67, cut up at Thompsons, Stockton-on-Tees 1/68.

92134

To traffic 24/5/57

Works

26/8/57-14/9/57**LC[EO]**	Crewe 8,001 Collision
28/7/58-8/8/58**NC[EO]**	Derby shed 33,793 Tubes
12/12/60-24/1/61**LC**	Crewe 110,950
4/9/62-18/10/62**LC**	Gorton
24/7/63-17/8/63**LC**	Crewe
22/7/64-8/9/64 **LI-HI**	Eastleigh 'W/E 29/8/64 awaiting material from Crewe, now received' Motion and brakework overhauled, small boiler tubes (136 replaced), superheater tubes (12 replaced), engine and tender frames straightened, cylinders rebored
5/65	Crewe

Annual Mileage
1957 18,118
1958 29,047
1959 35,138
1960 28,647

Sheds
Saltley 24/5/57
Wellingborough 21/12/57
Leicester [Midland] 10/2/64
Birkenhead 25/4/65

Tenders
BR1C no.1344 from new
BR1C no.1170 8/6/60 from 92120
BR1C no.1372 at Wellingborough, 6/9/60
BR1C no.1169 from 92080

Boiler
no.1681 from new

Condemned 10/12/66 stored at 8H Birkenhead 12/66-6/67 and Barry Docks 8/67-12/80, Engine preserved.

At last a 9F on a running in turn. Brand new 92133 on its unexpected arrival at Manchester's Ducie Street goods yard, on 28 May 1957. It was located at the side of Manchester London Road station and is now, inevitably, the car park for Piccadilly (London Road as was). The yard quite often produced an ex-works loco from Crewe running in and almost anything could turn up, from 8F to Royal Scot. Photographer Brian Green worked in the Manchester London Road Passenger Trains Office of the Eastern Region (Woodhead Line) alongside, and the office window looked directly out on to Ducie Street Yard, which used to have a regular pilot in the form of a 3F tank from Longsight. Photograph B.K.B. Green, Initial Photographics.

A wonderful 9F display on the Midland main line near Leicester, at Knighton North Junction, 30 August 1961. Photograph The Transport Treasury.

Saltley's 92135 at Derby on a westbound freight, 15 April 1959. The 9F was the perfect design for the block train which was seen as the salvation for BR goods working. Wagon load trains like these were inherently inefficient; dividing the number of journeys made by such wagons into 365, the number of days in the year, gave an astonishingly low average of *nine* days per journey! Photograph R.J. Buckley, Initial Photographics.

92135

To traffic 11/6/57

Works
17/6/58-7/7/58**NC[EO]**	Crewe 33,159 V and P exam
18/9/59-17/10/59**LI**	Crewe 77,416
8/12/59-2/3/60**LC[EO]**	Derby 2,080
8/2/61-14/3/61**LC**	Crewe 35,745
28/11/62-9/1/63**LC**	Crewe E4983 AWS
24/4/64-27/8/64	Eastleigh 'W/E 15/8/64 awaiting castings from Crewe' 'boiler-internal examination while on frames'

Annual Mileage
1957 20,880
1958 32,674
1959 25,942
1960 33,590

Sheds
Saltley 11/6/57
Croes Newydd 28/5/66
Wakefield 5/11/66

Tender
BR1C no.1345 from new

Boiler
no.1682 from new

Condemned 6/67, stored at 56A Wakefield 6/67-2/68, cut up at Drapers, Hull 3/68

92136

To traffic 18/6/57

Works
6/5/58-29/5/58**NC[EO]**	Crewe 32,235
26/11/59-2/1/60**HC[CB]**	Crewe 87,804
13/3/60-30/3/60	Cardiff [Canton]
5/4/62-19/5/62**LC**	Gorton

Annual Mileage
1957 18,852
1958 35,815
1959 33,178
1960 44,203

Shed
Saltley 18/6/57

Tender
BR1C no.1346 from new

Boilers
no.1683 from new
no.1902 2/1/60

Condemned 29/10/66, stored at 2E Saltley 10/66-1/67, cut up at Wards, Beighton, Sheffield 2/67.

Apart from a few of the Doncaster ones and those at Tyne Dock, Saltley's 92136 was just about the only other 9F to stay at one shed throughout its life. Here it is at an unlikely location, Salisbury station, on 17 August 1961 and blowing off in grand style. The oil train would be bound for Bromford Bridge on the 9F's home patch and would presumably have come from Fawley, near Southampton. Photograph J. Davenport, Initial Photographics.

92137

To traffic 24/6/57

Works
7/5/58-28/5/58**LC**	Crewe 32,774
18/5/60-2/7/60**GO**	Crewe 105,554
6/2/61-2/3/61**LC**	Crewe 23,584
19/10/62-20/12/62**LC**	Gorton
18/6/65-10/8/65**LI**	Crewe

Annual Mileage
1957 19,047
1958 37,080
1959 36,181
1960 33,447

Sheds
Saltley 24/6/57
Croes Newydd 6/8/66
Carlisle Kingmoor 31/12/66

Tender
BR1C no.1347 from new

Boilers
no.1684 from new
no.1435 2/7/60

Condemned 9/9/67, stored at 12A Kingmoor 9/67-1/68, cut up at Motherwell Machinery and Scrap Co., Wishaw 2/68.

92138

To traffic 25/6/57

Works
1/7/58-7/8/58**LC[EO]**	Crewe 32,732 V and P exam
21/6/60-6/8/60**LC**	Crewe 102,117
15/1/63-2/2/63**HI**	Crewe E4983 AWS
30/7/64-22/9/64**LI-HI**	Eastleigh 'W/E 5/9/64 awaiting oiling washers from Swindon and brake pull rod from Crewe'
10/64	Crewe
7/65	Crewe

Annual Mileage
1957 13,739
1958 35,744
1959 39,398
1960 30,995

Sheds
Saltley 25/6/57
Speke Jct. 20/8/66

Tender
BR1C no.1348 from new

Boiler
no.1685 from new

Condemned 8/7/67, stored at 8C Speke Jct 7-12/67, cut up at Birds, Long Marston 12/67-2/68.

York shed, and 92137 is off one of those long distance jobs that seemed to abound at Saltley. Their 9Fs had many fearsome jobs, but not so much of the unrelenting coal and iron ore of other sheds. This 9F was one of a couple that spent time at Croes Newydd, a shed that was probably not to the forefront of thinking when the initial allocations of the 9Fs were being worked out. Not least because the turntable was too small for them, so they could not enter the roundhouse. Photograph The Transport Treasury.

92139

To traffic 28/6/57

Works
8/7/58-14/8/58**LC[EO]**	Crewe 36,513
9/6/60-26/7/60**LC**	Crewe 101,557
Nov-Dec.1964	Crewe
Sept.1965	Crewe

Annual Mileage
1957 17,117
1958 35,501
1959 33,765
1960 31,144

Sheds
Saltley 28/6/57
Speke Jct 31/12/66
Carlisle Kingmoor 12/8/67

Tenders
BR1C no.1349 from new
BR1C no.1141 5/9/64 from 92020

Boiler
no.1686 from new

Condemned 9/9/67, stored at 12A Kingmoor 9/67-1/68, cut up at Motherwell Machinery and Scrap Co.Wishaw 2/68

92140

To traffic 5/7/57

Works
9/1/60-4/2/60**GO**	Darlington AWS
14/11/62-18/12/62**LC**	Crewe

Sheds
New England 5/7/57
Langwith Jct. 9/1/65

Tenders
BR1F no.1350 from new
BR1F no.1400 from 92191

Boiler
no.1687 from new

Condemned 11/4/65, stored at 41J Langwith Jct. 4-6/65, cut up at Cashmores, Great Bridge 7/65.

Saltley's 92139 at Leicester shed with new 2E shed plate (this makes the view post-September 1963 when the code was changed from 21A and before its transfer to Speke at the end of 1966). Usual agglomeration of white salts in the middle regions and the secret of where the spare lamps were stowed. Photograph J. Davenport, Initial Photographics.

92141

To traffic 29/7/57

Works
30/10/59-8/12/59**LI**	Darlington 90,500 AWS
4/1962	Darlington
6/1964	Crewe

Sheds
New England 29/7/57
Doncaster 23/9/62
New England 3/3/63
Langwith Jct. 9/1/65
Colwick 31/10/65

Tenders
BR1F no.1351 from new
BR1F no.1359 on 13/8/65 from 92149

Boilers
no.1688 from new
no.1691 8/5/62

Condemned 19/12/65, stored at 40E Colwick 12/65-3/66, cut up at Wards, Beighton, Sheffield 4/66.

92142

To traffic 29/7/57

Works
5/2/60-24/3/60**LC**	Darlington
3/9/62-31/10/62**LC**	Gorton

Shed
New England 29/7/57

Tender
BR1F no.1352 from new

Boiler
no.1689 from new

Condemned 21/12/65, stored at 34E New England 12/64-1/66 and 40E Colwick 2/66, [according to ERC sold to Cohen 5/4/65], cut up at Cohens, Kettering 4/66.

New England was the main home for 92140, which marked the start of a series for the GN after a long sequence for the Midland. Here it is at New England shed on 3 February 1962; somewhere along the line at Darlington it has acquired those enormous cabside numerals, which it didn't have in 1958, for instance. Truly heroic levels of grime and dirt. Photograph The Transport Treasury.

A freight to hardly dampen the brow of a 9F; 92141 out on the GN with an up train south of Rossington, Yorkshire, about 1958. Photograph The Transport Treasury.

A pounding approach to New Southgate by 92142 with a northbound freight. On the GN, as on the GC lines ceded to the LMR, the belief was in realistic engine diagrams so that engines got back to their home sheds every day; complex cyclic diagrams, on these duties at least, were eschewed, it seems. Photograph A. Scarsbrook, Initial Photographics.

92143

To traffic 10/8/57

Works
19/2/60-5/4/60**LI**	Darlington
23/1/61-22/3/61**LC**	Darlington
18/9/62-7/12/62**LC**	Gorton

Shed
New England 29/7/57

Tender
BR1F no.1353 from new

Boiler
no.1690 from new

Condemned 21/2/65, stored at 34E New England 12/64-4/65, cut up at Cohens, Kettering 5/65.

92145

To traffic 26/8/57

Works
27/8/59-10/10/59**GO**	Darlington AWS
24/2/61-25/3/61**LC**	Darlington Motion overhauled; frames straightened
17/4/62-15/6/62**GO**	Darlington Speedometer

Sheds
New England 21/9/57
Langwith Junction 3/1/65
Colwick 31/10/65
Immingham 19/12/65

Tenders
BR1F no.1355 from new
BR1F no.1395 10/4/62 at New England from 92185
BR1F no.1125 6/64

Boilers
no.1692 from new
no.1688

Condemned 6/2/66, stored at 40B Immingham 2-3/66, cut up at Wards, Beighton, Sheffield 4/66.

92147

To traffic 14/9/57

Works
15/4/59-22/5/59**LC**	Darlington
26/8/59-3/9/59**NC**	Darlington
8/6/61-8/7/61**GO**	Darlington

Sheds
New England 14/9/57
Immingham 3/3/63

Tender
BR1F no.1357 from new

Boiler
no.1695 from new

Condemned 4/4/65, stored at 36A Doncaster 4-7/65, cut up at Cashmores, Great Bridge 8/65.

92144

To traffic 19/8/57

Works
6/10/59-14/11/59**LI**	Darlington 89,350 AWS
19/2/62-29/3/62**GO**	Darlington
2/4/62-4/4/62**Adj**	Darlington
9/4/62-27/4/62**Adj**	Darlington

Sheds
New England 19/8/57
Immingham 23/9/62
New England 3/3/63
Langwith Jct. 3/1/65
Colwick 31/10/65

Tender
BR1F no.1354 from new

Boilers
no.1691 from new
no.1440

Condemned 19/12/65, stored at 40E Colwick 12/65-3/66, cut up at Wards, Beighton, Sheffield 4/66.

92146

To traffic 5/9/57

Works
26/5/59-17/6/59**LC**	Darlington AWS; tender frames
13/4/60-1/6/60**LI**	Darlington 101,200
13/6/60-25/6/60**Adj**	Darlington
4/7/60-28/7/60**Adj**	Darlington
2/4/63-1/5/63**GO**	Crewe

Sheds
New England 5/9/57
Langwith Jct. 3/1/65
Colwick 6/11/65
Doncaster 19/12/65

Tender
BR1F no.1356 from new

Boiler
no.1693 from new

Condemned 17/4/66, stored at 36A Doncaster 4-6/66, cut up at W. George, Station Steel, Wath 6-8/66.

Right. **Another snaking load of coal heads south out of Peterborough, August 1958 behind 92143. New England's coaling plant rises in the far distance. Photograph J. Davenport, Initial Photographics.**

92148

To traffic 21/9/57

Works
14/12/59-29/1/60**LI**   Darlington 89,970 AWS

Sheds
New England 21/9/57
Immingham 19/6/60
New England 17/9/61
Doncaster 3/3/63
Colwick 16/6/63
Staveley [Barrow Hill] 6/9/64
Langwith Jct. 3/1/65
Colwick 31/10/65

Tender
BR1F no.1358 from new

Boiler
no.1694 from new

Condemned 19/12/65, stored at 40E Colwick 12/65-3/66, cut up at Wards, Beighton, Sheffield 4/66.

92149

To traffic 1/10/57

Works
21/6/60-18/8/60**HI**   Darlington 105,000 AWS
26/8/60-12/9/60**Adj**   Darlington
7/2/63-5/4/63**LC**   Gorton

Sheds
New England 1/10/57
Langwith Jct. 3/1/65

Tender
BR1F no.1359 from new

Boiler
no.1696 from new

Condemned 27/6/65, stored at 41J Langwith Jct 6-9/65, cut up at Wards, Beighton, Sheffield 10/65.

92148 at Doncaster shed. Of the series of Crewe 9Fs allotted to the Eastern Region, 92140-92149, all ended their days (if in slightly straightened circumstances) on the same Region. Photograph J. Davenport, Initial Photographics.

Going home with empties, 92149 at Greenwood on 17 March 1962. Photograph B.W.L. Brooksbank, Initial Photographics.

92150

To traffic 5/10/57

Works
17/6/60-5/8/60**HC**	Crewe 82,219
22/9/61-24/10/61**LC[EO]**	Crewe 21,461
18/5/62-19/5/62**LC**	Eastleigh
25/1/63-27/2/63**LI**	Crewe E4983 AWS
19/10/64-20/11/64**LC**	Eastleigh 'boiler-internal examination on frames'

Annual mileage
1957 4,122
1958 22,752
1959 40,196
1960 32,076

Sheds
Westhouses 5/10/57
Saltley 3/2/59
Tyseley 23/5/64
Saltley 20/6/64
Wakefield 30/10/66

Tenders
BR1C no.1271 from new*
*was to have received 1360 which was instead converted for use with 71000. 1271, 71000's original tender, was then coupled with 92150
BR1C no.1314 18/8/61 from 92104

Boiler
no.1697 from new

Condemned 17/4/67, stored at 56A Wakefield 4-7/67, cut up at Drapers, Hull 7-11/67.

92151

To traffic 9/10/57

Works
9/12/60-21/1/61**LC**	Gorton 102,535
31/7/63-8/10/63**GO**	Crewe

Sheds
Saltley 9/10/57
Birkenhead 7/11/66

Tender
BR1C no.1361 from new

Boiler
no.1698 from new

Condemned 22/4/67, stored at 8H Birkenhead 4-10/67, 8C Speke Junction 10/67-4/68, cut up at Drapers, Hull 4/68.

92150 at Derby shed at an unknown date; while the 9Fs were familiar here of course, Derby was one of those Midland line sheds which barely had one allocated. There were only a couple, 92068 and 92096, very briefly at the end of 1965 – and these have all the look of the 'paper' allocations beloved of BR, and concocted to thwart us all years on. Photograph J. Davenport, Initial Photographics.

92151 in its undercoat in the Paint Shop yard at Crewe on 28 September 1957, a couple of weeks before it went into traffic. Photograph The Transport Treasury.

Toton shed, and local 9F 92153 stands in the yard, 27 September 1959. Photograph R.J. Buckley, Initial Photographics.

92152

To traffic 16/10/57

29/8/60-30/9/60**LC**	Gorton 98,457
24/12/64-17/2/65**LC**	Eastleigh 'boiler-internal examination on frames'

Annual mileage
1957 7,282
1958 35,416
1959 34,535
1960 28,443

Sheds
Saltley 16/10/57
Birkenhead 12/11/66

Tenders
BR1C no.1362 from new
BR1C no.1365 16/3/63 from 92155

Boiler
no.1699 from new

Condemned 11/11/67, stored at 8C Speke Jct. 11/67-2/68, cut up at Campbells, Airdrie 3/68.

92153

To traffic 21/10/57

Works
7/10/59-7/11/59**LC**	Crewe 44,862
21/3/61-27/3/61**LC**	Wellingborough shed 89,668
13/9/61-23/9/61**LC[EO]**	Gorton 99,694
5/11/62-25/1/63**LC**	Gorton
4/6/63-22/6/63**LC**	Crewe
4/11/63-20/11/63**LC**	Crewe
18/3/65-5/5/65**LI**	Eastleigh
26/5/65-1/6/65	Eastleigh

Annual mileage
1957 6,138
1958 28,561
1959 18,109
1960 30,990

Sheds
Toton 21/10/57
Westhouses 7/10/63
Speke Jct. 26/6/65

Tender
BR1C no.1363

Boiler
no.1700 from new

Condemned 16/1/68, stored at 8C Speke Jct. 4-5/68, cut up at Cashmores, Newport 6/68.

The shed at Grimesthorpe, Sheffield, nestled amongst the great steelworks (note the background) and its workings in the main were dependent on the iron and steel trade of the city. Oddly it never seems to have had 9Fs on the complement, perhaps because the turntable in the roundhouse was too small for a 2-10-0. The Midland put in a turntable outside and provided some stalls (one of which is occupied by Saltley's 92155) in anticipation of a second, larger, roundhouse but it never materialised. Photograph J. Davenport, Initial Photographics.

92154

To traffic 28/10/57

Works

14/11/58-23/11/58**NC[EO]**	Derby shed 40,388 Tubes
5/5/60-28/5/60**LC**	Gorton 83,519
26/6/61-19/8/61**LC**	Gorton 115,293
15/5/62-4/7/62**LC**	Gorton
26/7/63-28/8/63**HC**	Crewe
27/4/64-1/7/64**LC**	Crewe
8/6/66-10/8/66**HC**	Crewe Internal exam on frame

Annual mileage
1957 5,313
1958 38,389
1959 35,115
1960 24,697

Sheds
Wellingborough 28/10/57
Annesley 4/5/58
Wellingborough 19/9/58
Annesley 10/2/64
Kirkby-in-Ashfield 28/6/65
Speke Jct. 18/7/65

Tenders
BR1C no.1364 from new
BR1C no.1373 3/3/61 from 92164
BR1C no.1166 1/7/63 from 92077

Boiler
no.1701 from new

Condemned 22/7/67, stored at 8C Speke Jct. 7-12/67, cut up at Thompsons, Stockton-on-Tees 1/68.

92155

To traffic 5/11/57

Works

1/6/59-27/6/59**LC**	Crewe 57,300
30/11/60-31/12/60**LC**	Crewe 100,817
2/1/61-18/1/61**Return**	Crewe
8/1/63-2/2/63**LC**	Crewe
20/3/63-13/4/63**LC**	Crewe AWS
7/2/64-12/3/64**LC**	Crewe
22/2/65-9/4/65	Eastleigh 'boiler-internal examination on frames'

Annual mileage
1957 5,617
1958 40,033
1959 29,658
1960 25,509

Sheds
Saltley 5/11/57
Speke Jct. 14/8/66

Tenders
BR1C no.1365 from new
BR1C no.1362 at Saltley on 16/3/63 from 92152

Boiler
no.1702 from new

Condemned 19/11/66, stored at 8C Speke Jct. 11/66-3/67, cut up at Drapers, Hull 4/67.

A fresh 92156 in 1964 after a Light Intermediate. Toton, its home shed, had been re-coded 16A the previous year. There's no AWS, so perhaps Crewe had abandoned fitting it by now. Lamp irons altered, later type of front step. Photograph J. Davenport, Initial Photographics.

92156

To traffic 15/11/57

Works
2/7/59-18/8/59**LC[EO]**	Crewe 42,573
24/1/61-25/2/61**LC**	Gorton 83,290
12/3/64-8/5/64**LI**	Crewe
8/10/64-23/10/64**LC**	Eastleigh

Annual mileage
1957 3,890
1958 29,850
1959 20,878
1960 27,278

Sheds
Toton 15/11/57
Warrington 8/3/65

Tenders
BR1C no.1366 from new
BR1C no.1371 at Newton Heath on 14/7/64

Boiler
no.1703 from new

Condemned 22/7/67, stored at 8B Warrington 7/67-2/68, cut up at Drapers, Hull 3/68

92157

To traffic 20/11/57

Works
7/11/60-17/12/60**LC**	Gorton 93,721
23/1/62-24/2/62**LC**	Crewe
14/8/65-15/1/65**LI**	Crewe

Annual mileage
1957 3,413
1958 31,460
1959 34,923
1960 24,190

Sheds
Toton 20/11/57
Saltley 2/2/59
Birkenhead 18/4/64

Tender
BR1C no.1367 from new

Boiler
no.1704 from new

Condemned 19/8/67, stored at 8H Birkenhead 9-10/67, 8C Speke Jct. 11-12/67, cut up at Buttigiegs, Newport 1/68.

Not much that would reflect in that puddle from poor old 92157! Once one of the Toton and Saltley trailblazers, it had been at Birkenhead since 1964 and here at Kingmoor in 1967 looks pretty tired with it all. It got back to Merseyside and was withdrawn from Birkenhead in August 1967, going to South Wales for cutting up after a period in store. Photograph J. Davenport, Initial Photographics.

92158

To traffic 22/11/57

Works
18/4/61-15/5/61**LC**	Gorton
26/3/63-25/4/63**GO**	Crewe
July 1966	Crewe

Annual mileage
1957 3,445
1958 30,857
1959 25,348
1960 26,229

Sheds
Toton 22/11/57
Westhouses 21/9/63
Speke Jct. 13/6/64

Tender
BR1C no.1368 from new

Boiler
no.1705 from new

**Condemned 23/7/66, stored at 8C Speke Jct.
7-10/66, [despatched to Drapers
17/10/66] cut up at Drapers, Hull 11/66.**

92159

To traffic 27/11/57

Works
5/9/58-27/9/58**NC[EO]**	Derby shed 27,326 Tubes
3/3/61-5/4/61**LC**	Crewe 106,195
17/4/61-20/4/61**LC**	Crewe 106,670
28/11/61-5/1/62**LC**	Crewe
25/11/63-9/1/64**GO**	Crewe

Annual mileage
1957 2,621
1958 32,959
1959 36,203
1960 30,565

Sheds
Wellingborough 27/11/57
Cricklewood 1/12/58
Wellingborough 15/12/58
Rowsley 3/2/64
Kirkby-in-Ashfield 2/5/64
Newton Heath 4/10/64
Birkenhead 22/5/65

Tender
BR1C no.1369 from new

Boiler
no.1706 from new

**Condemned 22/7/67, stored at 8C Speke Jct.
7-12/67, cut up at Thompsons, Stockton-on-Tees 1/68**

92157 seems to have been active more or less to the bitter end. Here she is on the 12.55pm Stourton-Carlisle (these jobs would explain its presence at Kingmoor) passing through the closed Newley station on 29 April 1967. One bar to faster times was the vulnerability of the older stock to defects of one sort or another. On one Region about this time for instance, during four weeks three per cent of the freights had to be stopped for defective wagons. This sounds quite good until you realise the sheer scale of it all – that 3% amounted to nearly 1,500 trains and a total in only four weeks of *over 2,000 defective wagons*. And that was just one Region, and not the biggest either. Photograph Gavin Morrison.

92159 at Sileby on a mixed freight, in the Leicestershire countryside north of Leicester, 4 June 1962. Photograph B.W.L. Brooksbank, Initial Photographics.

92160 in a typical Toton line-up about 1958; a 9F alongside and another three in line behind, together with an 8F. Photograph B.K.B. Green, Initial Photographics.

92160

To traffic 29/11/57

Works
27/1/58-15/2/58**LC[EO]**	Crewe 4,762 New header
31/5/58-11/6/58**NC[EO]**	shed
29/10/60-9/1/61**LC**	Crewe 85,946
April 1961	Crewe

Annual mileage
1957 3,186
1958 27,933
1959 32,704
1960 22,123

Sheds
Wellingborough 29/11/57
Kettering 4/10/58
Warrington 13/3/65
Birkenhead 19/2/66
Carnforth 14/11/67
Speke Jct. 29/11/67
Carnforth 11/5/68

Tender
BR1C no.1370 from new

Boiler
no.1707 from new

Condemned 29/6/68, stored at 10A Carnforth 6-9/68, cut up at Campbells, Airdrie 10/68.

92161

To traffic 17/12/57

14/10/59-7/11/59**LC[EO]**	Crewe 44,117
9/5/61-3/6/61**LC**	Gorton 83,319
1/4/63-13/5/63**LC**	Gorton
27/1/64-26/2/64**GO**	Crewe

Annual mileage
1957 655
1958 26,067
1959 21,673
1960 29,717

Sheds
Westhouses 17/12/57
Newton Heath 12/7/58
Carlisle Kingmoor 22/5/65

Tenders
BR1C no.1371 from new
BR1C no.1366 ex 92156 11/7/64

Boiler
no.1708 from new

Condemned 10/12/66, stored at 12A Kingmoor 12/66-4/67, cut up at Motherwell Machinery and Scrap Co., Wishaw 5/67.

The splendid Gowhole and a perfect portrait of Newton Heath's 92162 in June 1961. It had worked its Central Division freight to this ancient boundary and, having duly handed it over to the Midland, it will now work back. Compare with 92016 at the same location earlier on, page 51. Photograph Dr A.H. Roscoe, The Transport Treasury.

92162

To traffic 19/12/57

Works
21/3/61-26/4/61**LC**   Crewe 81,832
31/7/63-21/9/63**GO**   Crewe

Annual mileage
1957   447
1958 26,559
1959 27,384
1960 22,438

Sheds
Westhouses 19/12/57
Newton Heath 12/7/58
Birkenhead 22/5/65

Tender
BR1C no.1360 from new
['repaired and renumbered from BR1E no.1271'*]
*actually a new tender to replace the 1360 assigned
to 92150 but converted for use with 71000

Boiler
no.1709 from new

Condemned 11/11/67, stored at 8C Speke Jct.
11/67-4/68, cut up at Campbells, Airdrie 5/68.

92163

To traffic 24/3/58

Works
14/4/58-1/5/58**LC[TO]**   Crewe 1,650 Damage
4/11/58-13/11/58**LC[EO]**   Derby shed 17,369 Tubes
3/11/61-7/12/61**LC**   Crewe
29/11/62-23/1/63**LC**   Crewe
26/2/63-16/3/63**LC**   Crewe
13/2/64-25/3/64**LC**   Crewe Internal exam
11/6/66-18/6/66**LI**   Crewe

Annual mileage
1958 21,028
1959 28,819
1960 26,824

Sheds
Kettering 24/3/58
Leicester [Midland] 19/6/59
Kettering 5/11/59
Warrington 13/3/65
Birkenhead 19/6/65

Tenders
BR1C no.1372 from new
BR1C no.1170 at 15A Wellingborough on 6/9/60 from 92134

Boiler
no.1710 from new

Condemned 11/11/67, stored at 8C Speke Jct.
11/67-4/68, cut up at Campbells, Airdrie 5/68.

92163 passing Hooton station at the base of the Wirral, 16 September 1965. A Birkenhead engine by now, it has the repositioned lamp irons, second step and AWS. Something got oddly mixed up at an overhaul at some stage in its career, for in June 1966 92163 was noted at Stockport Edgeley carrying a 'Built Crewe 1950' plate! Photograph B.W.L. Brooksbank, Initial Photographics.

92164

To traffic 1/4/58

Works
14/3/61-12/4/61 **LC**   Gorton 94,265
24/4/63-24/5/63 **HC**   Crewe

Annual mileage
1958 27,590
1959 30,782
1960 29,030

Sheds
Leicester [Midland] 1/4/58*
Saltley 25/6/62
*Noted by Tuplin (*Railway Magazine* 12/58)
as on loan from LM shed at Leicester to
the GC shed in August 1958 – see picture also

Tenders
BR1C no.1373 from new
BR1C no.1364 from 92154, 3/3/61 at Wellingborough

Boiler
no.1711 from new

**Condemned 30/7/66, stored at 2E Saltley
7-9/66, cut up at Drapers, Hull 10/66.**

THE BERKLEY STOKER

The Americans achieved much higher mileages with unpromising traffic like coal. They had many advantages, chiefly those of scale, hauling enormous quantities in enormous trains powered by vast, stoker-fed locomotives. The coal was cheaply won and travelled long distances in special wagons from a mechanised loading point to a mechanised discharge point. Geography – space, that is – and a much less recent and less crowded historical development, made this possible.

Little could be done to bring about any of this in Britain, except one. Why not fit mechanical stokers to 9Fs? The first announcement came in the summer of 1957, that five, 92163-92167, would appear with Berkley mechanised stokers, 'by which it is hoped to increase the Class "C" (up to 42 mph) loading for these engines from 37 to 53 loaded wagons'. This order for five was reduced within weeks to just three, which came out of Crewe April-May 1958. They were reported thus: *Three (instead of five, as originally announced) of these locomotives, numbered 92165, 92166 and 92167, have been experimentally fitted with Berkley mechanical stokers in addition to having double chimneys. Further locomotives will be equipped if the results prove worthwhile.*

The choice of the American Berkley stoker might be justified in terms of long experience with such stokers in the US (a number of influential visits had been paid across the Atlantic by British railway officers both before and after the Second World War) though Reed in his *Profile* reveals that it was not a widely applied type, even in its US homeland. The choice

Fame at last. Leicester Midland's 92164 at the GC shed in the city, where it was working on loan, 21 July 1958. Photograph Peter Groom.

came about because it was the one model with an effective 'Rep' in *this* country! There was experience closer to home, among others at Beyer Peacock for instance, a firm which had designed and built successful stokers, particularly in their articulated Beyer-Garratts, for customers abroad. Reed seems to condemn BR for choosing a foreign system that was undeveloped and complicated compared to others in use in North America. The Southern had run a Merchant Navy, 35005, for nearly 80,000 miles with a Berkley intermittently from 1948 to 1951 and could not really do much with it. If a stoker was to be tried, you'd think that the Berkley had had its chance and that another, more proven type would be given a try, such as Beyer Peacock's 'Standard' design. It was not to be.

It was little wonder that BR chose to build the stoker engines new rather than convert existing ones. There was, after all, a lot more work required, far beyond the mere 'fitting' of the equipment. At a cost of some £2,400, quite a bit more than you

might pay for a semi-detached house in a rather good London suburb at the time, 92165, 92166 and 92167 had to have a different firebox back with stays altered accordingly, and different tender front to accommodate the screw and its drive engine. There was even a reduction in water capacity.

The three descended upon Saltley shed in May 1958 and were put to work on the arduous Carlisle jobs where the benefits of the stoker might be expected to be most felt. There were problems from the first and later in the year 92166 was put through its paces at the Rugby Testing Plant. Coal consumption was higher, as should be, for the stoker's purpose lay in feeding coal into the grate at a rate way beyond the ability of the Fireman, so that greatly increased power should be available. The potential gain in extra power was, however, small in the 9F. The grate, at 40 square feet, was hardly big enough to warrant a stoker; certainly it would be dwarfed by those so fitted across the Atlantic. The problem with the BR Berkley

installation was that, though worthwhile improvements in steam generation were found on test, of the order of 12%, beyond that which a single man could provide, it came at a too-high price of increased coal consumption as much of the screw-produced dust went up the chimney while the stoker itself consumed much of the extra steam generated.

Again it was British conditions that made the Berkley stoker 'not worth the candle'. If we had had much bigger engines and very much more of them, running very heavy trains over longer distances with long periods of high output, and sheds were equipped with a suitably screened coal supply (too small, it flew through, too big and it jammed) there might just have been an overall gain but otherwise, it wasn't possible.

While the long distance work from Saltley might be thought of as suited to the stoker fitted trio and in principle it was, there were unforeseen difficulties and shortcomings, that rendered their working awkward in the extreme. With only three engines a specialised coal supply for each end of the journey would always be problematic, at best; the screw was found to be too short for the bunker and Firemen had alarming experiences clearing the coal forward from the rear.

There is every sign that Saltley after a while was happy to get shot of them. As early as the summer of 1958, apparently, there was talk of a transfer to Toton (this would have been fought tooth and nail – at Toton). The WR nonetheless agreed to a limited trial period with a stoker 9F. On '27 August 1959 92166 arrived at Ebbw Junction for a fortnight's evaluation on main line and local freights, but especially on the iron ore workings between Newport Docks

The business part of the Berkley stoker, the trough and its screw sitting inside. In the days long before the Trade Descriptions Act was even dreamed of, the manufacturer's notes claimed, puzzlingly (or maybe not so puzzlingly) that: *The Berkley Stoker takes the hardest run-of-mine coal and crushes it to the proper size without powdering the coal* and, bizarre as it must seem to us now, that because of its design and construction, it made *no noise*. The idea that it made no noise was laughable and as for the proper size, what was crucial was the size of the stuff going in. It had to be *graded* and in the absence of mechanical means, two men were employed at Carlisle (Canal apparently) and Saltley for 2½ hours breaking up the coal *for every trip made by a stoker-fired locomotive*. The problem was recognised, however, and soon a pebble-sized supply was made available at both Saltley and Carlisle. It would always be costly though.

and Ebbw Vale steel works'. There were fearsome gradients to be had and the 9Fs on iron ore work, as at Tyne Dock, had both to head and bank the trains as required. 92166 was first seen at work on the 3.30pm ore train from Newport Docks on 28 August. 'It returned to Saltley on September 11th' records *The Railway Observer*. This is at some variance with the Record Card which not only gives February 1960 as its return to Saltley but offers May 1959 as the departure from Saltley. It also shows it going to Canton for a month beforehand! Predictably, Ebbw Junction had no difficulty in listing plenty of reasons for its unsuitability. Apart from all the other difficulties and the minimal return in power/ steam generation, the labour required to 'grade' the coal – that is, break it up manually on shed, easily negated the theoretical labour saving on the footplate.

Just this extra labour alone might have suggested a rapid removal of the stokers but the engines stayed on at Saltley – some Fireman got the hang of it more than others no doubt. By 1961 it was decided that the Berkley screws and the tender mounted engines that drove them should be removed but the following year, in 1962 with the engines still stoker-fitted, the LM got Tyne Dock to try one out. 92167 duly travelled to the North East where, without air pumps, it was restricted to the banking role. As at Ebbw Junction, it was found to emit far too much ash, doubtless due to the old difficulty of grading the coal required. No shed, you'd think, was going to look kindly on a loco that in addition to everything else required a labourer to spend hours every day breaking up its coal, though *The Railway Observer* reported that 92167 was 'regarded as a considerable success'. It went back to Saltley after several months, though work suited to stoker operation was now much harder to

Right. The cab and the screw uptake, showing the engine with fire hole doors (steam operated) shut for screw operation and, secondly, with the butterfly doors open for hand firing. Notice the long white handle. While it was certainly possible to thus hand fire the engines the hole was high and small and awkward. In fact it was so small and awkward that it is hard to envisage any Fireman doing it except in the absolute direst necessity. The plate to the right marked JETS BERKLEY STOKER has five valve handles – the main jet steam valve and four for the individual jets of the stoker. There are two handles lower down, the larger one being the main steam cock for the stoker engine. The main throttle handle (forward to aft operation, as per standard) and reversing wheel are on the left.

find back in Birmingham. All three went to Bidston for the John Summers steel traffic, 92165 and 92166 in June 1962 and 92167 in December. When Bidston closed early the following year all three moved on to Birkenhead. It is hard to imagine that Bidston would have used the stokers and they may well have been little used, or not at all. Most likely they were manually fired whilst there. The Record Cards have the look of being 'filled in after the event' but Light Casuals immediately prior to transfer to Birkenhead give the game away. The Job No. was WH.110, when the 'material' was settled for the purposes of accountancy.

The gear, as unwrapped and laid out at Crewe. It shows the relationship of the engine with its drive shaft to the screw in its trough – this can be related to the lower picture, showing the equipment in place on the BR1K tender.

The front of a BR1K tender with stoker fitted – see the previous illustration to see how the visible parts are related. Note lever on right – **LIFT TO REVERSE** – which was supposed to come into play in the event of jamming. Recalling the earlier picture of that menacing screw in its trough, you can appreciate the warning DANGER REVOLVING SCREW.

92165

To traffic 17/4/58
Fitted with Berkley mechanical stoker

Works
4/1/61-16/2/61**LC**	Crewe 79,725
15/11/62-20/12/62**LC**	Crewe
21/4/65-14/6/65**LI**	Crewe
22/7/65-26/8/65**LC**	Crewe

Annual mileage
1958 29,650
1959 32,187
1960 17,737

Sheds
Saltley 17/4/58
Bidston 19/6/62
Birkenhead 9/2/63
Speke Jct.29/11/67

Tender
BR1K no.1375 from new

Boiler
no.1712 from new

**Condemned 16/3/68, stored at 8C Speke Jct.
3-5/68 cut up at Cashmores, Newport 6/68.**

92166

To traffic 24/5/58
Fitted with Berkley mechanical stoker

Work
10/12/62-5/1/63**LC**	Crewe E4983 AWS
	WH.118 For making good material
29/4/64-24/8/64**HC[CB]**	Crewe

Sheds
Saltley 24/5/58
Rugby Testing Station 11/9/58
Saltley 23/5/59
Cardiff [Canton] 5/9/59
Ebbw Jct. 3/10/59
Saltley 20/2/60
Bidston 23/6/62
Birkenhead 9/2/63

Tenders
BR1K no.1376 from new
BR1C no.1337 on 30/8/67 from 92127

Boiler
no.1714 from new

**Condemned 11/11/67, stored at 8H Birkenhead
11/67-1/68, 12A Kingmoor 2/68, cut up at
Campbells, Airdrie 3/68.**

92167

To traffic 9/5/58
Fitted with Berkley mechanical stoker

Works
25/2/59-13/3/59**LC[EO]**	Rugby 32,910
25/10/60-13/1/61 **LC[EO]**	Crewe 57,787
2/12/62	WH.118 For removal of Berkeley Stoker, for making a good material
August 1963	Crewe

Annual mileage
1958 30,282
1959 28,623
1960 16,882

Sheds
Saltley 9/5/58
Tyne Dock 12/5/62
Saltley 20/10/62
Bidston 8/12/62
Birkenhead 9/2/63
Carnforth 29/11/67

Tender
BR1K no.1377 from new

Boiler
no.1713 from new

**Condemned 29/6/68, stored at 10A Carnforth
6-9/68, cut up at Campbells, Airdrie 11/68.**

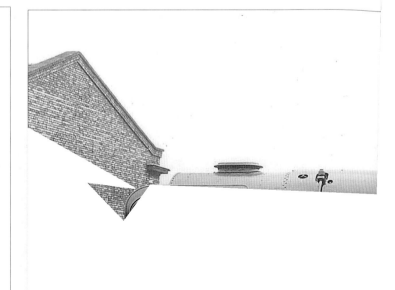

Above. 92166 during its sojourn at Ebbw Junction, in 1959. Saltley apparently 'flew the flag' and cleaned it up a bit for its trip. Photograph J. Davenport, Initial Photographics.

Below. 92167 new at Crewe in May 1958. The stoker promised much; the Class 'C' loading, it was hoped, would be increased from 37 to 53 loaded 16 ton minerals. It was this one, it turned out, that would be the last 9F in service, stoker long gone and famously running as a 2-8-2 with the trailing coupling rods removed. A 2-8-2 at last!

92168

To traffic 20/12/57

Works

18/9/59-29/9/59**NC**	Darlington AWS
5/7/60-2/9/60**LI**	Darlington 9,250
11/63	Crewe

Shed
Doncaster 20/12/57

Tender
BR1F no.1374* from new
*ran as 1377 to 5/58

Boiler
no.1715 from new

Condemned 27/6/65, stored at 36A Doncaster
6-10/65, cut up at Wards, Beighton Sheffield 11/65.

92169

To traffic 27/12/57

Works

15/10/59-26/10/59**NC**	Darlington AWS
25/4/60-15/6/60**LI**	Darlington 87,000
27/6/60-5/7/60**Adj**	Darlington

Shed
Doncaster 27/12/57

Tender
BR1F no.1378 from new

Boiler
no.1716 from new

Condemned 31/5/64, stored at 36A Doncaster
5-12/64, cut up at Wards, Killamarsh 1/65.

Back to Normal

Above. Useful detail of the big BR1F tender, so diagnostic of the Eastern Region; 92169 at Doncaster shed, March 1958. Photograph Brian Hilton, The Transport Treasury.

Bottom right. A magnificent portrayal of 92170 at Doncaster shed (then undergoing rebuilding) in June 1958. It looks like it's just had at least a wipe over (in itself extraordinary enough for a 9F), a theory given some weight by that cloth on the running plate by the steam pipe. The Fireman would brush that smokebox char off the front before they moved off – you didn't want it blowing back out on the road. Photograph J. Robertson, The Transport Treasury.

92170

To traffic 31/12/57

Works
29/9/59-7/10/59**NC**   Darlington AWS
10/5/60-24/6/60**LI**   Darlington 87,500
6/9/60-8/10/60**Adj**   Darlington

Shed
Doncaster 31/12/57

Tender
BR1F no.1379 from new

Boiler
no.1718 from new

Condemned 31/5/64, stored at 36A Doncaster 6-12/64, cut up at Wards, Killamarsh 1/65.

92171

To traffic 1/2/58

Works
8/12/59-16/12/59**NC**   Darlington AWS
31/1/61-23/3/61**LI**   Darlington 94,000

Sheds
Doncaster 1/2/58
New England 10/11/63

Tenders
BR1F no.1380 from new
BR1F no.1125 4/61
BR1F no.1395 6/64

Boiler
no.1717 from new

Condemned 31/5/64, stored at 34E New England 5/64-2/65, cut up at Wards, Killamarsh 3/65.

92172

To traffic 29/1/58

Works
24/11/59-1/12/59**NC**   Darlington AWS
25/10/60-2/12/60**LI**   Darlington 91,000
16/5/63-11/6/63**GO**   Crewe
9/12/64-10/2/65**LC**   Eastleigh 'boiler removed from frames for repair and replaced'

Shed
Doncaster 29/1/58

Tender
BR1F no.1381 from new

Boiler
no.1719 from new
no.1412 from 2/65

Condemned 17/4/66, stored at 36A Doncaster 4-6/66, cut up at W.George, Station Steel, Wath 6-7/66.

92173

To traffic 10/2/58

Works
27/10/59-9/11/59**NC**   Darlington AWS
3/11/60-21/12/60**LI**   Darlington 95,500
18/7/63-23/8/63**GO**   Crewe
25/3/64-24/4/64**LC**   Horwich

Sheds
Doncaster 10/2/58
Langwith Jct. 19/6/65
Colwick 6/11/65
Doncaster 19/12/65

Tender
BR1F no.1382 from new

Boiler
no.1720 from new

Condemned 6/3/66, stored at 36A Doncaster 3-4/66, cut up at Wards, Beighton, Sheffield 5/66.

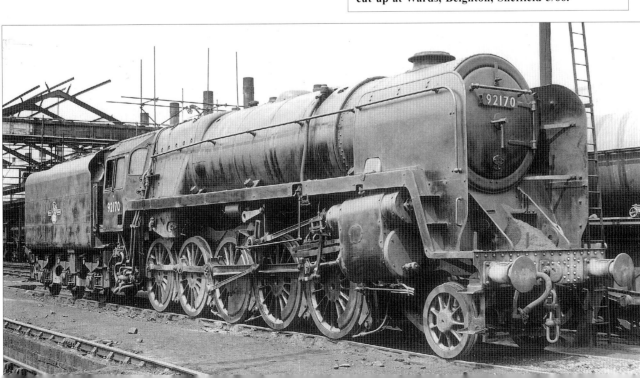

92170 was one of those few 9Fs which spent their entire lives (such as they were) at one particular shed – nearly always, it was Doncaster. Here it is back at 'Donny' after getting AWS at Darlington at the end of 1959; presumably this is where it acquired the 'Scottish' style large cabside numerals. No second type of front step yet, though. Photograph J. Davenport, Initial Photographics.

92171 at New England in May 1958. It was one of the ten stalwarts which went to Doncaster, part of a long series for the Eastern Region (the five intended – three actual – stoker examples got out of sequence) which began at 92168 and ended with 92202, from both Crewe and Swindon. Photograph B.K.B. Green, Initial Photographics.

92173 approaches York on the Down Main Doncaster line, past the old and crumbling Holgate excursion platform last used for race traffic before the Second World War, though it had later been visited by the RCTS (who else?). To the right are the reception sidings put in during the Great War; the lighting towers mark the site of Dringhouses Yard. The huge concrete beams are probably from Anglian Building Products, whose premises were on the remaining stub of the M&GN at Lenwade. That would make it quite a trip. Photograph The Transport Treasury.

92174

To traffic 14/2/58

Works
16/10/59-31/10/59**NC**	Darlington AWS
21/11/60-7/1/61**LI**	Darlington 100,100
24/10/63-10/12/63**GO**	Crewe

Shed
Doncaster 14/2/58

Tender
BR1F no.1383 from new

Boiler
no.1721 from new

Condemned 12/12/65, stored at 36A Doncaster 12/65-4/66, cut up at Wards, Beighton, Sheffield 5/66.

92175

To traffic 21/2/58

Works
26/10/59-5/11/59**NC**	Darlington AWS
21/6/61-16/8/61**LI**	Darlington 96,500

Shed
Doncaster 2/58

Tenders
BR1F no.1384 from new
BR1F no.1407 from 92197

Boiler
no.1723 from new

Condemned 31/5/64, stored at 36A Doncaster 5/64-1/65, cut up at Wards, Killamarsh 2/65.

92176

To traffic 4/3/58

Works
28/10/59-9/11/59**NC**   Darlington AWS
1/2/61-30/3/61**LI**   Darlington 97,500
4/4/61-5/4/61**Adj**   Darlington

Sheds
Doncaster 4/3/58
New England 10/11/63

Tenders
BR1F no.1385 from new
BR1F no.1380 on 1/4/61 from 92171

Boiler
no.1722 from new

Condemned 31/5/64, stored at 34E New England 5/64-2/65, cut up at Wards, Killamarsh 3/65.

92177

To traffic 12/3/58

Works
11/3/60-21/3/60**NC**   Darlington AWS
9/11/60-4/1/61**LI**   Darlington 97,400
30/5/62-28/6/62**LC**   Darlington Header down, repaired and replaced Crewe. Unrecorded but see picture – led to withdrawal?

c.1963

Shed
Doncaster 12/3/58

Tender
BR1F no.1386 from new

Boiler
no.1724 from new

Condemned 31/5/64, stored at Crewe Works 5-7/64, cut up Crewe Works 8/64.

Plawsworth viaduct, on the main line in County Durham, 18 August 1962, 92174 hurrying across with a fully fitted freight. Photograph A.R. Thompson.

92174 at home. It spent all its short life, from February 1958 to the end of 1965, at Doncaster shed. As if to match the waste of its charges, the shed was expensively rebuilt during the period of the 9Fs' tenancy and it too was prematurely redundant, though it did find use for diesels and stock. Photograph J. Davenport, Initial Photographics.

The modest, humble even, bridge in the background is in fact the A1, the country's main historic road artery. The M1 was being built over to the west and the A1 would follow in stages over the years. In the meantime, BR could still run mixed freights such as this, heading south behind 92176 on 7 September 1959 but, with road competition, the economic foundations of wagon load traffic were fast crumbling. Photograph Peter Groom.

An unusual view of a 9F, to say the least. This is 92177 in 1964, recognisable only from the stencilled reference numbers, at Crewe Works, actually on the diesel test roads. The footbridge visible beyond the EE Type 4 indicator box led to the 'Park Flats' as they were called and on to Victoria Road. The gap in the smokebox top is where a removable panel has been, well, removed, so that the superheater header can be taken off and attended to. Though it looks like it, 92177 is not exactly being broken up, and would not be broken up here anyway; it has obviously been taken out of 10 Shop. It was condemned in May 1964 but has been marked up for repair; it looks like 92177 went in as usual but something serious was discovered so it was then decided to condemn it and rob the carcass of parts. It would have to move soon to release the Type 4! It was 'stored' at Crewe for a while and then what was left was cut up for scrap. Photograph J.G. Walmsley, The Transport Treasury.

92177, always a Doncaster engine, in happier times on a down freight approaching Benningborough, on the main line north of York, Sunday 6 August 1961. It was half way through its working life. Photograph Gavin Morrison.

92178

To traffic 28/9/57

Works
2/57   Swindon
10/8/60-6/10/60**GO**   Darlington AWS
21/10/60-3/11/60**Adj**   Darlington

Sheds
New England 28/9/57
Swindon Testing Station 15/12/57
New England 9/3/58
Langwith Jct. 3/1/65

Tender
BR1F no.1388 from new

Boiler
no.1725 from new

Condemned 3/10/65, stored at 41J Langwith Jct. 8-11/65, cut up at Wards, Killamarsh 12/65.

92179

To traffic 7/10/57

Works
22/3/60-6/5/60**LI**   Darlington 90,700 AWS
10/62   Gorton
16/12/64-26/2/65**LC**   Eastleigh 'main steam pipe replaced'

Sheds
New England 7/10/57
Langwith Jct. 3/1/65
Colwick 31/10/65

Tenders
BR1F no.1389 from new
BR1F no.1410 11/65 from 92200

Boiler
no. 1726 from new

Condemned 14/11/65, stored at 40E Colwick 11/65-2/66, cut up at Hughes Bolckows Ltd., North Blyth 3-5/66

Something new here. This is 92178, the first to be equipped with a double chimney, out on controlled road tests between Reading and Stoke Gifford (this is Hullavington) in January-February 1958. The actual date is 30 January 1958. The passenger stock included the ex-GWR dynamometer car and was loaded up to 650 tons — brakes were partially applied to increase tractive resistance. A near 200 horsepower increase and a significant saving in coal was achieved. It was thought at first that the double chimney would obviate the need for smoke deflectors. On the road tests, 92178 was worked at speeds of up to 75 mph downhill but the deflectors were deemed to be 'still desirable'. The contraption on the tender is presumably something to do with the need to weigh coal.

92178 on the Swindon Test plant, November 1957. It was the work of S.O. Ell at Swindon that showed that so many classes had been working in Britain well below their maximum potential for years. The new arrangement gave a boost in maximum drawbar horse power at 36 mph of nearly 200 and so was adopted as standard for new construction, which meant from 92183 onwards.

The double chimney 92178, at New England shed in 1963. It had been the first of Swindon's new Lot 422, a series for the Eastern Region beginning in 1957 but by the time the tests were finished 92179, 92180, 92181 and 92182 had already flown the Swindon coop, so the 'production' series of double chimney 9Fs began with 92183. Photograph J.G. Walmsley, The Transport Treasury.

92180

To traffic 8/11/57

Works
21/1/60-26/2/60**GO**   Darlington
24/12/62-25/1/63**LC**   Crewe

Sheds
New England 8/11/57
Langwith Jct. 3/1/65

Tender
BR1F no.1390 from new

Boiler
no.1727 from new

Condemned 11/4/65, stored at 41J Langwith Jct. 4/65,
cut up at Cashmores, Great Bridge 7/65

92181

To traffic 22/11/57

Works
16/6/60-15/8/60**LI**   Darlington
26/10/61-9/11/61**LC**   Darlington
4/1/63-9/2/63**HI**   Darlington

Shed
New England 22/11/57

Tender
BR1F no.1391 from new

Boiler
no.1728 from new

Condemned 21/2/65, stored at 34E New England
1-6/65, cut up at Cohens, Kettering 7/65
[Sold Cohen 5/4/65]

The hand of Darlington can be detected once again in those large cabside numbers on 92180, up to north London for the day in August 1962. That's definitely a couple of leaks that have sprung in the tender! Photograph B.H. Fletcher, The Transport Treasury.

92182

To traffic 2/12/57

Works
25/8/59-2/9/59**NC**	Darlington AWS
2/9/60-21/10/60**LI**	Darlington 104,250
23/10/63-28/11/63**GO**	Crewe

Sheds
New England 2/12/57
Langwith Jct. 3/1/65
Colwick 6/11/65
Doncaster 19/12/65

Tender
BR1F no.1392 from new

Boiler
no.1729 from new

Condemned 17/4/66, stored at 36A Doncaster 4-6/66, cut up at W.George, Station Steel, Wath 6-7/66.

92184

To traffic 10/1/58

Works
May 1960	Darlington AWS
25/9/64-29/10/64**LC**	Eastleigh

Sheds
New England 10/1/58
Frodingham 14/1/59
New England 14/6/59
Colwick 9/6/63
New England 3/11/63
Immingham 5/1/64

Tenders
BR1F no.1394 from new
BR1F no.1123 on 1/9/61 from 92034
BR1F no.1394 on 1/10/61 from 92034
BR1F no.1131 on 9/2/63 from 92042

Boiler
no.1731 from new

Condemned 21/2/65, stored at 40B Immingham 2-5/65, cut up at Drapers, Hull 6/65

92183

To traffic 20/12/57

Works
3/9/58-10/9/58**NC**	Darlington
4/8/60-17/9/60**LI**	Darlington
1/11/61-15/12/61**LC**	Darlington
5/4/62-5/7/62**HC**	Darlington
19/11/63-2/1/64**HC**	Crewe

Sheds
New England 20/12/57
Colwick 9/6/63
Doncaster 10/1/65

Tender
BR1F no.1393 from new

Boiler
no.1730 from new

Condemned 3/4/66, stored at 36A Doncaster 4-6/66, cut up at W.George, Station Steel, Wath 7/66.

92185

To traffic 15/1/58

Works
7/3/60-13/4/60**GO**	Darlington
31/12/62-22/2/63**LC**	Gorton
2/64	Crewe

Sheds
New England 15/1/58
Colwick 9/6/63
New England 3/11/63
Immingham 5/1/64

Tenders
BR1F no.1395 from new
BR1F no.1355 on 12/4/61 from 92145
BR1F no.1406 on 25/2/65 from 92193

Boiler
no.1732 from new

Condemned 21/2/65, stored at 40B Immingham 2-5/65, cut up at Drapers, Hull 2/65

Big numbers for 92185, not long out of Darlington Works and still in near-dazzling (for a 9F) condition, backing into the yard at Hornsey shed, 1 June 1960. Readers of *British Railways Illustrated*, the October 1998 issue, might remember this part of the yard as being parallel to Wightman Road (an important local thoroughfare) and the cause of particular smoke complaints. Photograph Peter Groom.

92186 at York on a parcels train, 19 August 1961. The nameplate of that Jubilee alongside can only be MARS. Photograph A.G. Forsyth, Initial Photographics.

92186

To traffic 27/1/58

Works
2/6/60-27/7/60**LI**	Darlington AWS
20/12/62-25/1/63**HC**	Crewe

Sheds
New England 27/1/58
Colwick 9/6/63
Doncaster 10/1/65
Langwith Jct. 19/6/65

Tender
BR1F no.1396 from new

Boiler
no.1733 from new

Condemned 29/8/65, stored at 41J Langwith Jct. 8/65, cut up at Drapers, Hull 2/66.

92187

To traffic 12/2/58

Works
8/8/58-15/8/58**NC**	Darlington
9/10/58-28/10/58**NC**	Darlington
5/12/58-2/1/59**C**	Darlington
15/3/61-27/4/61**HI**	Darlington
8/5/61-15/5/61**ADJ**	Darlington

Sheds
New England 12/2/58
Grantham 8/6/58
New England 21/9/58
Colwick 9/6/63

Tenders
BR1F no.1397 from new
BR1F no.1401

Boiler
no.1734 from new

Condemned 21/2/65, stored at 40E Colwick 1-4/65, cut up at Drapers Hull 5/65.

92188

To traffic 27/2/58

Works
8/7/58-8/8/58**LC**	Darlington
21/12/59-21/2/60**NC**	Darlington
8/12/60-21/1/61**LI**	Darlington
3/2/64-13/2/64**LC**	Crewe

Sheds
New England 27/2/58
Grantham 8/6/58
New England 21/9/58
Colwick 9/6/63

Tender
BR1F no.1398 from new

Boiler
no.1735 from new

Condemned 21/2/65, stored at 40E Colwick 1-4/65, cut up at Drapers, Hull 5/65.

92189

To traffic 14/3/58
AWS 8/59

Works
15/1/61-11/2/61	Darlington
August 1962	Darlington

Sheds
Mexborough 30/3/58
Darnall 13/4/58
Doncaster 11/5/58
Frodingham 4/1/59
Doncaster 19/4/59
Colwick 8/9/63
Langwith Jct. 10/1/65
Colwick 31/10/65

Tenders
BR1F no.1399 from new
BR1F no.1123 6/65

Boiler
no.1736 from new

Condemned 9/12/65, stored at 40E Colwick 12/65-3/66, cut up at Wards, Beighton, Sheffield 4/66.

Grantham's 92187, AWS fitted, at Kings Cross waiting to leave with an express – about 1959/60 at a guess. Photograph The Transport Treasury.

AWS fitted 92189 runs through Grantham; the period would be 1963-64, when the 9F was a Colwick (40E) engine. Photograph The Transport Treasury.

92190

To traffic 28/3/58

Works

28/8/58-3/10/58**LC**	Darlington
24/8/59-1/9/59**NC**	Darlington
24/3/61-13/5/61**HI**	Darlington
8/8/61-28/9/61**LC**	Darlington
4/10/62-28/11/62**LC**	Gorton

Sheds

Mexborough 28/3/58
Darnall 13/4/58
Doncaster 11/5/58
Frodingham 4/1/59
Doncaster 26/4/59
Colwick 14/9/63
Doncaster 20/6/64

Tenders

BR1F no.1400 from new
BR1F no.1385

Boiler

no.1737 from new

Condemned 10/10/65, stored at 36A Doncaster 10-12/65 as a stationary Boiler, cut up at Wards, Beighton, Sheffield 1/66.

92191

To traffic 15/4/58

Works

2/60	AWS (presumed Darlington)
11/11/61	Darlington

Sheds

Darnall 15/4/58
Doncaster 11/5/58
Colwick 8/9/63
Langwith Jct. 10/1/65
Colwick 31/10/65

Tenders

BR1F no.1401 from new
BR1F no.1400 from 92140
BR1F no.1350 on 7/5/65

Boiler

no.1738 from new

Condemned 19/12/65, stored at 40E Colwick 12/65-4/66, cut up at Wards, Beighton, Sheffield 4/66.

92192

To traffic 1/5/58

Works

15/11/58	Darlington
10/59	AWS (presumed Darlington)
8/7/61	Darlington
June 1963	Crewe

Sheds

Doncaster 1/5/58
Colwick 8/9/63
Frodingham 24/11/63

Tender

BR1F no.1402 from new

Boiler

no.1739 from new

Condemned 21/2/65, stored at 36A Doncaster 2-4/65, cut up at Wards, Beighton, Sheffield 5/65.

92193

To traffic 23/5/58

Works

28/10/58-4/11/58**NC**	Darlington
22/6/59-24/6/59**NC**	Darlington
10/8/59-27/8/59**NC**	Darlington
11/12/59-9/2/60**LC**	Darlington
21/3/60-25/3/60**NC**	Darlington
24/3/61-7/4/61**LC**	Darlington
5/9/61-6/10/61**GO**	Darlington
24/9/62-13/10/62**LC**	Crewe

Sheds

Doncaster 23/5/58
Immingham 1/2/59

Tenders

BR1F no.1403 from new
BR1F no.1406 from 92196
BR1F no.1355 on 25/2/65 from 92185
BR1F no.1384

Boiler

no.1740 from new

Condemned 13/6/65, stored at 40B Immingham 6-10/65, cut up at Drapers, Hull 11/65.

92190, another Colwick 9F, at Holbeck shed on Friday 4 October 1963. Large numbers and that access panel low down on the cabside has a locally-altered look to it. Photograph Gavin Morrison.

92191 at Doncaster shed; it looks more or less new but this would be the occasion of its return home to 'Donny' after attention at Darlington in February 1960 where it got the AWS and the large numbers. Ashpan doors open. Photograph J. Davenport, Initial Photographics.

AWS fitted 92192, undergoing some big end attention in the sunshine at what could be New England, or maybe Doncaster Works. She looks very recently out of works anyway, so may have gone back for 'rectification' as the big end got a bit warm perhaps. Photograph The Transport Treasury.

Fine portrait at Doncaster shed, June 1958. Ashpan raking doors hanging open in typical fashion. Photograph J. Robertson, The Transport Treasury.

92194

To traffic 10/6/58

Works
11/6/59-16/6/59**NC**	Darlington
2/9/59-10/9/59**NC**	Darlington
21/1/60-11/3/60**NC**	Darlington
3/10/61-18/11/61**LI**	Darlington
22/3/62-2/4/62**ADJ**	Darlington

Sheds
Doncaster 20/6/58
Immingham 1/2/59

Tender
BR1F no.1404 from new

Boiler
no.1741 from new

Condemned 5/12/65, stored at 85B Gloucester [Horton Road] 12/65-1/66, cut up at Arnott Young, Parkgate and Rawmarsh 3/66.

92195

To traffic 27/6/58

Works
2/7/59-6/7/59**NC**	Darlington
24/10/61-2/12/61**GO**	Darlington

Sheds
Doncaster 27/6/58
Immingham 1/2/59
New England 20/6/64
Langwith Jct. 3/1/65

Tender
BR1F no.1405 from new

Boiler
no.1742 from new

Condemned 9/5/65, stored at 41J Langwith Jct 5-8/65, cut up at Drapers, Hull 11/65.

92196

To traffic 15/8/58

Works
27/7/59-6/8/59**NC**	Darlington
14/2/61-8/4/61**GO**	Darlington
15/5/61-30/5/61**ADJ**	Darlington

Shed
Doncaster 15/8/58
Immingham 1/2/59

Tenders
BR1F no.1406 from new
BR1F no.1403 from 92193

Boiler
no.1743 from new

Condemned 6/12/64, stored at 40B Immingham 10/64-12/65, cut up at Wards, Beighton, Sheffield 1/66.

92197

To traffic 11/9/58

Works
15/1/60-22/1/60**NC**	Darlington AWS
5/6/61-29/7/61**LI**	Darlington
19/3/65-5/5/65**LC**	Eastleigh 'complete overhaul of one or more valve gears'

Sheds
Doncaster 11/9/58
Frodingham 1/2/59
Doncaster 2/5/59
Immingham 11/9/60

Tenders
BR1F no.1407 from new
BR1F no.1384 from 92175
BR1F no.1355

Boiler
no.1744 from new

Condemned 19/9/65, stored at 40B Immingham 9-12/65, cut up at Wards, Beighton, Sheffield 1/66.

92198

To traffic 6/10/58

Works
20/3/60**LI**   Darlington AWS
10/3/62   Darlington

Sheds
Doncaster 6/10/58
Frodingham 1/2/59
Doncaster 14/6/59
Colwick 8/9/63
Frodingham 24/11/63

Tender
BR1F no.1408 from new

Boiler
no.1877 from new

Condemned 2/8/64, stored at 36C Frodingham 7/64-5/65, cut up at Wards, Beighton, Sheffield 6/65.

92199

To traffic 29/10/58

Works
10/60   AWS (presumed Darlington)
13/1/61 Darlington

Sheds
Doncaster 29/10/58
Colwick 8/9/63
Frodingham 24/11/63

Tender
BR1F no.1409 from new

Boiler
no.1745 from new

Condemned 2/8/64, stored at 36C Frodingham 7/64-5/65, cut up at Wards, Beighton, Sheffield 6/65

Last on the checklist – tie your shoelaces! 92199, in terrible freight working condition, ready to leave Kings Cross with an express about 1960. Photograph The Transport Treasury.

92200

To traffic 18/11/58

Works
1/9/59-11/9/59**NC** Darlington
15/9/61-3/11/61**LI** Darlington Ball joint
20/6/63-9/8/63**HC** Crewe

Sheds
Doncaster 18/11/58
Immingham 14/9/63
Doncaster 20/6/64
Langwith Jct. 19/6/65

Tender
BR1F no.1410 from new

Boiler
no.1746 from new

Condemned 3/10/65, stored at 41J Langwith Jct. 10-11/65, cut up at Wards, Killamarsh 12/65.

92201

To traffic 5/12/58

Works
7/9/59-16/9/59**NC**   Darlington
22/10/59-29/10/59**NC**   Doncaster
27/2/62-6/4/62**LI**   Darlington
9/4/63-11/5/63**HC[CB]**   Crewe

Sheds
Doncaster 5/12/58
Immingham 14/9/63
Doncaster 20/6/64

Tender
BR1F no.1411 from new

Boiler
no.1747 from new

Condemned 27/3/66, stored at 36A Doncaster 3-6/66, cut up at W.George, Station Steel, Wath 7/66.

A shiny new 92201 amidst the pannier tanks at Swindon, 30 November 1958. The 'F' of the '9F' on the cabside was frequently absent in this batch. Photograph Ivo Peters, courtesy Julian Peters.

92202

To traffic 27/12/58

Works
29/5/59-3/6/59**NC**	Darlington
14/9/59-22/9/59**NC**	Darlington
11/60	Swindon
11/1/62-1/3/62**LI**	Darlington

Sheds
Doncaster 27/12/58
Immingham 5/4/59

Tender
BR1F no.1412 from new

Boiler
no.1748 from new

**Condemned 19/12/65, stored at 40B Immingham
12/65-2/66, cut up at Wards, Beighton, Sheffield 3/66.**

92203

To traffic 6/4/59

Works
11/60	Swindon
16/11/62-19/12/62**LC**	Crewe
22/8/63-26/9/63**LC**	Crewe
4/5/64-29/7/64 **HC[CB]**	Crewe
19/10/66-31/12/66 **HC[CB]**	Crewe
Mileage at 7/7/62 91,434	

Annual mileage
1960 24,399
1961 22,523
1963 16,006

Sheds
Bristol St Philips Marsh 6/4/59
Old Oak Common 8/10/60
Banbury 6/4/63
Birkenhead 11/9/66

Tender
BR1G no.1510 from new

Boiler
no.1749 from new

**Condemned 11/11/67, engine preserved on
Glos. and Warwickshire Rly. Toddington.**

As a St Philip's Marsh (Bristol) 9F, 92204 would not have been any stranger in London; there is no date or location for this photograph but it is surely Old Oak Common and the 2-10-0 is on the 'firepit' on the goods engine side of the coal stage. In its laughably short existence it moved within a few months from Bristol to Southall and then almost immediately to Old Oak, then off to Banbury to see out its days on the LMR.

92204

To traffic 21/4/59

Works
25/6/62-1/11/62**HI**   Swindon
12/7/63-3/8/63**LC**   Crewe
Mileage at 7/7/62 103,190

Annual mileage
1960 33,525
1961 30,217
1963 15,122

Sheds
Bristol St.Philips Marsh 21/4/59
Southall 8/10/60
Old Oak Common 5/11/60
Banbury 6/4/63
Tyseley 14/9/63
Speke Jct. 20/8/66

Tenders
BR1G no.1511 from new
BR1G no.1535

Boiler
no.1879 from new

**Condemned 9/12/67, stored at 8C Speke Jct.
12/67-2/68, cut up at Wards, Beighton, Sheffield 3/68.**

92205

To traffic 4/59

Works
5/9/61-23/9/61**LC**   Eastleigh 67,179 '26 small
                           boiler tubes
                           replaced, new, steel; 4 or more
                           wheels
                           turned up and axleboxes
                           refitted to
                           horns and journals'
9/10/62-10/11/62**LC**   Eastleigh 95,406 Test 2337
                           [new]
30/7/64-15/8/64**LC**   Crewe
9/2/65-23/3/65**LI**   Crewe

Sheds
Bristol St. Philips Marsh 16/4/59
Westbury 8/10/60
Eastleigh 17/1/61
Feltham 24/6/63
York 8/9/63
Wakefield 5/11/66

Tender
BR1G no.1512 from new

Boiler
no.1880 from new

In fact 92204 spent even less time at St Philip's Marsh than the allocation record suggests, for much of that first summer was spent on loan to Bath Green Park for work on the Somerset & Dorset. Here she breasts Masbury Summit with the 9.55am (SO) Bournemouth-Leeds on 2 July 1960. Photograph Ivo Peters, courtesy Julian Peters.

Another St Philip's Marsh 9F on loan that summer to the S&D, 92205 passing Broadstone on the 9.35am Sheffield-Bournemouth, 23 July 1960. Photograph J. Davenport, Initial Photographics.

St Philip's Marsh got the first five of the last 9F Lot, 429 from Swindon, which culminated in 92220 EVENING STAR. This series began with 92203 in April 1959, after Crewe's final Lot E497 had ended, with 92250 in December 1958. There was a reversion to the BR1G tender for this Lot. The Bristol ones were not well received, or work of the right category could not be found for them, for all five St Philip's Marsh 9Fs had moved on within a few months. So this is an unusual photograph of one on a Bristol job, with a down freight approaching Teignmouth in August 1959. It's fairly new, but completely filthy. Photograph R.S. Carpenter Photos.

92206

To traffic 5/59

Works

12/9/60	Bristol Barrow Road Pistons
13/1/61-3/2/61**LC**	Eastleigh 73,016
17/5/62-9/6/62**LI**	Eastleigh 81,179
27/12/62-19/1/63 **NC-LC**	Eastleigh 93,133 'T2337 [new]; 25 small boiler tubes replaced, new, steel, 14 superheater tubes replaced'
11/9/64-23/1/65**LC**	Crewe

Sheds
Bristol St.Philips Marsh 16/5/59
Westbury 8/10/60
Eastleigh 17/1/61
Feltham 24/6/63
York 8/9/63
Wakefield 5/11/66

Tender
BR1G no.1513 from new

Boiler
no.1880 from new

Condemned 9/5/67, stored at 56A Wakefield 5-8/67, cut up at Arnott Young, Parkgate and Rawmarsh 9/67.

92207

To traffic 6/59

Works

28/1/60-11/2/60**LI**	Laira	
20/5/61**LI**		Caerphilly
4-5/63	Crewe	

Sheds
Bristol St.Philips Marsh 13/6/59
Southall 27/2/60
Ebbw Jct. 22/11/64

Tender
BR1G no.1514 from new

Boiler
no.1882 from new

Condemned 26/12/64, preserved at Shillingstone, Dorset.

92207 brand new at Swindon, 24 May 1954. This was the last of the St Philip's Marsh five and their famously-brief stay. Photograph Norman Preedy Archive.

92207 on 2 September 1962, now a Southall engine and bearing the white smokebox door hinges which appeared around that time. At the end of 1964 she was unexpectedly sent to Ebbw Junction, to eke out a few more months of work. Photograph Peter Groom.

North of the Border. With the Moffat branch moving away in the foreground, 92208 with a down fitted freight passes a Black Five on an up one. On 21 September 1967, towards the end of its life, this particular 9F was noted passing northwards (south of Carlisle near Upperby) hauling 'three clean but condemned 46400, 46433 and 46499'. Photograph The Transport Treasury.

92208

To traffic 11/6/59

Works
12/4/62-25/6/62**HI**	Swindon
9/1/65-10/1/65	Tender change with 92023
12/1/66-11/3/66**HI**	Crewe

Mileage at 7/7/62 79,419

Annual mileage
1960 25,591
1961 25,231
1963 1,883

Sheds
Laira 11/6/59
Southall 26/3/60
Cardiff Canton 2/12/61
Cardiff East Dock 8/9/62
Newton Heath 6/10/63
Carlisle Kingmoor 27/6/64

Tenders
BR1G no.1515 from new
BR1C no.1334 from 92023, 10/1/65

Boiler
no.1883 from new

Condemned 28/11/67, stored at 12A Kingmoor 10/67-1/68, cut up at McWilliams, Shettleston 2/68.

92209

To traffic 6/59

Works
August 1962   Swindon

Sheds
Bristol St.Philips Marsh O/L 7/59
Laira 7/11/59
Cardiff Canton 5/9/59
Ebbw Jct. 20/5/62
Cardiff East Dock 28/9/63
Southall 13/6/65
Cardiff East Dock 11/7/65
Bristol Barrow Road 9/10/65
Bath Green Park 6/11/65

Tender
BR1G no.1516 from new

Boiler
no.1884 from new

Condemned 31/12/65, stored at 82E Bristol [Barrow Road] 12/65-2/66, cut up at Cashmores, Newport 3/66.

Stately progress for shining new 92209 with a Plymouth-Crewe train passing Teignmouth in June 1959. It was one of two that summer to go direct to Laira, a shed that obviously knew what to do with them. Photograph Stanley Creer, The Transport Treasury.

92210

To traffic 8/59

Sheds
Cardiff Canton 8/8/59
Bristol Barrow Road 10/9/60
Bath Green Park 14/7/62
Cardiff Canton 11/8/62
Cardiff East Dock 8/9/62
Southall 28/12/63
Ebbw Jct. 22/6/64

Tender
BR1G no.1517 from new

Boiler
no.1885 from new

Condemned 11/64, stored at 86B Ebbw Jct. 11/64-2/65, cut up at Buttigiegs, Newport 3/65.

92211

To traffic 9/59

Works

13/10/61-4/11/61**LC**	Eastleigh 58,908 'superheater header taken down and replaced'
29/6/62-10/8/62**LC**	Crewe
4/3/63-30/3/63**LC**	Crewe
23/12/64-16/3/65**LI**	Crewe
8/8/66-21/9/66**NC**	Crewe

Sheds
Old Oak Common 31/10/59
Westbury 17/6/61
Eastleigh 23/8/61
Feltham 24/6/63
York 8/9/63
Wakefield 5/11/66

Tender
BR1G no.1518 from new

Boiler
no.1886 from new

Condemned 22/5/67, stored at 56A Wakefield 5-11/67, cut up at Drapers, Hull 12/67.

92210 at Canton shed, though without a date or the shed plate it is hard to tell which period we are looking at. The clue is 70019 LIGHTNING in the background; the Britannia went away from Canton and the Western Region in September 1961 and had been there since before 92210 had been built. Photograph J. Davenport, Initial Photographics.

Summer holidays. 92210 leaving Devonshire Tunnel on the Somerset & Dorset with the 8.15am down local from Bath, 11 August 1962. Photograph Ivo Peters, courtesy Julian Peters.

92211 at Westbury shed; the lack of shed plate suggests it has just arrived at its new home, which would make the period about June-July 1961. We are back now of course, in the land of the sideways lamp iron. Photograph J. Davenport, Initial Photographics.

92212

To traffic 22/9/59

Works
6/11/61-2/4/62**HC**   Swindon
23/6/64-20/8/64**LI**   Crewe
22/6/65-2/9/65   [Works not identified]
Mileage at 30/12/62 55,407

Annual mileage
1960 24,273
1961 14,119
1963 22,759

Sheds
Banbury 22/9/59
Bath Green Park 17/6/61
Ebbw Jct. 10/9/61
Tyseley 14/7/62
Carnforth 29/10/66

Tender
BR1G no.1519 from new

Boiler
no.1887 from new

Condemned 6/1/68, engine preserved on the Mid-Hants Railway.

92213

To traffic 22/10/59

Works
16/7/60**LC**   Caerphilly
29/7/63-28/8/63**LC**   Crewe
Mileage at 30/12/62 68,303

Annual mileage
1960 29,816
1961 21,382
1963 13,597

Sheds
Bristol St.Philips Marsh 22/10/59
Banbury 28/11/59
Carlisle Kingmoor 15/10/66

Tender
BR1G no.1520 from new

Boiler
no.1888 from new

Condemned 5/11/66, stored at 12A Kingmoor 10/66-1/67, cut up at McWilliams, Shettleston 2/67.

92214

To traffic 10/59

Works
23/1/63-21/2/63**NC**   Caerphilly
17/6/63-30/7/63**LC**   Crewe

Sheds
Banbury 5/11/59
Ebbw Jct. 2/12/61
Severn Tunnel Jct. 20/7/64

Tender
BR1G no.1521 from new

Boiler
no.1889 from new

Condemned 9/8/65, preserved at the Midland Railway Centre.

92215

To traffic 17/11/59

Works
30/7/61   Swindon
7/3/63-17/4/63**LC**   Gorton
3/6/63-19/7/63**LC**   Crewe
Mileage at 30/12/62 65,526

Annual mileage
1960 29,744
1961 15,305
1963 11,023

Sheds
Banbury 17/11/59
Tyseley 14/9/63
Wakefield 5/11/66

Tenders
BR1G no.1522 from new
BR1G no.1515 from 92208
BR1B no.977

Boiler
no.1890 from new

Condemned 8/6/67, stored at 56A Wakefield 5/67-2/68, cut up at Drapers, Hull 3/68.

92216

To traffic 12/59

Works
30/7/61　　　　Swindon

Sheds
Cardiff Canton 26/12/59
Cardiff East Dock 8/9/62
Neath 2/11/63
Southall 12/10/64
Severn Tunnel Jct. 20/8/65

Tender
BR1G no.1523 from new

Boiler
no.1891 from new

Condemned 10/65, stored at 81F Oxford 10/65-3/66, cut up at Cashmores, Newport 4/66.

92217

To traffic 22/12/59

Works
16/9/61　Wolverhampton
Mileage at 7/7/62 83,680

Annual mileage
1960 46,165
1961 23,562
1963 21,883

Sheds
Cardiff Canton 22/12/59
Bristol St.Philips Marsh 30/1/60
Banbury 30/3/63
Tyseley 14/9/63

Tender
BR1G no.1524 from new

Boiler
no.1892 from new

Condemned 30/7/66, stored at 2A Tyseley 8-9/66, cut up at Drapers, Hull 10/66.

92218

To traffic 18/1/60

Works
15/12/61-13/2/62**LC**　　　Swindon
16/2/62-8/3/62　　　Swindon [continuation of above **LC**]
12/6/63-19/7/63**LC**　　　Crewe
5/66　　　Crewe
Mileage at 7/7/62 77,436

Annual mileage
1961 23,528
1963 17,314

Sheds
Bristol St. Philips Marsh 18/1/60
Banbury 6/4/63
Warrington 15/10/66
Speke Jct. 25/3/67
Carlisle Kingmoor 12/8/67
Speke Jct. 27/1/68

Tender
BR1G no.1525 from new

Boiler
no.1893 from new

Condemned 5/68, stored at 9H Patricroft, cut up at Arnott Young, Parkgate and Rawmarsh 7/68.

92219

To traffic 1/60

Works
24/9/61　　　　Swindon
April 1962　　　　Tyseley

Sheds
Bristol St.Philip's Marsh 1/60
Cardiff Canton 27/2/60
Cardiff East Dock 8/9/62

Tender
BR1G no 1526 from new

Boiler
no.1894 from new

Condemned 9/8/65, preserved at The Midland Railway Centre.

Top right. An up part-fitted freight comes in to Birmingham Snow Hill on 16 December 1961 behind 92213. She carries the 84C plate of Banbury which in a year and a half will pass to the LMR. Photograph Michael Mensing.

Middle right. 92215 passing Grimes Hill station on the GW lines south of Birmingham, 17 September 1964. A Tyseley engine, by now it is the 2A code of the LMR. Photograph R.J. Buckley, Initial Photographics.

Below. 92218 at Banbury. A small shed in the middle of the country, Banbury nevertheless played an important role in the steel traffic to and from South Wales and the north and east of England. Photograph B.K.B. Green Collection, Initial Photographics.

EVENING STAR

The last steam locomotive completed for British Railways (it even made the *Tonight* programme with Cliff Michelmore – *The next tonight, tomorrow night* – on the BBC) was named in a special ceremony at Swindon on 18 March 1960, with Mr R.F. Hanks (WR Board Chairman) presiding. Again, as is well known, the appropriate name was chosen by popular competition in the Western Region *Magazine*; it was a natural choice given the STAR connections on the Western and three members of staff picked the name and all won a cash prize. Less well known is that an exhibition of stock was also held to coincide with the naming ceremony, and locos included shunter D2136, D817 FOXHOUND, D818 GLORY, 6003 KING GEORGE IV, 5057 EARL WALDEGRAVE, CITY OF TRURO, the Caledonian Single 123, GW railcar No.4 and various items of stock. Unofficially present was Vale of Rheidol No.9 PRINCE OF WALES in 'A' Shop. Guests were conveyed to and from Swindon in a special train hauled by 7007 GREAT WESTERN. A few weeks later 92220 was in charge of an LCGB special and worked back to its South Wales home on a freight to Cardiff. It was to take up residence at Canton but would not be lost on coal and ore jobs (it would, after all, be a shame to waste that painting and nameplate) and was soon on the best summer trains to London and back. Fairly soon, however, EVENING STAR was something of an embarrassment. With a fleet of perfectly sound locomotives going to the breakers as pathetic filthy scrap decades before their time it might have been better if 92220 was just another anonymous black engine...

92220 EVENING STAR

To traffic 25/3/60
(actually complete by 7/2/60!)

Works
24/1-26/2/64-24/3/64**LC**   Swindon

Sheds
Cardiff Canton 25/3/60
Bath Green Park 11/8/62
Old Oak Common 6/10/62
Oxford 3/11/62
Bath Green Park 31/8/63
Cardiff East Dock 2/11/63

Tender
BR1G no.1527 from new

Boiler
no.1895 from new

Condemned 29/3/65, preserved at the NRM, York.

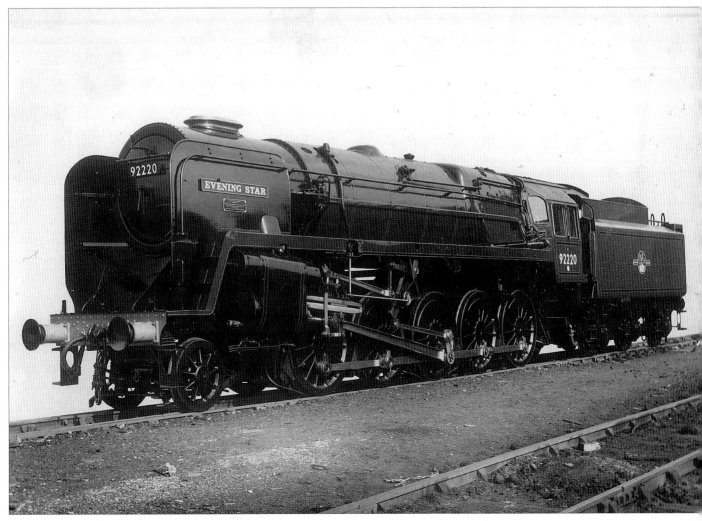

The official portrait.

The official 'do', or its aftermath at least, at Swindon. Photographs The Transport Treasury.

The plaque. Mr Hanks may have presided, but Mr Grand did the naming. Photograph The Transport Treasury.

Out in the yard at Swindon a couple of days after the ceremony – it has still not been steamed yet since naming. Strangely enough, 92220 had originally been finished in black. No special treatment had been envisaged and it came into the world just another anonymous 9F. It was observed in this condition on the Works weighbridge on 7 February, one of the official guides remarking to a visiting party that 'they are going to do something with it'. A further works visit on 14 February found 92220 still lingering in the yard though it later gravitated to the Newburn Carriage Shed – still in black. Matters got moving and on 7 March 92220 was observed in 'A' Shop finished in green; it was duly named and given the ceremonial send-off on 18 March 1960. Photograph The Transport Treasury.

EVENING STAR at Old Oak shed a few weeks after its unveiling, on 2 April 1960. On an LCGB special the day before, it would work a freight to get to its intended home, Cardiff. It was famously in passenger green, lined with a copper capped chimney – GW livery in effect. Photograph R.C. Riley, The Transport Treasury.

To mark the Golden Jubilee of the Institution of Locomotive Engineers, the British Transport Commission arranged an exhibition of locomotives and rolling stock at Marylebone parcels depot on 11-14 May 1961. Among the diesels were MALLARD, DUKE OF GLOUCESTER and EVENING STAR. Canton was still 86C when EVENING STAR appeared but it doesn't seem to have carried a plate until the shed became 88A later on in 1960.

At Canton in its pomp. EVENING STAR seems to have been a regular on passenger work in the summer, though whether it was specially selected before any other 2-10-0s on the shed's books is hard to say. Our last steam locomotive would typically be found on a Friday Cardiff-Portsmouth passenger train, for instance. Photograph J. Davenport, Initial Photographics.

Beautifully turned out for a special working at Paddington, over on the Metropolitan side, with Southern coaches, about 1962-63. Photograph J.G. Walmsley, The Transport Treasury.

At Old Oak, September 1962. That access door on the cabside is a replacement; when built the lining ran across it. WR route colour disc on cab – yellow for this class. Photograph Prorail UK (Durrant), The Transport Treasury.

Looking scruffy for once, EVENING STAR at Templecombe on the Somerset & Dorset during 1962. The locomotive was condemned at the end of March 1965 and then seemed to spend periods of store (it was inside Barrow Road roundhouse at Christmas 1965, for instance) here, there and everywhere, in ever increasing decrepitude until it was finally restored. Its own Golden Anniversary is now not too far off. Photograph P.J. Coster.

Back to Normal

George Heiron's wonderful composition of 92222, while a Banbury engine, in amongst the locals at Canton shed. Quite perfect. Photograph George Heiron, courtesy Mrs Shirley Heiron, The Transport Treasury.

92221

To traffic 30/5/58

Works
3/59	Wolverhampton
20/10/59-20/11/59**LI**	Laira
30/12/61	Wolverhampton

Sheds
Banbury 10/6/58
Laira 11/7/59
Banbury 26/3/60
Laira 18/6/60
Westbury 10/9/60
Banbury 8/10/60
Bristol Barrow Road 5/11/60
York 8/9/63

Tender
BR1G no.1532 from new

Boiler
no.1912 from new

Condemned 10/5/65, stored at 50A York 5-8/65, cut up at Hughes Bolckows Ltd., North Blyth 9/65.

92222

To traffic 2/6/58

Works
29/10/59-16/11/59**LI**	Old Oak Common
2/62	Swindon
10/3/64-16/4/64**LC**	Swindon

Sheds
Banbury 2/6/58
Laira 11/7/59
Banbury 26/3/60
Laira 18/6/60
Ebbw Jct 5/11/60
Neath 30/11/63
Southall 12/10/64

Tender
BR1G no.1533 from new

Boiler
no.1913 from new

Condemned 26/3/65, stored at 81C Southall 3-6/65, cut up at Cashmores, Newport 7/65.

92223

To traffic 6/6/58

Works
16/9/58-19/9/58**NC**	Swindon AWS
30/8-13/10/61**HC**	Swindon
12/10/62-10/1/63**LC**	Gorton
22/5/64-24/12/64	Swindon
25/7/66-8/9/66	Crewe Attention to Boiler
Mileage at 17/5/64 94,248	

Annual mileage
1960 17,917
1961 19,804

Sheds
Banbury 6/6/58
Laira 11/7/59
Banbury 26/3/60
Laira 18/6/60
Westbury 10/9/60
Ebbw Jct. 25/3/61
Bromsgrove 2/11/63
Tyseley 28/5/64
Saltley 7/11/66
Carlisle Kingmoor 29/11/66
Carnforth 27/1/68

Tender
BR1G no.1534 from new

Boiler
no.1914 from new

Condemned 13/4/68, stored at 10A Carnforth 4-7/68, cut up at Arnott Young, Dinsdale 9/68.

92224

To traffic 16/6/58

Works
22/1/60-9/2/60**LI**	Laira
23/4/60-26/5/60**LC**	Swindon
8/62	Swindon
26/3/65-28/4/65**LC**	Crewe

Sheds
Banbury 12/6/58
Laira 11/7/59
Southall 16/6/60
Oxford 3/11/62
Bath Green Park 31/8/63
Bristol Barrow Road 28/9/63
Cardiff East Dock 2/11/63
Banbury 7/11/64
Warrington 13/8/66

Tender
BR1G no.1535 from new
BR1G no.1552 at 8B Warrington

Boiler
no.1915 from new

Condemned 30/9/67, stored at 12A Kingmoor 9/67-5/68, cut up at McWilliams, Shettleston 6/68.

92223 scurries for lower altitudes and relative shelter with a southbound freight as a late season snow storm sweeps across Ribblehead viaduct and Whernside, 6 April 1967, The dear old thing lasted until 1968, at Carnforth, despite being officially condemned by the Western Region (the first 9F to be so dealt with) back in February 1964. It had arrived as Lickey banker the previous year and a periodical examination disclosed severe scoring of the both cylinders. An inspector was summoned from Swindon and the 9F was withdrawn. Nonetheless 92223 was reinstated and went to Tyseley. It then did the rounds of LMR sheds to find itself, late in life, in the Pennines. Photograph Paul Cotterell.

The WR 9Fs that survived the end of steam on that Region did so because their home sheds, such as Banbury, Tyseley and so on, were taken over by the LMR. One that made it to the North West was 92224 – here it is, a Warrington engine, taking water at Preston in June 1967, three months before withdrawal. The Driver is trying to get the injector to work! Photograph A.W. Battson.

92225

To traffic 20/6/58

Works
14/9/59-2/10/59**NC**	Laira
24/12/59-11/1/60**NC**	Taunton
4/11/61**HC**	Caerphilly
5/62**LI**	Caerphilly
3-7/64	Swindon

Sheds
Banbury 20/6/58
Laira 11/7/59
Ebbw Jct. 26/3/60
Neath 2/11/63
Ebbw Jct. 22/6/64

Tender
BR1G no.1536 from new

Boiler
no.1916 from new

Condemned 7/65, stored at 86B Ebbw Jct., cut up at Cashmores, Newport 9/65

92226

To traffic 26/6/58

Works
30/9/59-24/10/59**NC**	Banbury
28/5/61	Swindon

Sheds
Banbury 26/6/58
Southall 16/7/60
Ebbw Jct. 5/11/60
Old Oak Common 4/11/61
Ebbw Jct. 3/12/62
Southall 5/11/63
Ebbw Jct. 22/6/64
Severn Tunnel Jct. 20/7/64
Ebbw Jct. 1/11/64
Severn Tunnel Jct. 11/7/65

Tender
BR1G no.1537 from new

Boiler
no.1917 from new

Condemned 10/9/65, stored at 86E Severn Tunnel Jct 9-11/65, cut up at Cashmores, Newport 12/65-2/66.

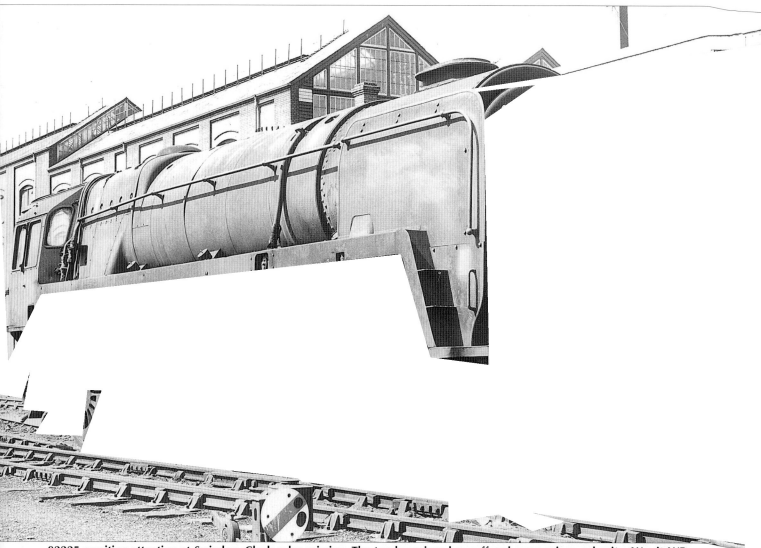

92225 awaiting attention at Swindon. Clack valve missing. The top lamp iron has suffered some minor calamity. Was it WR custom to remove the shed plate on sending an engine to works? Photograph J. Davenport, Initial Photographics.

92226 at its first shed, Banbury, 19 August 1958. In a short life it had an inordinate number of shed transfers, a reflection of the rapid rundown of steam. Photograph Peter Groom.

92226, date and location undisclosed. The Old Oak shed plate indicates that the period is late 1961-late 1962. The presence of 2-8-0 3861 suggests South Wales and the 9F is freshly painted; it wasn't one of those dealt with at Caerphilly so it can be surmised that 92226 has been in Swindon (the Record Card doesn't help) and has reached the Principality on a goods; the turntable and trees in the distance suggest we might be at Severn Tunnel Junction; other situations could be conjured up, but this is the best we can do. Photograph The Transport Treasury.

92227

To traffic 3/7/58

Works
8/10/58-9/10/58**NC**	Swindon
11/7/60-13/10/60**LC**	Swindon
26/1/62-1/6/62**HI**	Wolverhampton
4/9/63-12/10/63**LC**	Crewe
15/4/64-25/6/64**LC**	Crewe
1/3/66-20/4/66**LI**	Crewe

Mileage at 30/12/62 82,422

Annual mileage
1960 16,768
1961 26,177
1963 12,893

Sheds
Banbury 3/7/58
Cardiff Canton 28/1/61
Banbury 11/8/62
Warrington 9/10/66
Speke Jct 25/3/67

Tenders
BR1G no.1538 from new
BR1G no.1522 from 92215

Boiler
no.1919 from new

Condemned 4/11/67, stored at 8C Speke Junction 10-12/67, cut up at Wards, Beighton, Sheffield 1/68.

92228

To traffic 12/7/58

Works
8/10/59-31/10/59**LI**	Banbury
6-8/62	Swindon
8/11/65-23/12/65**LI**	Crewe V and P exam

Mileage at 30/12/62 92,250

Annual mileage
1960 15,031
1961 27,593
1963 25,699

Sheds
Banbury 12/7/58
Speke Jct. 9/10/66

Tender
BR1G no.1539 from new

Boiler
no.1920 from new

Condemned 28/2/67, stored at 8C Speke Jct 1-5/67, cut up at Wards, Beighton, Sheffield 6/67.

Transformation of a 9F, a job which seems to have involved fitting a new roof. 92227 is just west of the traverser at Crewe Works, on the stripping pits. After stripping what was left would be moved, via the traverser, eastwards for reassembly to commence. Photograph A. Scarsbrook, Initial Photographics.

92227, with Banbury's LM code 2D painted on, at Gloucester Central with iron ore tipplers, 8 July 1965. New lamp iron positions, second front step; an ash raking door hangs nonchalantly open. Photograph Norman Preedy.

92228 at Canton, a visitor from Banbury; it was the iron and steel traffic that brought the Banbury engines down into South Wales. Photograph J. Davenport, Initial Photographics.

92228 meets 92139 at Tramway Junction, Gloucester, 19 June 1965. Photograph Norman Preedy.

On a summer Saturday, 6 August 1960, Old Oak Common has turned out its own 92230, with customary coating of white, for the 11.35 Carmarthen train. Photograph R.C. Riley, The Transport Treasury.

92229

To traffic 18/7/58

Works
24/2/62   Caerphilly 'Heavy repair'

Sheds
Banbury 18/7/58
Old Oak Common 1/11/58
Ebbw Jct. 30/1/60
Southall 30/11/63
Ebbw Jct. 22/6/64

Tender
BR1G no.1540 from new

Boiler
no.1921 from new

Condemned 4/11/64, stored at 81C Southall 11/64-2/65, cut up at Cox and Danks, Park Royal, North Acton 2/65.

92230

To traffic 1/8/58

Works
6/62   Swindon

Sheds
Banbury 1/8/58
Old Oak Common 1/11/58
Ebbw Jct. 30/1/60
Old Oak Common 6/10/62
Ebbw Jct. 3/11/62
Bromsgrove 25/1/64
Ebbw Jct. 20/7/64
Gloucester Horton Road 7/11/65

Tender
BR1G no.1541 from new

Boiler
no.1922 from new

Condemned 31/12/65, stored at 86B Ebbw Jct. 12/65-2/66, cut up at Cashmores, Newport 3-7/66.

A scruffy 92231 at Ebbw Junction shed; some pipework has sagged and is showing about mid-way under the running plate. This engine was one of the five 9Fs sent to Eastleigh (see 92239) where it became a particular favourite, among crews which in any event took to the 9Fs with considerable enthusiasm. The 9Fs were intended for the Bromford Bridge oil trains but were used on anything that might turn up — on pigeon specials, for instance, the Southern men soon discovering their high speed potential. It was one of several that appeared spasmodically in 1961-62 between Exeter and Salisbury, usually on stone trains. A particularly notable day was 22 September 1962 when it arrived at Exeter Central on the 3.5pm Salisbury-Exeter stopper. It returned on the 10.18pm local to Honiton and continued on to Salisbury hauling a stone train berthed at Honiton.

92231

To traffic 1/8/58

Works
17/10/58-21/10/58**NC**	Swindon AWS
11/59	Worcester
20/3/61-6/5/61**LI-HI**	Eastleigh 78,641 'Mechanical lubricator gear modified; 3 ring piston heads; UK piston rod packing; Front cylinder covers modified, 4 or more new tyres, 34 small boiler tubes replaced, 5 super-heater tubes welded, piston valves renewed, cylinders rebored
4/3/63-4/4/63**GO**	Crewe
21/9/64-7/11/64**NC**	Crewe
13/11/64**NC**	Crewe

Sheds
Pontypool Road 1/8/58
Severn Tunnel Jct. 24/1/59
Cardiff Canton 21/2/59
Ebbw Jct. 31/10/59
Cardiff Canton 27/2/60*
Bristol Barrow Road 8/10/60
Eastleigh 17/1/61
Feltham 24/6/63
York 8/9/63
*On loan in May to Bromsgrove

Tenders
BR1G no.1542 from new
BR1C no.949 from 92000

Boiler
no.1922 from new

Condemned 17/11/66, stored at 50A York 11/66-3/67, cut up at Drapers, Hull 4/67

92232

To traffic 6/8/58

Works
16/10/59-30/10/59**NC**	Banbury
26/1/60-1/3/60**NC**	Banbury
10/12/60-14/4/61**HC**	Swindon
15/10/62-19/12/62**LC**	Gorton
23/1/64-17/4/64**LC**	Swindon

Sheds
Pontypool Road 6/8/58
Severn Tunnel Jct. 24/1/59
Cardiff Canton 21/2/59
Banbury 3/10/59
Cardiff East Dock 8/9/62

Tender
BR1G no.1543 from new

Boiler
no.1923 from new

Condemned 12/64,, stored at 88A Cardiff East Dock 12/64-2/65, cut up at Woodhams, Barry 3/65.

Extravagantly coaled for the forthcoming haul over the Mendips, 92233 is ready for the Pines at Bath Green Park shed, 7 September 1962. Photograph Peter Groom.

92233

To traffic 11/8/58
Increased cylinder lubrication

Works

22/10/58-24/10/58**NC**	Swindon
18/11/59-7/12/59**NC**	Banbury
8/8/60-7/10/60**LC**	Caerphilly
19/10/61-30/1/62**HI**	Swindon
2/12/63-18/1/64**LC**	Crewe
15/9/64-13/11/64 **HC[CB]**	Crewe
8/2/66-5/3/66**LI**	Crewe
21/3/66-30/3/66**Ret**	Crewe

Mileage at 7/7/62 100,866

Annual mileage
1960 21,986
1961 19,134
1963 1,790

Sheds
Pontypool Road 11/8/58
Severn Tunnel Jct. 24/1/59
Cardiff Canton 21/2/59
Banbury 21/9/59
Cardiff Canton 28/1/61
Bath Green Park 14/7/62
Ebbw Jct. 10/10/63
Newton Heath 12/10/63
Carlisle Kingmoor 12/7/64
Speke Jct. 27/1/68

Tenders
BR1G no.1544 from new
BR1G no.1551 from 92240
BR1B no.970 on 21/2/65 from 92021

Boiler
no.1924 from new

Condemned 3/2/68, stored at 8C Speke Jct. 2-7/68, cut up at Wards, Beighton, Sheffield 8/68.

92234

To traffic 19/8/58

Works

27/10/58-31/10/58**NC**	Swindon AWS
27/10/60-11/11/60**LC**	Caerphilly
18/4/61-15/8/61**HI**	Swindon
23/5/63-15/6/63**LC**	Crewe
4/10/63-29/11/63**HC**	Crewe
3/6/65-7/7/65**LI**	Crewe
2/8/66-10/10/66 **HC[CB]**	Crewe

Mileage at 30/12/62 93,949

Annual mileage
1960 22,886
1961 9,507
1963 12,418

Sheds
Pontypool Road 19/8/58
Severn Tunnel Jct. 24/1/59
Cardiff Canton 21/2/59
Banbury 21/9/59
Bromsgrove 7/10/61
Banbury 2/12/61
Tyseley 11/8/62
Banbury 19/9/64
Saltley 8/10/66
Birkenhead 15/11/66

Tender
BR1G no.1545 from new

Boiler
no.1925 from new

Condemned 11/11/67, stored at 8H Birkenhead 11-12/67, 8C Speke Jct. 1/68, cut up at Campbells, Airdrie 2/68.

With characteristic white staining, 92235 arrives at Bristol Temple Meads, 'with empty stock', August 1959. It is carrying express lights so is likely enough going to work the train out (this is probably a Saturday). Note also the frame for the WR train reporting numbers. Photograph B.W.L. Brooksbank, Initial Photographics.

92235

To traffic 22/8/58

Works
18/5/60-31/5/60**LC**   Caerphilly
6-8/62   Swindon

Sheds
Pontypool Road 22/8/58
Severn Tunnel Jct. 24/1/59
Cardiff Canton 21/2/59
Ebbw Jct. 3/10/59
Bristol Barrow Road 7/11/65

Tender
BR1G no.1546 from new

Boiler
no.1926 from new

Condemned 18/11/65, stored at 81F Oxford 12/65-3/66, cut up at Cashmores, Newport 4/66.

92236

To Traffic 4/9/58

Works
29/10/59-27/11/59**NC**   Didcot
4/62   Caerphilly 'Heavy repair'

Sheds
Ebbw Jct 4/9/58
Cardiff Canton 29/11/58
Cardiff East Dock 8/9/62
Severn Tunnel Jct. 8/11/64

Tender
BR1G no.1547 from new

Boiler
no.1927 from new

Condemned 5/4/65, stored at 82C Swindon 8/65, cut up at Birds, Bridgend 8-10/65.

92237

To traffic 9/9/58

Works
1/12/59-14/12/59**NC**   Canton
11/60   Swindon
2/62   Swindon

Sheds
Ebbw Jct. 9/9/58
Cardiff Canton 29/11/58
Cardiff East Dock 8/9/62
Severn Tunnel Jct. 8/11/64
Ebbw Jct. 7/3/65

Tender
BR1G no.1548 from new

Boiler
no.1928 from new

Condemned 10/9/65, stored at 86B Ebbw Jct. 9-10/65, cut up at Cashmores, Newport 11/65.

92238

To traffic 22/9/58

Works
28/11/59-14/12/59**NC**   Old Oak Common
11/60   Swindon
2/12/61   Caerphilly
4/64   Swindon
11/6/64-1/7/64**LC**   Eastleigh

Sheds
Ebbw Jct. 22/9/58
Old Oak Common 10/12/58
Southall 10/9/60
Ebbw Jct. 2/12/61
Bristol Barrow Road 2/11/63
Severn Tunnel Jct. 8/8/65
*was wearing 82F Bath Green Park
plate in summer of 1965

Tender
BR1G no.1549 from new

Boiler
no.1929 from new

Condemned 10/9/65, stored at 86E Severn Tunnel Jct. 9-10/65, cut up at Cashmores, Newport 12/65.

92238 at Bournemouth Central, 12 June 1965, after arrival with a Warwickshire Railway Society special via the S&D from Birmingham. The weather was miserable and performance described as absolutely abysmal (reduced to walking pace uphill). Return was up the SR main line so the 2-10-0 went back light. It had been 'specially imported for the occasion'. Photograph The Transport Treasury.

92239 at an unknown location – it could be any shed on the oil trains' path northward, Didcot for instance. It was odd that the Southern by this time had none of the plentiful WD 2-8-0s, and that it took so long to get any 9Fs. Yet it had a history of using heavy freight engines from elsewhere. It had turned out that the ever-increasing Fawley oil traffic was being worked by WR and LMR engines, with Eastleigh men. The idea behind the five 9Fs coming to Eastleigh was that Eastleigh would run these heavy trains itself, on the basis that, if you took the job, then you should be responsible for the locomotives. Yet a portion of the work still remained with 'foreign' engines; indeed it was one of the few circumstances in which a Lancashire or Birmingham 9F, say, could find itself near the Solent. The Fawley-Bromford Bridge tanks were worked by Eastleigh's 'Didcot Gang' via the Didcot, Newbury & Southampton line. The 9Fs in fact had become everyday fare at Eastleigh before the five arrived and were still familiar after they had left; freight jobs for Southampton brought them in from the Western and beyond. Then there was the unlooked-for development of 9Fs coming to Eastleigh Works for overhaul. Throughout much of 1964 and 1965, 9Fs were coming to Eastleigh at the rate of two or three a month. Photograph P.J. Coster.

In 92239 (pictured at Bollo Lane Crossing near Acton, south-west London; the line runs away from us south-westwards under the LT District and Piccadilly lines running north-west to south-east, right to left on the bridge above) we have a *Southern* 9F. It is running light engine northbound and carries an SR headcode, Feltham-Brent (LM) via Kew East, so it is going to fetch a train from the LMR. Five of the 2-10-0s were transferred from the WR to Eastleigh for the 1,200 ton oil trains (the 'railcars' as they were termed, oddly) from Fawley to the West Midlands over the Didcot, Newbury and Southampton line. They were not used exclusively on the oil workings and could turn up on unexpected jobs, as here. The quintet was 92205, 92206 and 92231 in January 1961 and 92211 and 92239 in August, though the first three were recorded as 'on loan' from the latter part of 1960. Principal trains were the Fawley-Bromford Bridge tanks (an afternoon job), the Fawley-Scunthorpe (Scanton Sidings) tanks and Fawley-Spondon tanks (1.0pm). There was a Fawley-Northampton tank job, and freights from Eastleigh to Washwood Heath and Tyseley. 9Fs off the Western Region also played a regular part, and 92221 of Barrow Road and 92225 of Ebbw Junction seemed such 'regulars' that they could almost have been loaned. See '(Expletive Deleted) 9Fs at Eastleigh' in *British Railways Illustrated* Vol.7 No.1, October 1997. *The Railway Observer* for February 1961 recorded that: *'The 2-10-0s have been specially sanctioned to work over the DNS section. The tank wagon traffic formerly went via Bristol and the Midland main line to Birmingham, but owing to heavy delays encountered in the Bristol area this revised route was agreed.'* Working, the *Observer* recorded, 'commenced 1 January 1961' but this was later corrected, and as at 20 February, the trains were still running via Salisbury, Westbury and Bristol. 92239 had arrived from the WR in August 1961 and, along with the other four, transferred to Feltham in June 1963. It might already be working from Feltham – which was not far off – by the time of this picture. All five moved on to York in September. Notice yet again the inevitable combination of lamp irons. Photograph The Transport Treasury.

92239

To traffic 25/9/58

Works
13/11/58-18/11/58**NC**	Swindon AWS
6/1/61-10/2/61**LC**	Wolverhampton
17/11/61-16/12/61**LC**	Eastleigh 89,431
16/2/62-24/2/62**LC**	Eastleigh 89,561
17/5/62-19/5/62**LC**	Eastleigh 89,924
2/4/63-4/5/63**GO**	Crewe

Sheds
Ebbw Jct. 25/9/58
Old Oak Common 10/12/58
Southall 10/9/60
Westbury 15/7/61
Eastleigh 23/8/61
Feltham 24/6/63
York 8/9/63

Tender
BR1G no.1550 from new

Boiler
no.1930 from new

Condemned 17/11/66, stored at 50A York 11/66-2/67, cut up at Drapers, Hull 4/67

92240

To traffic 1/10/58

Works
19/11/58-21/11/58**NC**	Swindon
17/11/61-2/3/62**HI**	Swindon 'Increased cylinder lubrication'
16/7/63-17/8/63**LC**	Crewe
20/8/64-4/9/64**LC**	Eastleigh '4 or more wheels turned up and axleboxes refitted to horns and journals, coupled 1st, 2nd, 3rd, 4th, 5th engine wheels'

Sheds
Ebbw Jct. 1/10/58
Old Oak Common 29/11/58
Southall 10/9/60

Tenders
BR1G no.1551 from new
BR1G no.1544 from 92233

Boiler
no.1931 from new

Condemned 8/65, preserved on the Bluebell Railway.

92240 in the shed yard at Southall, 9 September 1962. Photograph Peter Groom.

92241

To traffic 6/10/58

Works
9/61 Swindon

Sheds
Ebbw Jct. 6/10/58
Old Oak Common 29/11/58
Cardiff Canton 5/11/60
Cardiff East Dock 8/9/62
Southall 30/11/63

Tender
BR1G no.1552 from new

Boiler
no.1932 from new

**Condemned 2/7/65, stored at 81C Southall 7-8/65,
cut up at Cashmores, Newport 9-12/65.**

The 9Fs were prey to deflector hand rail damage, though by what cause is unknown. 92241's last shed was Southall, where it was condemned in July 1965 and afterwards carted off to South Wales for scrap. Near to the end, it has obviously found its way north; this is Crewe South shed, and if it had visited the works, it went unrecorded. Those chalk marks *suggest* that it might have been in for attention, though it's been used for a while, sufficient to gather a film of grime over the chalk. Photograph The Transport Treasury.

Ebbw Junction's 92242 up in London in May 1959, at Old Oak Common. Photograph J. Davenport, Initial Photographics.

92242

To traffic 13/10/58

Works
2-3/59   Swindon
12/62   Gorton
1/63   Crewe

Sheds
Ebbw Jct 1/11/58
Severn Tunnel Jct 1/11/64

Tender
BR1G no.1553 from new

Boiler
no.1933 from new

Condemned 21/5/65, stored at 86E Severn Tunnel Jct. 5-7/65, cut up at Cashmores, Newport 8/65.

92243

To traffic 21/10/58

Works
19/2/60-11/4/60NC   Ebbw Jct
6-10/62   Swindon

Sheds
Ebbw Jct. 21/10/58
Old Oak Common 17/11/62
Cardiff East Dock 28/9/63
Severn Tunnel Jct. 8/11/64
Cardiff East Dock 7/2/65
Ebbw Jct. 8/8/65
Bristol Barrow Road 7/11/65

Tender
BR1G no.1554 from new

Boiler
no.1934 from new

Condemned 31/12/65, stored at 82F Bath Green Park 12/65-3/66, cut up at Cashmores, Newport 4/66.

92244

To traffic 28/10/58

Works
4/1/60-12/2/60**NC** Southall

Sheds
Ebbw Jct. 28/10/58
Old Oak Common 29/11/58
Canton 5/11/60
Cardiff East Dock 8/9/62
Oxford 3/11/62
Cardiff East Dock 17/11/62
Ebbw Jct. 8/8/65
Gloucester Horton Road 7/11/65

Tender
BR1G no.1555 from new

Boiler
no.1935 from new

Condemned 31/12/65, stored at 85B Gloucester Horton Road 12/65-3/66, cut up at Cashmores, Newport 4-7/66.

92245

To traffic 4/11/58

Works
13/12/59-4/1/60**NC**   Old Oak Common
3-5/61   Swindon
5/62**LI**   Caerphilly

Sheds
Old Oak Common 4/11/58
Cardiff Canton 5/11/60
Bath Green Park 16/6/62
Oxford 6/10/62
Southall 3/11/62

Tender
BR1G no.1556 from new

Boiler
no.1936 from new

Condemned 12/64, stored at 81C Southall 1-6/65, presently preserved at Barry, South Wales.

An odd combination at Llanelly shed, fuelled with the despised compacted 'cobbles', widely known by an obscene but nonetheless amusing epithet.   Photograph L. Turner, The Transport Treasury.

An unusual view of 92245, undergoing some preparatory work at Swindon on 9 April 1961 before going into the works. An interesting conjunction of 9F with GWR tender! Photograph H.D. Ramsey, Initial Photographics.

Its 1961 overhaul made 92245 a good choice for a summer on the Somerset & Dorset the following year. On 7 July 1962 the 9F had the 9.25am Saturdays Only Bournemouth to Manchester train, near Midford. In a sense, the 9Fs were a perfect mixed traffic locomotive for many BR lines; they exactly suited the S&D and the GC, so why not the Waverley, Carlisle-Newcastle or the Cambrian? Photograph Ivo Peters, courtesy Julian Peters.

92245 in standard 9F state, 7 April 1964; ashpan raking doors gape open. Mind you, that double chimney still looked the business. Photograph Peter Groom.

92246

To traffic 20/11/58

Works
20/11/59-11/12/59**NC**	Old Oak Common
28/1/61**LC**	Caerphilly
6/62	Swindon
8/63	Swindon
7/65	Crewe

Sheds
Old Oak Common 20/11/58
Cardiff Canton 5/11/60
Cardiff East Dock 8/9/62
Southall 30/11/63
Severn Tunnel Jct. 19/9/65
Gloucester Horton Road 7/11/65

Tender
BR1G no.1557 from new

Boiler
no.1937 from new

Condemned 31/12/65, stored at 2A Tyseley 12/65, 85B Gloucester Horton Road 12/65-3/66, cut up at Cashmores, Newport 4/66.

92247

To traffic 2/12/58

Works
1/62	Oswestry
6/63	Crewe
6/65	Crewe

Mileage at 30/12/62 95,175

Annual mileage
1960 28,372
1961 25,378
1963 15,880

Sheds
Old Oak Common 2/12/58
Cardiff Canton 24/2/62
Banbury 11/8/62
Newton Heath 17/9/66

Tender
BR1G no.1558 from new

Boiler
no.1938 from new

Condemned 8/10/66, stored at 8H Birkenhead 10/66-3/67, cut up at Drapers, Hull 4/67.

A compelling, informal portrait of a 9F; 92247 on a down freight at Severn Tunnel Junction in May 1961. Photograph J. Davenport, Initial Photographics.

Super study of 92247 at Banbury shed in June 1966, a few months short of closure; one of the original stars of the Ebbw Junction debacle back in 1954, 92004 stands ahead on the same 'firepit'. By this time Banbury's work was fast disappearing; in a startling illustration of the nature of changing times, it was through diesel workings from Carlisle to Eastleigh that would see off the last of the local 9Fs. In the event, 92247 had a brief further lease of life at Newton Heath. Photograph J.A.C. Kirke, The Transport Treasury.

Adieu. 92249, by now a Kingmoor engine, rolls the Long Meg empties across Garsdale viaduct on 30 May 1967. Photograph Paul Cotterell

92249

To traffic 10/12/58

Works
25/3/63-19/4/63**LI**   Crewe
17/1/65   Tender change at Carlisle
27/10/65-11/12/65**HI[CB]** Crewe
Mileage at 7/7/62 80,905

Annual mileage
1960 22,868
1961 18,659
1963 4,602

Sheds
Ebbw Jct. 10/12/58
Laira 18/6/60
Ebbw Jct. 8/10/60
Newton Heath 6/10/63
Carlisle Kingmoor 27/6/64
Speke Jct. 27/1/68

Tenders
BR1G no.1560 from new
BR1B no.973from 92024

Boiler
no.1940 from new

Condemned 4/5/68, stored at 8C Speke Jct. 5-8/68, cut up at Arnott Young, Parkgate and Rawmarsh 9/68.

92248

To traffic 2/12/58

Works
6/63   Crewe

Sheds
Ebbw Jct. 2/12/58
Saltley 12/9/59
Ebbw Jct. 5/11/59
Bristol Barrow Road 10/9/60
Cardiff East Dock 7/2/65

Tender
BR1G no.1559 from new

Boiler
no.1939 from new

Condemned 24/5/65, stored at 88A Cardiff East Dock 5-7/65, cut up at Cashmores, Newport 8/65.

So there remains one last 9F for us to look at, one which was notable in two ways. It was the last steam engine to be built at Crewe (it would in fact have been *the* last, an EVENING STAR, had production schedules not got out of kilter at Swindon) and it famously bore the Giesl ejector. Indeed it first saw the light of day conventionally fitted with a double chimney and ran thus at Banbury for some months. Before any hint of the Giesl (Bond was not keen but lobbying at Board level resulted in a command to try out the ejector) this is 92250 as the subject of an official ceremony at Crewe as the last steam locomotive to be built at the mighty works. The chap in the bowler is presumably His Worship the Mayor and the lovely Vivien Leigh-like lady his wife, clothed in suitably film star mink. It was December, after all, and very cold.

GIESL

The principle of the Oblong Ejector was the reduction of the 'shock loss' as the exhaust gases met the exhaust steam. This was done by accelerating the exhaust gases before they came into contact with the steam. It was thus the latest, and last, in a series of 'draughting appliances' as Cox put it, going back through Kylala, Kylchap, LeMaître and the rest. Its noticeable feature was the row of seven nozzles and the severely oblong nature of the 'smoke stack' itself. It succeeded in the straightforward essential of increasing the draught in the fire (putting it very simply) which was, after all, the purpose of such 'appliances'.

Roland Bond was not too keen on the idea apparently but after some lobbying in high places he was induced to make a 9F available. The last Crewe-built one, 92250 recently in traffic with a double chimney, was chosen. The ejector, it was claimed, was responsible for considerable savings in coal and improvements in performance on Dr Adolf Giesl-Gieslingen's native heath and, as with the Crosti episode, an agreement was drawn up with payment dependent on the savings attained. The conversion of even a few thousand engines would have made the Herr Doktor a wealthy man, we presume.

92250 was on test at Rugby in 1959 ('May etc' it says in the Engine Cards) but by July it was clear that anticipated economies would not be forthcoming. The main purpose had been to economise by using lower grade coals; this was not achieved and, moreover, with declining mileages in prospect for the 9Fs it seemed unlikely that the cost of fitting, some £500, would be recouped over two years (part of the agreement apparently) and that was that, in the story of the Giesl ejector. It was supposed to go back to the makers but their interest evaporated along with the prospect of future sales and BR settled on its retention for another year. The cost of conversion back to double chimney arrangement was barely worth it and Dr Giesl's creation stayed on 92250 to the end.

92250

To traffic 16/12/58
Subsequently fitted with Giesl Oblong Ejector

Works
1/64 Swindon

Sheds
Banbury 16/12/58
Rugby Testing Station 5/59
Ebbw Jct. 28/11/59
Southall 30/11/63
Ebbw Jct. 22/6/64
Severn Tunnel Jct. 20/7/64
Gloucester Horton Road 7/11/65

Tender
BR1G no.1561 from new

Boiler
no.1941 from new

Condemned 12/65, stored at 85B Gloucester [Horton Road] 12/65-5/66, cut up at Cashmores, Newport 7/66.

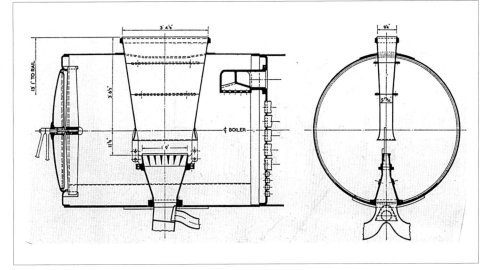

On shed at Southall about 1964; two more 9Fs behind (including 92246) and 6841 MARLAS GRANGE alongside. Photograph J.G. Walmsley, The Transport Treasury.

92250 (which surely should have been named too) went to Rugby for tests about June 1960 with the ejector, presumably fitted at Crewe along the way. These, as is well known, failed to show the hoped-for improvements in fuel economy and so a 9F was to disappoint yet a second foreign doktor. The oblong ejector would remain in place for a year, it was agreed but by the time July 1960 came and went no one remembered and the ejector stayed in place, in the event, till the engine went for scrap. Observe the crude cut-away in the running plate to improve access to the anti-vacuum valve, on top of the cylinder. Why 92250 wasn't presented to Crewe council for preservation on a pedestal somewhere in the town escapes one. Surely all they had to do was ask. Photograph Prorail UK (Durrant), The Transport Treasury.

92250 at Barrow Road shed, Bristol. Photograph The Transport Treasury.

Some Giesl detail; the front gardens are believed to be in South Wales, somewhere in the vicinity of Ebbw Junction shed. There was an interesting postscript to the Giesl story; in a riposte to assertions by Dr Tuplin in *Trains Illustrated* in 1962, Dr Giesl-Gieslingen was somewhat frosty. 'If front end problems were a matter of such simple arithmetic as Dr Tuplin presents to us, we would long ago have ceased to worry about them' he wrote. And that was about the end of it. As a postscript, it could be noted that the 'Nines' ducked the smoke deflector hand rail removals that beset many Britannias. Photograph Prorail UK (Durrant), The Transport Treasury.